Exploring
the Letters
of John
& Jude

Exploring
the Letters
of John
& Jude

A DEVOTIONAL COMMENTARY

GEORGE R. KNIGHT

REVIEW AND HERALD® PUBLISHING ASSOCIATION
Since 1861 | www.reviewandherald.com

The author assumes full responsibility for the accuracy of all facts and quotations as cited in this book.

All Bible texts quoted are the author's unless otherwise noted.

Bible texts credited to ESV are from the *English Standard Version* of the Bible, copyright © 2001, by Crossway Bibles, a division of Good News Publications. Used by permission.

All texts credited to Message are from *The Message.* Copyright © 1993, 1994, 1995, 1996, 2000, 2001, 2002. Used by permission of NavPress Publishing Group.

Scripture quotations from NASB are from the *New American Standard Bible,* copyright © 1960, 1962, 1963, 1968, 1971, 1972, 1973, 1975, 1977, 1994 by the Lockman Foundation. Used by permission.

Scripture quotations marked NEB are from *The New English Bible.* © The Delegates of the Oxford University Press and the Syndics of the Cambridge University Press 1961, 1970. Reprinted by permission.

Texts credited to NIV are from the *Holy Bible, New International Version.* Copyright © 1973, 1978, 1984, International Bible Society. Used by permission of Zondervan Bible Publishers.

Texts credited to REB are from *The Revised English Bible.* Copyright © Oxford University Press and Cambridge University Press, 1989. Reprinted by permission.

Bible texts credited to RSV are from the Revised Standard Version of the Bible, copyright © 1946, 1952, 1971, by the Division of Christian Education of the National Council of the Churches of Christ in the U.S.A. Used by permission.

Bible texts credited to TEV are from the *Good News Bible*—Old Testament: copyright © American Bible Society 1976, 1992; New Testament: copyright © American Bible Society 1966, 1971, 1976, 1992.

Texts credited to Wuest are from Kenneth S. Wuest, *The New Testament: An Expanded Translation.* Grand Rapids: Eerdmans, 1961. Reprinted 1994. Originally *Wuest's Expanded Translation of the Greek New Testament,* 1956-1959.

This book was
Edited by Gerald Wheeler
Cover designed by Left Coast Design
Cover illustration by Jerry Blank
Typeset: 11/14 Bembo

PRINTED IN U.S.A.

13   12   11   10   09   5   4   3   2   1

Library of Congress Cataloging-in-Publication Data
Knight, George R.
  Exploring the letters of John and Jude: a devotional commentary / George R. Knight.
     p. cm.
  1. Bible. N.T. Epistles of John—Commentaries. 2. Bible. N.T. Jude—Commentaries.
I. Title.
  BS2805.53.K65 2009
  227'.94077—dc22

                              2008049317

ISBN 978-0-8280-2444-0

Dedicated to

Bruce Johnston,
whose love and ministry reflect
that of the apostle John

Contents

Exploring the "Exploring" Idea

Exploring the Letters of John and Jude is the fifth volume in a series of user-friendly commentaries aimed at helping people understand the Bible better. While the books have the needs and abilities of laypeople in mind, they will also prove beneficial to pastors and other church leaders. Beyond individual readers, the "Exploring" format will be helpful for church study groups and in enriching participation in midweek meetings.

Each volume is best thought of as a devotional commentary. While the treatment of each passage seeks to develop its exegetical meaning, it does not stop there but moves on to practical application in the daily life of believers in the twenty-first century.

Rather than focusing on the details of each verse, the "Exploring" volumes seek to give readers an understanding of the themes and patterns of each biblical book as a whole and how each passage fits into its context. As a result, they do not attempt to solve all of the problems or answer all the questions related to a given portion of Scripture.

In an effort to be user-friendly these devotional commentaries on the Old and New Testaments present the entire text of each biblical book treated. The volumes divide the text into "bite-sized" portions that are included immediately before the comments on the passage. Thus readers do not have to flip back and forth between their Bibles and the commentary.

The commentary sections aim at being long enough to significantly treat a topic, but short enough for individual, family, or group readings.

The translation of each New Testament book is my own, and claims no special merit. Although I have based it on the original languages, in making it I have conferred with several English versions. While not being a "technical achievement," the translation has sought to take every significant translational problem and issue into consideration and to remain as close as possible to the original text of the Bible. In order to accomplish that goal the translation employs word-for-word translation wherever possible but utilizes thought-for-thought translation when word-for-word fails adequately to carry God's message from the original languages and cultures into modern English.

George R. Knight
Rogue River, Oregon

Foreword

The letters of John and Jude have all registered in my thinking over the years, but the impression varied from letter to letter. First John has always been one of my favorite Bible books. Its engaging style, the warmth of its message, its promise of forgiveness, and its significant discussions of sin and the atonement have all found a large place in my heart and thinking.

I can't say the same thing for John's two shorter epistles. To me they generally registered a zero. I knew that they belonged to the 27 books of the New Testament canon, but they never really stimulated my interest.

And then there was Jude. With his little letter my attitude was neither positive nor neutral, but rather one of negativity and avoidance. His reports of angels "reserved in everlasting chains under darkness," the esoterics of the apocryphal sayings of Enoch, and beastly people behaving like waterless clouds and twice-dead trees just didn't do much for my daily walk with Jesus.

Given my attitude, I tended to neglect Jude and 2 and 3 John, while spending a great deal of time studying and preaching from 1 John. The last two years have witnessed a reevaluation. As one might expect, I continue to hold onto John's first letter as one of my favorites. But, surprise of surprises, once I embedded myself in Jude I came to see both his logic and the crucial importance of his message for the twenty-first century. Beyond that, I found that the two shorter letters of John took on life when read in the context of the larger one and in relationship to each other.

What struck me most about the combined study of these documents was how much the church in our day needs their counsel. Both authors wrote to congregations flooded with strange philosophic ideas that undercut not only apostolic authority and teaching but Christian theology and morality in every age. The four letters taken together have a message second to none for a church living in a secularizing society inundated by postmodern attitudes, Eastern and New Age religious concepts, and moral laxity.

Having spent two years with these little books, I am absolutely certain of their importance for twenty-first century Christians. And that is especially true of Jude. He thundered his judgments for a reason. And that reason in the end was redemptive. Because he cared, he could not be silent. But all of his thundering is contexted in an understanding of God's saving gospel second to no other New Testament author.

One can read this devotional commentary as a freestanding book or it can be utilized with the on-line study guide developed to accompany it. The study guide to *Exploring the Letters of John and Jude* will provide those who use it with an opportunity to let the biblical books speak to them personally through a number of structured questions before they turn to the commentary itself. (To download and print the free study guide, go to www.AdventistBookCenter.com, find the book *Exploring the Letters of John and Jude*, then click on Click for Details and follow the instructions for downloading the study guide.)

I would like to express my appreciation to my wife, who typed my handwritten manuscript; and Gerald Wheeler and Jeannette R. Johnson, who shepherded the manuscript through the publication process.

I trust that *Exploring the Letters of John and Jude* will be a blessing to its readers as they seek to learn more of their Lord and as they put that knowledge into practice in daily living.

Exploring
First John

Introduction to the
First Letter of John

Iow plain, how full, and how deep a compendium of Christianity!"
(Wesley, vol. 3, p. 146). John Wesley's description of 1 John speaks
to all of us who love that little book.

Our Bibles tell us that 1 John is a letter. But it doesn't look like one.
After all, it has no address, addressee, or reference to a specific author.
Beyond that, it contains no names of either persons or places, and it indicates no special destination. "In fact," G. M. Burge tells us, "of all twenty-
one letters" in the New Testament, 1 John "is the least like a first-century
letter" (in Martin, p. 596). Another notable feature of 1 John is that it
never quotes from the Old Testament. From that perspective, it is worlds
apart from the letters authored by Paul, Peter, and James.

But for all its peculiarities John's first letter is brimming to the full with
some of Christianity's most edifying and informing teachings. It is one of
the most rewarding books to read in all of Scripture. Before turning to the
letter itself, it will be helpful to examine a few background issues.

Author, Date, and Recipients

Even though the three letters assigned to John do not bear his name,
both the records of the early church and very definite thematic connections
with the Fourth Gospel firmly suggest that their author is the "beloved"
apostle John, the son of Zebedee and one of Christ's original 12 disciples.

While John began his ministry in Jerusalem, he spent his latter years in
the Greek world. Not only would he be exiled to the island of Patmos off

of the coast of Asia Minor (today's Turkey), but he would lead the church in nearby Ephesus for many years.

That location is significant, since Ephesus in the latter New Testament period was a fertile breeding ground for the Greek philosophic ideas that would eventually cause the difficulties in the Christian church in that area of the Roman Empire that would call forth John's three letters. And it is significant that the first letter in the book of Revelation (also authored by John) was to Ephesus. Although invaded by false apostles, the church had overcome the teachings of the Nicolaitans (Rev. 2:1-7; cf. verses 14, 15), who had apparently been teaching some form of lawless indulgence on the basis that "the human body was evil . . . and only the spirit was good. A Christian, therefore, could do whatever he desired with his body because it had no importance" (Tenney, vol. 4, pp. 435, 436; see also Irenaeus *Against Heresies* 3. 11. 1). That anti-law teaching would be targeted in 1 John.

The apostle John most likely wrote his three epistles to the church in the Ephesus area sometime between A.D. 80 and A.D. 90. By that time the Greco-Roman philosophic ideas that would later be known as Gnosticism, Docetism, and Nicolaitanism would have had time to germinate and develop. As we will see, forms of all three of those related and problematic concepts would be central in the false teachings that John would combat in his epistles.

Occasion and Background

All students of 1 John agree that its author composed it to address a situation brought about by a schism in the Christian community. The dissidents were Christians who had formerly belonged to the church, but who had recently "went out" from the fellowship to start a movement of their own (1 John 2:19, RSV). But even though they had left the church, they were still communicating with its members "and were causing considerable uncertainty among them regarding the true character of Christian belief and whether the members of the church could truly regard themselves as Christians" (Marshall, p. 14).

A series of warnings found throughout the document reveals the nature of the opposition:

- "If we say that we have fellowship with Him yet are walking in the darkness" (1:6).

- "If we say that we have no sin" (1:8).
- "The one saying 'I have come to know Him, yet is not keeping His commandments" (2:4).
- "The one claiming to live in Him" but doesn't walk like Him (2:6).
- "Who is the liar but the one who denies that Jesus is the Christ?" (2:22).
- "If anyone says, 'I love God,' and hates his brother" (4:20).

At the core of the schism stood teachings related to the nature of Christ. For example, the schismatics denied that Jesus was the Christ (2:22) and that He had come in the flesh (4:2). On the other side of these issues are 1 John's repeated affirmations that Jesus was the Son of God and the Christ who had come in the flesh (1:3, 7; 2:23; 3:8, 23; 4:2, 9, 10, 15; 5:1, 11).

It appears that the dissidents had no problem accepting the idea of a divine Christ or Messiah but doubted that such a divine being became flesh and, more specifically, that the man Jesus was the incarnation of God. Thus as G. B. Caird puts it, "We are not to conclude . . . that they were Jews or Judaizers who denied [Christ's] Messiahship, but that they were Christians who denied the Incarnation" (in Buttrick, vol. 2, p. 947). Their teaching represents the idea, later called Docetism (from the Greek *dokein*, which means "seemed"), that Christ didn't really come in the flesh but only appeared to do so. That perspective reflected a Greek philosophic position holding the idea that spirit was good, while the material aspects of existence (including the flesh) were evil. Thus the teaching that the divine Christ would appear in flesh was both foolish and impossible.

Closely related to the separatists' Christological problem was its ethical outcome. Having separated their understanding of the divine Christ from the human Jesus, they found it only natural to deny the significance of Jesus' earthly teachings. Thus they boasted that they were free from sin (1:8, 10), that they had fellowship with God even as they walked in darkness (1:6), that they knew God even though they were disobedient (2:4), that they were in the light in spite of the fact that they hated their fellow Christians (2:9), and that they loved God even as they hated their earthly brothers and sisters (4:20).

Undergirding the theories of the separatists were prominent Greek philosophic concepts centering on the ideas that matter was evil and that the way to God was through special knowledge available to only an elite minority. A few decades after the writing of 1 John such ideas would become fully developed in the teaching that came to be known as Gnosticism.

The word "Gnosticism" derives from *gnōsis*, the Greek word meaning knowledge. In the Christian community of 1 John the separatists, with their superior airs and claims to special knowledge, had apparently shaken the confidence of many of those still faithful to the church. Their's, the implication ran, was the true prophetic voice that had superceded the primitive and unsophisticated ideas of the *old* apostle who was leading their church. As a result, those still faithful to the teachings of the church had come to doubt not only their understanding of Christianity but their personal spirituality.

Purpose of 1 John

The aim of John in his first epistle was obviously to meet the challenges of those troubling the church. But neither that epistle nor the other two can accurately be called polemical writings since they do not speak directly to those who have caused the trouble. Rather, we should view them as pastoral letters to those who have remained faithful.

As Colin Kruse points out, "the author's purpose . . . was not to correct the secessionists . . . , but to show his readers that the secessionist claims were false. By doing this he wanted to prevent them from being deceived by secessionist teachings" (Kruse, p. 27).

In the process, one of John's central aims was to attack the authority of the false teachers troubling the church. Thus the significance of his command to test the spirits. "Beloved," he wrote, "do not believe every spirit, but test the spirits to see whether they are of God; for many false prophets have gone out into the world. By this you know the Spirit of God: every spirit which confesses that Jesus Christ has come in the flesh is of God, and every spirit which does not confess Jesus is not of God. This is the spirit of the antichrist, of which you heard that it was coming, and now it is in the world already" (4:1-3, RSV).

The apostle not only unmasked the false prophets, but went on to note that faithful believers had nothing to fear since they "are of God" (verse 4). They were not only of God but they had been "anointed by the Holy One" (2:20, RSV), and they had "no need that any one should teach" them since they "abide in him" (verse 27, RSV). In short, the faithful members had nothing to fear from the dissidents. Not only did the latter have a false spirit, but the faithful had both the Holy Spirit and God's truth.

John set forth at least three tests by which to expose the false teachers (see Law, pp. 21-24).

- The test of truth—that those who are from God hold that Christ came in the flesh (4:1-6).
- The test of righteousness—that those who are from God confess their sins (1:9), walk in the light (2:6), and keep God's commandments (2:4).
- The test of love—that those who are from God love their fellow church members (2:10, 11; 3:14; 4:20).

After applying those tests to both the dissidents and themselves, John's readers will know that they are the ones who know God, have fellowship with Him, and have eternal life. The apostle's "tests" not only expose the secessionists but at the same time confirm the faith and status of his faithful parishioners. Thus his presentation agrees with the letter's one explicit statement of purpose: "I write this to you who believe in the name of the Son of God, so that you may know that you have eternal life" (5:13, RSV).

1 John's Major Themes

First John is rich in its teachings. While it does not present a systematic view of theology or Christian living, its responses to the secessionists highlight several themes that stand at the heart of a sound Christian understanding and ethics.

1. *Apostolic Authority*. The first words in 1 John raise the issue of authority. John buttresses his teachings with an assertion that his is a first-person witness. He *knows* because he has *heard, seen,* and *touched.* And those things that he has experienced he is passing on to his readers (1:1-4). Throughout his letter John repeatedly claims that the foundation for belief is the apostolic witness "which you heard from the beginning" (3:11; 1:1; 2:7, 13, 14, 24). Gary Burge points out that he "is not merely writing in defense of tradition, as if 'older is better' or any innovation is suspect." Rather John "is pointing elsewhere. By 'the beginning' he refers to the historic coming of Jesus Christ and the preservation of that revelation" through the authoritative apostolic witness (Burge, p. 35). Thus he asserts

that believers must test the new "prophetic" and philosophic ideas of the dissidents he is combating against that historical witness (4:1-6). Foundational to his message is John's belief that "the church is accountable to the historic revelation given in Jesus Christ and passed down through the apostles" (Martin, p. 593).

2. *The nature of Christ*. Because the central attack of the dissidents dealt with the person of Christ, 1 John in its answer to them is especially helpful in what it teaches about Jesus the Christ. Robert Kysar is on target when he writes that "no other NT writing stresses the importance of the humanity of Jesus for Christian faith" as do 1 and 2 John (in Freedman, vol. 3, p. 909). Because the false teachers had uplifted Christ's divinity at the expense of His humanity, even going so far as to distinguish between the divine Christ and the human Jesus, John asserts that "Jesus is the Christ" (5:1), that He came in the flesh (4:2), and that He is the Son of God (1:3, 7; 2:23; 3:8, 23; 4:9, 10, 14, 15). A correct understanding of the nature of Christ became for the apostle the litmus test of Christianity. Those who were wrong on that point should not be trusted (4:1-3).

3. *The saving work of Christ*. It is logical that those who denigrated the humanity of Christ would also fail to realize the significance of His life and death. Thus John sets forth Jesus as the propitiation or "atoning sacrifice for our sins" and "also for the sins of the whole world" (2:2, NIV; cf. 4:10). The fact that Jesus died in our place as "the Lamb of God, who takes away the sin of the world!" (John 1:29, RSV) was the foundation of John's understanding of the plan of salvation. Because of His death for humanity, those who accept Him become children of God (1 John 5:1), are born into God's family (3:1, 2; cf. John 1:12, 13), and receive the gift of eternal life (5:13). More specifically, the death of Christ provides the grounds for the forgiveness of sin (1:9). It is "the blood of Jesus His Son" that "cleanses us from all sin" (1:7). The sacrificial death also forms the foundation for His advocacy before the Father on behalf of sinners (2:1). As a result, John sets forth Jesus as the "Savior of the world" (4:14), an expression found only here and in John 4:42.

4. *The nature of sin*. Another highlight of 1 John is its description of sin. Sin is a big item in the apostle's agenda. He uses the noun form for sin (*hamartia*) 17 times and its verbal equivalent (*hamartanō*) 10 times. The letter defines sin as "lawlessness" (3:4). Central to its discussion is the seem-

ing contradiction between the statement that Christians "cannot sin" (3:9, RSV) and the assertion that Christians who say that they do not sin are liars (1:8) and make God into a liar (1:10). As we will see in the commentary, the inability to sin of chapter 3 reflects on sin as a self-centered, anti-God way of life, while the first chapter is speaking to lapses in behavior which can be confessed and thus forgiven (1:9). John therefore pictures confessed sins as "not unto death" but sin as a way of life as "unto death" (5:16, 17, KJV) since it is not repented of or confessed.

5. *The moral life.* Closely related to John's definition of sin as "lawlessness" (3:4) or "the transgression of the law" (KJV) is the issue of living the Christian life. William Barclay points out that "no New Testament writer makes a stronger ethical demand than John does, and no New Testament writer more strongly condemns a so-called religion which fails to issue in ethical action. God is righteous and every one who knows God must reflect in his life the righteousness of God (2:29)" (Barclay, p. 20). If the false teachers he is combating walk in darkness (1:6) and are disobedient (2:4), the true followers of Christ must walk as He did (2:6) and keep His commandments (2:3). After all, "he who says 'I know him' but disobeys his commands is a liar, and the truth is not in him" (2:4, RSV). At the very center of the obedient life in 1 John is the duty to love (4:8).

6. *The centrality of love.* Augustine (354-430) was only slightly exaggerating when he wrote in the preface to his commentary that 1 John "speaks at length and almost the whole time about love" (in R. Brown, p. 116). Words related to *agapē* (love) occur 62 times in John's brief letters. Leon Morris makes a profound point when he writes that "we will never find what love means if we start from the human end" (Morris, *Theology, p.* 290). John begins with the divine perspective. Not only does he define God as love (4:8) but he specifically relates God's love to humans in the cross of Christ: "This is love: not that we loved God, but that he loved us and sent his Son as an atoning sacrifice for our sins" (4:10, NIV; cf. 3:16).

Human love from John's perspective is a response to divine love. Only because we see and experience His love toward us in sending Christ do we love in turn. His love for us inspires us to love Him and other people (2:10; 3:23; 4:7, 21; 5:2). Keeping His commandments is one expression of our reciprocating love to God. "For this is the love of God, that we keep his commandments" (5:3, RSV). Morris notes that "it is striking that these letters, which put such stress on love, have more references to God's commandments than any other New Testament book (*entolē*, 'command,' occurs 18 times, whereas Paul has the word only 14 times in all his epistles)" (Morris, *Theology,* p. 290). John's teaching on the topic is an expansion of Christ's which highlighted love to God and other people as the very center of the law (Matt. 22:36-40). As does the Fourth Gospel (John 13:35), John's first epistle makes love the defining characteristic of true Christianity (3:14; 4:20), while showing hate to others is the mark of those who walk in darkness (2:9).

It is no accident that John put such an emphasis on love, given the divisive and unloving ways of the false teachers who were disrupting the church or churches that he was writing to. Unity and fellowship could be achieved only through God-inspired love.

7. *The assurance of God's children.* One dominating theme in 1 John is the Christian's assurance of salvation and eternal life (see Boice, p. 9). We see that theme reflected in the author's only explicit statement of purpose: "*I write these things* to you who believe in the name of the Son of God *so that you may know that you have eternal life*" (5:13, NIV). Such assurance is also at the heart of the Fourth Gospel, which asserts that "he who hears my word and believes him who sent me, has eternal life" (John 5:24, RSV; cf. John 3:36).

The key word for 1 John's doctrine of assurance is "know." Thus true believers may have confidence because they

- "know" that they are in Him because they keep His commandments (2:3, 5).
- "know" that they have passed from death to life because they love fellow believers (3:14).
- "know" that they abide in Him because He has given them His Spirit (4:13).
- "know" that they are the children of God because they love and obey Him (5:2).
- "know" that they are born of God because they do not live in a state of sin (5:18).

Please note that assurance for John is not "merely believe and be saved," but is related to how people live their lives. While belief is important, as James Montgomery Boice puts it, John "works on a more practical level, showing that the Christian can be assured of his salvation in that God has brought about fundamental changes in his life. He has given him a sure knowledge of himself in Jesus Christ. This involves *truth*. He has given him a desire to pursue and obey the commandments of Christ. This involves *righteousness*. He has given him a new relationship with other believers. This involves *love*" (Boice, p. 9).

Thus 1 John's understanding of assurance is not once saved/always saved. After all, the secessionists that the apostle aimed his letter at had definitely moved into darkness even though they had once belonged to the community. In 1 John assurance rests upon the tests of believing the *truth* about Jesus, *righteous* living, and *loving* others. On all three counts, the dissidents had failed. They may have been right that knowledge (*gnōsis*) was central to Christianity, but they had the wrong *gnōsis*. On the other hand, genuine Christians, claims 1 John, have not only the true *gnōsis* but they also "know" that they have eternal life (5:13).

8. *The nature of God and antichrist.* First John has three very specific things to say about God: (1) "that God is light and in him is no darkness at all" (1:5, RSV), (2) that "God is love" (4:8), and (3) that He is righteous (2:29; 3:7; 2:1). The apostle sets forth those qualities as essential attributes of both God and those who follow Him.

Opposed to God is "antichrist," translated from a Greek word used only five times in the New Testament—all by John (1 John 2:18, 22; 4:3; 2 John 7). Antichrist stands for the opposite of the characteristics of God and Christ. Thus the spirit of antichrist consists of those attributes that lead to living in darkness, unrighteousness, and hate (2:9; 3:10). In addition, it "denies that Jesus is the Christ" (2:22; 4:3). It is along the frontier of the characteristics of God and antichrist that 1 John formulates its argument.

The Relationship Between
1 John, 2 and 3 John, and the Fourth Gospel

On the relationship between the Fourth Gospel and the three letters, I. Howard Marshall concludes that they "stand closer . . . in style and content than do any other writings to one another in the New Testament" (Marshall, p. 33). Or, as Alfred Plummer puts it, "the lesson of both is one and the same; faith in Jesus Christ leading to fellowship with Him, and through fellowship with Him to fellowship with the

Father and with one another: or, to sum up all in one word, Love" (Plummer, *Gospel*, p. 51). Central to their shared concepts are an overshadowing interest in the incarnation, the new birth experience, and a host of shared theological vocabulary.

Yet differences do exist between the gospel and the letters. And there should be. After all, they have different purposes. John, for example, wrote his Gospel for unbelievers to create a conviction "that Jesus is the Christ, the Son of God" (John 20:30, 31, RSV), while he penned the first letter to deepen assurance of salvation for Christians (1 John 5:13). As a result, the Fourth Gospel contains "signs" to develop faith (John 20:30), while the letter provides "tests" by which to judge its validity (1 John 2:4; 4:2, 3, 20). In addition, the enemies of the truth in the Gospel are unbelieving Jews, while in the letters they are professing Christians who have gone astray.

Consequently, John wrote his first letter to people who already know the truth (2:20) and who needed to remember what they already knew (2:21). The presentation in 1 John presupposes a knowledge of the content of the Fourth Gospel, even if the readers had it only in oral form. While it is impossible to tell which one John actually penned first, Plummer has aptly described the letter as "a comment on the Gospel, 'a sermon with the Gospel for its text'" (Plummer, *Epistles*, p. xlv). In other words it appears that the letters presuppose an understanding of the teachings of the Fourth Gospel.

As with 1 John and the Gospel, the various ties between the three epistles point to a common author. Among the several similarities between 2 John and 3 John is the fact that they were both sent by "the elder." And 1 John and 2 John are united by the common problem of the "antichrist" (1 John 2:18, 22; 4:3; 2 John 7). Beyond those facts, the three epistles deal with the same issues and utilize overlapping vocabularies. For example, 86 percent of the words of the second letter and 70 percent of those in the third appear in 1 John (Freedman, vol. 3, p. 907).

The more difficult issue is not that of common authorship but of their relationship to each other. While we cannot determine it with certainty, one possibility is that 1 John is a general tract dealing with the issues, while 2 John and 3 John are cover letters to a specific congregation (or congregations) in the apostle's area of responsibility.

Structure and Outline of 1 John

Students of 1 John have repeatedly noted the impossibility of discovering a structural outline that doesn't run into problems of inconsistency. Part of the problem seems to be that John sets forth his ideas in a spiral form in which he introduces themes and then repeatedly returns to them for additional treatment in terms of amplification and/or application.

One of the more helpful approaches to an outline develops a structure around the letter's statements about the nature of God. Thus the basic outline has the following divisions:

Prologue (1:1-4)
   I. God is light (1:5-2:27)
  II. God is righteous (2:28-4:6)
 III. God is love (4:7-5:12)
Epilogue (5:13-21)

While such a summary offers insights into the general progression of 1 John, it runs into definite problems because of the spiral nature of John's style in accounting for all the details in the flow of the text. It is more helpful to view the book as a progression of associated ideas rather than as a document whose larger sections fit the traditional outline format (see Marshall, p. 26). The following proposal takes that approach:

    I. Prologue—witness to the Word of life (1:1-4)
   II. God's children walk in the light (1:5-2:2)
  III. God's children walk in obedience to the commandments (2:3-11)
  IV. The status of believers as God's children and their relation to the world (2:12-17)
   V. Warning to God's children to beware of antichrists (2:18-27)
  VI. The hope of God's children (2:28-3:3)
 VII. The sinlessness of God's children (3:4-10)
VIII. The love of God's children (3:11-18)
  IX. The assurance of God's children confirmed by their belief in the Son and their obedience (3:19-24)
   X. Tests for God's children in defining truth and falsehood (4:1-6)
  XI. The love of God's children as a response to God's love (4:7-12)

1 John's Relevance for the Twenty-first Century

While some might question the relevance of such Bible books as Obadiah or the Song of Solomon for twenty-first-century living, few would harbor doubts about 1 John. Even at a surface level it is clear that 1 John deals with issues central to Christian faith and life.

Who, for example, can possibly question the importance of Godlike love in corporate living or the issues dealing with sin, salvation, and moral living highlighted in John's short but forceful letter. And who can fail to grasp the importance of the incarnation, Christ's death on the cross, and His ministry as our Advocate to the basic core of Christian understanding. And where are those that don't thrill to the fact that we can "know" that we have eternal life. All of those topics have been central to vital Christianity throughout its history. And they will continue to be so in the future.

Beyond those broad-ranging, forever-relevant concerns is the very practical issue that the church on earth will always face the threat of schism. One of the most important of 1 John's contributions is its counsel for dealing with those who have moved away from the central core of Christian theology and living, all the while proclaiming that they have it right. The three-fold test of truth, righteousness, and love that John sets forth continues to have the utmost value as the church and individual Christians deal with those whose "new light" and human philosophies put them at odds with the apostolic witness.

List of Works Cited in 1, 2, and 3 John

Akin, Daniel L. *1, 2, 3 John*. The New American Commentary. Nashville: Broadman and Holman, 2001.
Alexander, Neil. *The Epistles of John*. Torch Bible Commentaries. London: SCM Press, 1962.
Ante-Nicene Fathers, 10 vols. Ed. Alexander Roberts et al. Peabody, Mass.: Hendrickson, 1994.
Apostolic Fathers. Trans. J. B. Lightfoot and J. R. Harmer. Ed. Michael W. Holmes. 2nd ed. Grand Rapids: Baker, 1989.

Balz, Horst, and Gerhard Schneider, eds. *Exegetical Dictionary of the New Testament*. 3 vols. Grand Rapids: Eerdmans, 1990-1993.

Barclay, William. *The Letters of John and Jude*. 2nd ed. The Daily Study Bible. Edinburgh: Saint Andrew Press, 1960.

Barker, C. J. *The Johannine Epistles*. A Lutterworth Commentary. London: Lutterworth, 1948.

Barker, Glenn. "1 John." In *The Expositor's Bible Commentary*. Grand Rapids: Zondervan, 1981, vol. 12, pp. 291-358.

Barton, Bruce B., et al. *1, 2, & 3 John*. Life Application Bible Commentary. Wheaton, Ill.: Tyndale House, 1998.

Bauer, Walter. *A Greek-English Lexicon of the New Testament* and *Other Early Christian Literature*. Rev. Frederick William Danker. 3rd ed. Chicago: University of Chicago Press, 2000.

Beale, G. K., and D. A. Carson, eds. *Commentary on the New Testament Use of the Old Testament*. Grand Rapids: Baker, 2007.

Berkouwer, G. C. *Faith and Santification*. Grand Rapids: Eerdmans, 1952.

Black, C. Clifton. "The First, Second, and Third Letters of John." In *The New Interpreter's Bible*. Nashville: Abingdon, 1998, vol. 12, pp. 363-469.

Boice, James Montgomery. *The Epistles of John: An Expositional Commentary*. Grand Rapids: Zondervan, 1979.

Bray, Gerald, ed. *James, 1-2 Peter, 1-3 John, Jude*. Ancient Christian Commentary on Scripture. Downers Grove, Ill.: InterVarsity, 2000.

Bromiley, Geoffrey W., ed. *Theological Dictionary of the New Testament*. Abridged ed. Grand Rapids: Eerdmans, 1985.

Brooke, A. E. *A Critical and Exegetical Commentary on the Johannine Epistles*. International Critical Commentary. Edinburgh: T & T Clark, 1912.

Brown, Colin, ed. *The New International Dictionary of New Testament Theology*. 3 vols. Grand Rapids: Zondervan, 1978.

Brown, Raymond E. *The Epistles of John*. The Anchor Bible. New York: Doubleday, 1982.

Bruce, F. F. *The Epistles of John*. Grand Rapids: Eerdmans, 1970.

Brunner, Emil. *The Mediator*. New York: Macmillan, 1934.

Burge, Gary M. *The Letters of John*. The NIV Application Commentary. Grand Rapids: Zondervan, 1996.

Buttrick, George Arthur, ed. *The Interpreter's Dictionary of the Bible*. 4 vols. Nashville: Abingdon, 1962.

Calvin, John. *Commentaries on the Catholic Epistles*. Trans. John Owen. Grand Rapids: Baker, 1999.

Dodd, C. H. *The Johannine Epistles*. Moffat New Testament Commentary. New York: Harper and Brothers, 1946.

Douglass, Herbert E. *Why Jesus Waits*. Rev. ed. [Riverside, Calif.]: Upward Way, 1987.

Findlay, George G. *Studies in John's Epistles: Fellowship in the Life Eternal*. Grand Rapids: Kregel, 1989.

Freedman, David Noel, ed. *The Anchor Bible Dictionary*. 6 vols. New York: Doubleday, 1992.

Grayston, Kenneth. *The Johannine Epistles*. New Century Bible Commentary, Grand Rapids: Eerdmans, 1984.

Green, Gene L. *The Letters to the Thessalonians*. Pillar New Testament Commentary. Grand Rapids: Eerdmans, 2002.

Guthrie, Donald. *New Testament Introduction*. 4th ed. Downers Grove, Ill.: InterVarsity, 1990.

Hoon, Paul W. "Exposition" of 1, 2, 3 John. In *The Interpreter's Bible*. Nashville: Abingdon, 1957, vol. 12, pp. 216-313.

Houlden, J. L. *A Commentary on the Johannine Epistles*. Harpers New Testament Commentaries. Peabody, Mass.: Hendrickson, 1973.

Jackman, David. *The Message of John's Letters: Living in the Love of God*. The Bible Speaks Today. Downers Grove, Ill.: InterVarsity, 1988.

Johnson, Thomas F. *1, 2, and 3 John*. New International Biblical Commentary. Peabody, Mass.: Hendrickson, 1993.

Keener, Craig S. *The IVP Bible Background Commentary: New Testament*. Downers Grove, Ill.: InterVarsity, 1993.

Kelley, Dean M. *Why Conservative Churches Are Growing: A Study in Sociology of Religion*. New York: Harper and Row, 1972.

Kittel, Gerhard, and Gerhard Friedrich, eds. *Theological Dictionary of the New Testament*. 10 vols. Grand Rapids: Eerdmans, 1964-1976.

Knight, George R. *Angry Saints*. Washington, D.C.: Review and Herald, 1989.

———. *The Cross of Christ: God's Work for Us*. Hagerstown, Md.: Review and Herald, 2008.

Kraemer, Hendrik. *Why Christianity of All Religions?* Philadelphia: Westminster, 1962.

Kruse, Colin G. *The Letters of John*. The Pillar New Testament Commentary. Grand Rapids: Eerdmans, 2000.

Kysar, Robert. *I, II, III John*. Augusburg Commentary on the New Testament. Minneapolis: Augsburg, 1986.

Laurin, Roy L. *First John: Life at its Best*. Grand Rapids: Kregel, 1987.

Law, Robert. *The Tests of Life: A Study of the First Epistle of St. John*. 3rd ed. Grand Rapids: Baker, 1968.

Lenski, R.C.H. *The Interpretation of the Epistles of St. Peter, St. John, and St. Jude*. Minneapolis: Augsburg, 1966.

Lewis, C. S. *Mere Christianity*. New York: Macmillan, 1960.

———. *The Problem of Pain*. New York: Macmillan, 1962.

Lewis, Greville P. *The Johannine Epistles*. Epworth Preacher's Commentaries. London: Epworth, 1961.

Lloyd-Jones, Martyn. *Children of God: Studies in 1 John*. Wheaton, Ill.: Crossway, 1993.

———. *Fellowship With God: Studies in 1 John*. Wheaton, Ill.: Crossway, 1993.

———. *The Love of God: Studies in 1 John*. Wheaton, Ill.: Crossway, 1994.

————. *Walking With God: Studies in 1 John*. Wheaton, Ill.: Crossway, 1993.

MacLaren, Alexander. *John, Jude and Revelation*. Expositions of Holy Scripture. Grand Rapids: Eerdmans, 1938.

Marshall, I. Howard. *The Epistles of John*. New International Commentary on the New Testament. Grand Rapids: Eerdmans, 1978.

Martin, Ralph P., and Peter H. Davids., eds. *Dictionary of the Later New Testament and Its Developments*. Downers Grove, Ill.: InterVarsity, 1997.

Morris, Leon. "1 John." "2 and 3 John." In *The New Bible Commentary*. Rev. ed. Grand Rapids: Eerdmans, 1970, pp. 1259-1273.

————. *New Testament Theology*. Grand Rapids: Zondervan, 1986.

————. *The Atonement: Its Meaning and Significance*. Downers Grove, Ill.: InterVarsity, 1983.

Nichol, Francis D., ed. "The First Epistle General of John." In *The Seventh-day Adventist Bible Commentary*. Washington, D.C.: Review and Herald, 1953-1957, vol. 7, pp. 621-680.

Plummer, Alfred. *The Epistles of St John*. The Cambridge Bible for Schools and Colleges. Cambridge: Cambridge University Press, 1886.

————. *The Gospel According to St John*. The Cambridge Bible for Schools and Colleges. Cambridge: Cambridge University Press, 1896.

Reeves, Thomas C. *The Empty Church: The Suicide of Liberal Christianity*. New York: Free Press, 1996.

Rensberger, David. *1 John, 2 John, 3 John*. Abingdon New Testament Commentaries. Nashville: Abingdon, 1997.

————. *The Epistles of John*. Westminster Bible Companion. Louisville: Westminster John Knox, 2001.

Richardson, Alan, ed. *A Theological Word Book of the Bible*. New York: Collier, 1950.

Roberts, J. W. *The Letters of John*. The Living Word Commentary. Austin, Tex.: R. B. Sweet, 1968.

Rogers, Cleon L., Jr., and Cleon L. Rogers III. *The New Linguistic and Exegetical Key to the Greek New Testament*. Grand Rapids: Zondervan, 1998.

Ross, Alexander. *The Epistles of James and John*. The New International Commentary on the New Testament. Grand Rapids: Eerdmans, 1954.

Schnackenburg, Rudolf. *The Johannine Epistles*. Tunbridge Wells, Kent, Eng.: Burns and Oates, 1992.

Smalley, Stephen S. *1, 2, 3 John*. Word Biblical Commentary. Dallas: Word, 1984.

Smith, David, "The Epistles of John." In *The Expositor's Greek Testament*. Grand Rapids: Eerdmans, n.d., vol. 5, pp. 149-208.

Smith, D. Moody. *First, Second, and Third John*. Interpretation: A Bible Commentary for Teaching and Preaching. Louisville: John Knox, 1991.

Spicq, Ceslas. *Theological Lexicon of the New Testament*. 3 vols. Peabody, Mass.: Hendrickson, 1994.

Stott, John R. W. *The Letters of John*. 2nd ed. Tyndale New Testament Commentaries. Grand Rapids: Eerdmans, 1988.

Tenney, Merrill C., ed. *The Zondervan Pictorial Encyclopedia of the Bible*. 5 vols. Grand Rapids: Zondervan, 1976.

Thatcher, Tom. "1 John," "2 John," "3 John." In *The Expositor's Bible Commentary*. Rev. ed. Grand Rapids: Zondervan, 2006, vol. 13, pp. 413-538.

Thayer, Joseph H. *Thayer's Greek-English Lexicon of the New Testament*. Peabody, Mass.: Hendrickson, n.d.

Thompson, Marianne Meye. *1-3 John*. The IVP New Testament Commentary Series. Downers Grove, Ill.: InterVarsity, 1992.

Vine, W. E. *The Epistles of John: Light, Love, Life*. Grand Rapids: Zondervan, 1956.

Wesley, John. *The Works of John Wesley*. 14 vols. 3rd ed. Peabody, Mass.: Hendrickson, 1984.

Westcott, Brooke Foss, *The Epistles of St John*. Grand Rapids: Eerdmans, 1952.

White, Ellen G. *Steps to Christ*. Mountain View, Calif.: Pacific Press, 1956.

————. *The Desire of Ages*. Mountain View, Calif.: Pacific Press, 1940.

White, R.E.O. *Open Letter to Evangelicals: A Devotional and Homiletic Commentary on the First Epistle of John*. Grand Rapids: Eerdmans, 1964.

Wilder, Amos N. "Exegesis" of 1, 2, 3 John. In *The Interpreter's Bible*. Nashville: Abingdon, 1957, vol. 12, pp. 216-313.

Williams, R. R. *The Letters of John and James*. The Cambridge Bible Commentary. Cambridge: Cambridge University Press, 1965.

Witherington, Ben, III. *Letters and Homilies for Hellenized Christians: A Socio-Rhetorical Commentary on Titus, 1-2 Timothy and 1-3 John*. Downers Grove, Ill.: IVP Academic, 2006.

Wuest, Kenneth S. *Wuest's Word Studies From the Greek New Testament*. 3 vols. Grand Rapids: Eerdmans, 1973.

Yarbrough, Robert. "3 John." In *Zondervan Illustrated Bible Backgrounds Commentary*. Grand Rapids: Zondervan, 2002, vol. 4, pp. 220-227.

Part I

Setting the Stage

1 John 1:1-4

1. Witness to the Word of Life

1 John 1:1-4

> *¹That which was from the beginning, which we have heard, which we have seen with our eyes, which we gazed upon and touched with our hands, concerning the Word of Life. ²And the life was revealed and we have seen it and testify and proclaim to you the eternal life which was with the Father and was revealed to us. ³We proclaim that which we have seen and we have heard even to you, that you also may have fellowship with us. And our fellowship is with the Father and with His Son Jesus Christ. ⁴And we write these things that our joy may be filled up.*

That which was from the beginning" (1:1). It is almost impossible not to think of the first words of the Fourth Gospel when reading the letter's first words: "In the beginning was the Word, and the Word was with God, and the Word was God" (John 1:1, RSV). Yet "the beginning" in each document is not the same. The Gospel refers to the pre-incarnate Christ who existed with the Father throughout eternity and was an active agent in creation. First John, on the other hand, is speaking of the incarnate Christ whom John and the other apostles had heard, seen, and touched (1 John 1:1-3).

The real parallelism between the Gospel and 1 John is not found in "the beginning" but in that Jesus "the Word was God" (John 1:1) and that "the Word became flesh and dwelt among us" as "the only Son from the Father" (John 1:14, RSV). It was the incarnation and the fact that Jesus of Nazareth was the divine Christ that the dissidents whom John wrote against in his letter were denying (1 John 4:2; 2:22). And it was the reality that Jesus was the divine Christ and had truly taken on human flesh that 1 John will pound home repeatedly throughout the letter (1:1, 2; 2:23; 3:8, 23; 4:2, 9, 10, 11, 15; 5:1). That the recipients of 1 John had those truths from "the beginning" of their Christian experience (2:24) implies that they had been instructed regarding the incarnation, life, and death of Jesus on the basis of the content of the Fourth Gospel, even if the apostle only presented his recollections to them in oral form.

Be that as it may, the important point is that John and his fellow apostles had had personal experience with the incarnate Christ. Their knowledge of Jesus was not some figment of their imagination, not something they had made up. To the contrary, they had "heard" Him (1:1, 3). It was from the incarnate Christ that John had received the gospel message that he had taught his converts from the beginning of their Christian experience (2:7, 24; 3:11).

Having heard was good, but John's personal contact with the incarnate Christ extended beyond the auditory. He had actually seen Christ with his own eyes. Four times in three verses the apostle tells us that he had viewed the God who had incarnated Himself in human flesh.

First John uses two quite different words for the apostle's visual witness to Jesus. The first is *horaō,* which signifies seeing something with one's physical eye. But the second is *theaomai,* which I have translated as "gaze upon." To gaze at someone, or at something, signifies not merely the act of seeing but of taking a long look until one has grasped "the meaning and the significance of that person or thing" (Barclay, p. 27; cf. C. Brown, vol. 3, p. 512). It means to "view attentively" or to "contemplate" (Wuest, vol. 2, sec. 3, p. 92). Thus it was that in his prologue to the Fourth Gospel John says "we have beheld [*theaomai*] his glory" (John 1:14, RSV). Or as Kenneth Wuest renders it in his *Expanded Translation,* "we gazed with attentive and careful regard and spiritual perception at his glory." The idea underlying *theaomai* is not that of a quick glance, but of a "steadfast searching gaze." Barclay notes that "a quick glance at Christ never made a man a Christian" (Barclay, p. 27).

Now hearing, seeing, and gazing upon Christ may have been good and helpful, but they weren't enough to satisfy all of the questions that had led to the problem in John's congregation. As John Stott points out, "to have *heard* was not enough; people 'heard' God's voice in the Old Testament. To have *seen* was more compelling. But to have *touched* was the conclusive proof of material reality, that the Word 'became flesh, and lived for a while among us'" (Stott, p. 65). Once again, the Greek word used for "touched" implies more than momentary contact, but has the sense of "examine closely" (Brooke, p. 5).

All in all, the apostle is claiming that he and his fellow disciples had had significant and in-depth experiences in hearing, seeing, and touching the earthly Jesus Christ. Those experiences were of the utmost importance in the context in which John was writing. As noted in the introduction to 1 John, the acids of Greco-Roman philosophy had eaten into the belief structure and social fabric of the Christians in John's Ephesian sphere of influence. The apostle Paul had told the church in Ephesus at the conclusion of his final visit with them that "I know that after my departure fierce wolves will come in among you, not sparing the flock; and from among your own selves will arise men speaking perverse things, to draw away the disciples after them" (Acts 20:29, 30, RSV).

That time had arrived. The problem that John was facing was that members had departed from the Christian fellowship (1 John 2:19). They had not only disrupted things by leaving it themselves, but they were aggressively and abrasively promoting further schism by claiming to have superior and essential knowledge to those who remained, even more advanced than that of the apostle himself. The particular focus of that knowledge centered on the idea that Jesus could not possibly be the Christ, since God would never take human form (2:22; 4:2). Only a simpleton, they implied, could accept something so irrational. After all, spirit is good and matter is evil, and therefore the good representative of God (Christ) could not possibly come in human flesh. Thus Jesus was not Christ. The divine Christ only appeared to have taken genuine flesh.

In response, George Findlay asserts, "the Apostle John confronts the Gnostic metaphysicians of his time, and the Agnostic materialists of ours, with his impressive declaration" of personal experience. "Of what use was it for men at a distance," he claims, "to argue that this thing and that thing could not be? 'I tell you,' says the great Apostle, 'we have seen it with our eyes, we have heard Him with our very ears; we have touched and tested and handled these things at every point, and we know that they are so'" (Findlay, p. 104).

John writes that he not only knows the truth about the incarnation of

Christ, but that his mission is to "testify and proclaim . . . the eternal life [i.e., Jesus] which was with the Father and was revealed to us" (1 John 1:2). Here is an important point. John didn't receive his understanding of the person and message of Christ to enjoy to himself. Positively not! He was to testify and proclaim its truth. And that same commission is for every other minister throughout history. In fact, it is for every Christian.

It is the loss of the certainty of the message on the person and atoning work of Christ in our era, Martyn Lloyd-Jones asserts, "that accounts for so much of the present state of the Church." Whereas dogmatism is out of place in many areas, he points out that it is quite appropriate to be dogmatic regarding what was clearly revealed to the apostles regarding Christ and His atoning ministry. "We should be modest about our own opinions and careful as to how we voice our own speculations, but here, thank God, we are not in such a realm. . . . The gospel, according to the New Testament, is a herald; it is like a man with a trumpet who is calling people to listen. There is nothing tentative about what he has to say; something has been delivered unto him, and his business is to repeat it" (Lloyd-Jones, *Fellowship*, p. 46).

John realized the centrality of the incarnation and the atoning work of Jesus Christ. He recognized that to lose or downplay those teachings was ultimately to destroy the Christian message.

The apostle witnessed the problem in its early years. We are seeing it today in full bloom. Our postmodern fear of asserting claims of absolute Truth and the New Age mentality that suggests that all religions lead to the same place are attitudes that have shipwrecked much of modern Christianity. We see their results reflected by such insightful books as Dean Kelley's *Why Conservative Churches Are Growing* and Thomas Reeves' *The Empty Church: The Suicide of Liberal Christianity*.

Hendrick Kraemer in *Why Christianity of All Religions?* caught the essence of the message of 1 John 1:1-4 when he wrote that Christians have too often confused truth with "bigheartedness." He penned a sentence that John could agree with when he noted that "the absolutely distinctive and peculiar and unique element in Christianity is the *fact* of Jesus Christ" (Kraemer, pp. 39, 80).

The apostle knew that the truth of the incarnate Christ who died for our sins (1 John 2:2) and mediates for us before the Father (verse 1) is the very core of Christianity. To destroy and downplay those insights will dis-rupt the fellowship of Christians (1:3) and fracture the joy of salvation for individual church members (1:4).

We will return to the topic of fellowship and the filling up of Christians with joy in subsequent discussions, since John tells us that the reason he wrote his letter is directly related to those topics (1:3; 5:13). In the meantime, we need to shift our focus to themes of light and darkness as we follow the apostle into verses 5-7 of his first chapter.

Part II

God Is Light

1 John 1:5-2:27

2. Walking in the Light

1 John 1:5-7

⁵This is the message which we have heard from Him and proclaim to you, that God is light and there is absolutely no darkness in Him. ⁶If we say that we have fellowship with Him yet are walking in the darkness, we lie and are not practicing the truth. ⁷But if we walk in the light as He is in the light, we have fellowship with one another and the blood of Jesus His Son cleanses us from all sin.

One of the most universal human activities is that of creating God in our own image. Or as one person put it: "If God made man in his own image, . . . then man has returned the compliment" (Jackman, p. 26).

And I must admit that having a god like us has certain advantages. After all, such a god would think like us, hold our value system, and act like us. Thus, for example, we find many people in our day who fervently claim to believe in god (or their "higher power"), and pray daily, yet have no problem having a sexual partner out-

> "If God made man in His own image, . . . then man has returned the compliment."
> —David Jackman

side of a marriage relationship. Of course, some are quick to add, even regarding their homosexual relationships, that it must be a "responsible" relationship.

The good news is that they have a convenient god, one who fits their desires and needs perfectly. The bad news is that such a deity has no roots in reality. It is purely an extension of its creator's thoughts and values.

There is nothing new or modern about such projections. Most of the people whom John was writing to had been taught in their pre-Christian life to worship Zeus and Hermes (Acts 14:12); Artemis of the Ephesians (Acts 19:34); Dionysus (or Bacchus), the god of wine and revelry; and Aphrodite, the many-breasted goddess of love. The deities of the Greco-Roman world could lie, cheat, commit adultery with one another, and be spiteful toward each other and humans. In short, the gods were like sinful people, only more powerful. Thus they were mixtures of good and evil, kindness and cruelty, darkness and light.

It was into such a world that the apostle shot his message "that God is light and there is absolutely no darkness in Him" (1:5). Perhaps nothing he had to say was more revolutionary. To set forth a God who is absolute rectitude, wisdom, and love should have produced nothing but relief and worship in the human mind. To know such a God would be to pass out of darkness into marvelous light.

But what should have been and reality are not the same thing. You see, a God of goodness creates a problem. And that problem finds its roots in sinful human nature. Most of us don't really want that kind of a God, especially if we are expected to be like Him. As a result, we construct and substitute a deity more in line with our desires, one who doesn't frown on a little hanky panky on the side, or even at the center. And thus it is that idol worship continues on into the postmodern age. David Jackman is profoundly astute when he writes that "all sin is in essence an attack upon the character of God" (Jackman, p. 26).

John's revolutionary proclamation is that "God is light and there is absolutely no darkness in Him" (1:5). The contrast between light and darkness runs throughout the Bible. It associates light with such things as splendor and glory, radiance, purity, and guidance into truth, whereas it identifies darkness with chaos, unfruitfulness, hostility, error, and godlessness.

The Fourth Gospel is big on light and darkness. The apostle not only sets forth Jesus as the "true light that enlightens" every person (John 1:9, RSV), but ties the divine light to ethical living when he writes that "men loved darkness rather than light, because their deeds were evil. For every one who does evil hates the light, and does not come to the light, lest his deeds should be exposed. But he who does what is true comes to the light, that it may be clearly seen that his deeds have been wrought in God" (John 3:19-21, RSV).

First John portrays the same connection between light/darkness and ethical living. "If we say we have fellowship with Him yet are walking in the darkness, we lie and are not practicing the truth" (1 John 1:6). "Here," Alexander Ross writes, "the 'son of thunder' speaks" as "he hurls a shattering thunderbolt against the deadly heresy of Antinomianism" or lawlessness (Ross, p. 142). John isn't beating around the bush. Political correctness is not his strong suit. To him people who claim to be Christians while living a life of sin are nothing but liars. We should note that the metaphor of walking in its present tense signifies a way of life rather than an occasional act that is repented of. It is those who are not repentant, who see nothing wrong with their lives, who fall under the apostle's condemnation.

In using the phrase "if we say" (1:6) John is reflecting upon the claims of those who were tearing apart the churches with their false theologies. He will repeat the same phrase in verses 8 and 10. Apparently the secessionists were not only claiming to have fellowship with God even

> **Doing the Truth**
>
> "The 'truth' has no exclusive reference to the sphere of the intellect. It expresses that which is highest, most completely in conformity with the nature and will of God, in any sphere of being. In relation to man it has to do with his whole nature, moral and spiritual as well as intellectual. 'Speaking' the truth is only one part of 'doing' the truth, and not the most important. To 'do the truth' is to give expression to the highest of which he is capable in every sphere of his being" (Brooke, p. 14).

as they lived sinful lives, but also that they had not committed sinful acts that they needed to repent of (1:8-10). John has only one word for such an attitude: "darkness" (1:6). They were in the dark, confused, and didn't know where they were going either intellectually or ethically.

By way of contrast, the apostle viewed practicing or doing the truth (1:6) and walking in the light as a way of life and as the path of honesty and hope (1:7). But that is too much for those who want fellowship with God on easy terms—their own terms. Their solution is to divorce religion and ethics. They are happy to have a caring God, just as long as he doesn't get into their business and tell them what to do or what not to do. Such was the gnostic heresy of not only the early church, but of every age.

John wants nothing to do with such darkness of mind and spirit. To him, all who propound such theological drivel are nothing short of being liars. The unity of religion (a correct relationship to God) and theology (a correct understanding about God) are intimately and necessarily tied to ethical living. "For our author there is no hard-and-fast line between be-lief and behavior, between theology and ethics. Ethics is just putting one's theology into practice, doing the truth" (Witherington, p. 451). Put in an-other way, "Whereas, for Gnostics, 'God is light' is merely a mystical no-tion to 'get lost in,' for John it immediately spells God's absolute ethical demand upon men" (Alexander, p. 47). That is, God's light helps us see how we should live.

And once we see, we need to do the truth, to practice it, to live a life of walking in the light. And when "we walk in the light as He is in the light, we have fellowship with one another and the blood of Jesus His Son cleanses us from all sin" (1:7).

According to verse 7, walking in the light has two important results. First, it puts us in fellowship with other Christians. That statement comes as a surprise to the careful reader. Since it is fellowship with God that is denied those who walk in darkness, we would naturally expect to find that walking in the light leads to fellowship with God rather than with one an-other. But we find an important truth here. The way John puts it high-lights the fact that "there is no real fellowship with God which is not expressed in fellowship with other believers" (Kruse, p. 64). Too many Christians act as if they can be right with God while at the same time treat-ing other people unkindly and unlovingly (see 1 John 2:9). Such can never be. Those who have fellowship with God *will* have a healthy respect for and relationship with other people. That is one of the implications of Jesus' discussion of the two great commandments (Matt. 22:36-40), and it under-girds the unity of the two tables of the Decalogue. A correct relationship to God *necessitates* a caring relationship with other people. Any separation of the two is darkness rather than light.

A second benefit from walking in the light is cleansing from all sin by the blood of Jesus (1 John 1:7). While this is the only explicit reference to blood in 1 John, we find it also implied in the fact that Jesus came to be the "Savior of the world" (4:14, RSV) and that He is the "atoning sacrifice for our sins" (4:10, NIV; cf. 2:2). Beyond that, the blood undergirds the ongoing forgiveness and justification of 1 John 1:9. The blood of the "Lamb of God" takes away the sins of the world and is foundational to each and every major metaphor for salvation in the Bible (see Knight, *Cross*, pp. 78, 79).

In its context, cleansing from sin in verse 7 seems to suggest not only forgiveness but empowerment for holy living. And the best news is that the cleansing work is not a once-for-all-time event but an ongoing process expressed in the Greek by the present tense. Thus John Calvin, the great sixteenth-century reformer, notes that "this passage shews that the gratuitous pardon of sins is given us not only once, but that it is a benefit perpetually residing in the Church, and daily offered to the faithful" (Calvin, p. 165).

We can thank God daily for His continuing grace, a topic that we will treat more fully in our next reading.

3. Facing Up to My Sins

1 John 1:8-10

⁸If we say that we have no sin, we deceive ourselves and the truth is not in us. ⁹If we confess our sins, He is faithful and just, He forgives our sins and cleanses us from all unrighteousness. ¹⁰If we say that we have not sinned, we make Him a liar and His word is not in us.

In verses 8-10 John deals with the problem of those who were claiming to be in fellowship with God even as they walked in darkness and were not living according to the truth. Such people, he writes in no uncertain terms, were liars (1:6). In order to grasp the unity of the passage that begins at verse 5 and runs into chapter 2, it is helpful to examine its structure. The most obvious element tying the section together is the three denials of the secessionists:

1. "*If we say* that we have fellowship with Him yet are walking in the darkness" (1:6).
2. "*If we say* that we have no sin" (1:8).
3. "*If we say* that we have not sinned" (1:10).

To each of those boasts John affixes a result:

1. "*We lie* and are not practicing the truth" (1:6).
2. "*We deceive ourselves* and the truth is not in us" (1:8).
3. "*We make Him a liar* and His word is not in us" (1:10).

Both the denials and the results indicate a progression of thought. For example, their walking in darkness led the secessionists into the self deception that they were not guilty of committing sins. We likewise find a progression in boasting, except it is even more explicit. First, the passage says that those who make such claims are liars. Second, it claims that they have believed their own lie and have thereby managed to deceive themselves. And finally, worst of all, the boasters have made God out to be a liar. "Here," Ben Witherington points out, "is a description of . . . regress into darkness, involving both arrogance and wickedness" (Witherington, p. 450). John's analysis points to the fact that sin leads step by step from bad to worse. Such people as he is writing about, of course, have no hope of fellowship with God. Then again, who can have hope, given the fact that "all have sinned" (Rom. 3:23, RSV)?

But, but, but! "But" may be one of the most important words in all of Scripture. John's analysis doesn't stop with sin's results. He consistently moves beyond its dire consequences to hope in all three of his sequences:

1. "*But if* we walk in the light as He is in the light" (1:7).

2. But "*if we confess our sins*" (1:9).

3. "*But if* anyone sins" (2:1).

Here we find shades of the gospel, with John saving the best for last in each sequence. His logic follows a pattern: (1) people have boasted falsely, (2) serious results followed their arrogance, (3) "but" all is not lost if they take action to correct the problem, and (4) such action leads to redemptive healing and to fellowship with God and others.

Thus the second set of conditional statements also has results—good ones this time. If we walk in the light and confess our sins:

1. a. "We have fellowship with one another"

   b. and "the blood of Jesus His Son cleanses us from all sin" (1:7).

2. a. "He forgives our sins"

   b. and He "cleanses us from all unrighteousness" (1:9).

3. a. "We have an Advocate with the Father" (2:1)

   b. and "He is the atoning sacrifice for our sins" (2:2, NIV).

In concluding our examination of the unity and flow of the passage beginning in 1 John 1:5, we need constantly to keep in mind the problem afflicting the apostle's congregations: Those with false understanding of the nature of Christ were also living out of harmony with God's will. To put it bluntly, they were lost in darkness. They needed help. But, as we noted earlier, John isn't writing to the dissenters. He penned his letter to those who were still in the church, but were becoming confused and required guidance. It is to those faithful ones that the apostle provides some of the most helpful discussion in the Bible concerning God's redemptive plan of reconciliation. Of course, the dissenters could also come back on board by accepting and following John's counsel. And beyond just hope for those two groups is the good news that the healing hope John sets forth in 1 John 1:5-2:11 is for us also. That passage is pregnant with promise for you and me. It's as meaningful today as it was 2,000 years ago.

At this point we must examine more fully the implications of 1 John 1:8-10. When verse 8 notes that the secessionists claimed to "have no sin" they were not asserting that they had a sinless human nature, but rather that they were not guilty of committing acts of sin. The result of their claim is that they were suffering from ongoing self-deception which, as we shall see in verse 9, shut them out from any real hope.

Verse 9 indicates the depth of their hopelessness, and by way of contrast, the abundant hope of those who remain faithful to the gospel message. "If we confess our sins."

No one confesses sins that they deny. Thus the desperate situation of those opposing John.

On the other hand, those who continually confess their sinful acts will be both justified and cleansed. The tense of the Greek verb indicates the ongoing nature of the confession. Confession and forgiveness are not once-for-all sorts of things. Rather, the bountiful nature of God's forgiving grace is of the seventy times seven sort that Jesus taught (see Matt. 18:22). God's amazing grace has an astounding depth to it. As many times as we confess, God extends forgiving grace. That's the gospel truth!

> ## Better and Better Eyesight
>
> "In fellowship with Christ our eye becomes ever keener and keener for sin, especially for *our* sin. It is precisely the mature Christian who calls himself a great sinner" (Findlay, p. 123).

But, please note, the apostle said we needed to confess "*our* sins." Most of us would rather talk about other people's problems. Whether we like it or not, we are all a bit deceived and tempted toward denial regarding our personal shortcomings (1 John 1:8). That's why God gave us the Holy Spirit: to wake us up, to convict us of sin, and to lead us to repentance (John 16:8).

When we confess, the apostle writes, God "is faithful and just, He forgives our sins and cleanses us from all unrighteousness" (1 John 1:9). Here the word "faithfulness" reminds us of God's new covenant promise: "I will forgive their iniquity, and I will remember their sin no more" (Jer. 31:34. RSV; cf. Heb. 8:12). Forgiving sin is a part of the covenant blessing.

Thus John describes God as being faithful in that act. That is plain enough. "But," John Stott asks, "how can he also be described as *just* when he forgives us our sins?" (Stott, p. 83). After all, sinners by definition have rebelled against God and deserve to be punished by the God who "will by no means clear the guilty" (Ex. 34:7, RSV).

Here is the divine dilemma. On what basis can God forgive the guilty and still remain just and righteous? Leon Morris notes that in the face of such forgiveness "you can argue that this shows God to be merciful, or compassionate, or kind, or forbearing, or loving. But you cannot argue that it shows him to be *just*" (Morris, *Atonement*, p. 195). It is a problem, Colin Kruse notes, "which the apostle Paul had to deal with when explaining his gospel in Romans 3:21-26, and his resolution of the problem was that God can be both just and the justifier of sinners because he set forth Christ as the atoning sacrifice (*hilastērion*) for their sins. The author of 1 John does not state the matter as clearly as Paul does, but it is plain that he, too, understands God to be righteous [i.e., just] in forgiving those who confess their sins because he sent his Son to be the atoning sacrifice [*hilasmos*] for their sins [2:2]" (Kruse, p. 70). With that thought in mind, it is contextually significant that John's next few verses turn to the atoning work of Christ, whom he sets forth in the Fourth Gospel as the "Lamb of God, who takes away the sin of the world" (John 1:29, RSV).

Meanwhile, 1 John 1:10 tells us that "if we say that we have not sinned, we make Him a liar and His word is not in us." As in verses 8 and 9, John is still referring to acts of sin. The difference between verses 8 and 10 is not the nature of sin, but who is being implicated as a liar. In verse 8 it is those who are making the claim that they don't commit acts of sin, while in verse 10 it is God.

The question that begs to be asked is how is it that a human denial of committing sin makes God a liar? While John does not explain his argument, the logic is clear enough. It goes something like this:

1. God says all human beings are sinners (see Paul's documented argument in Romans 1:18-3:23, especially 3:9-20, 23).

2. The dissenters claim that they don't commit sins.
3. If they are right, then God is wrong.
4. Therefore, by making the claim not to sin they are making God a liar.

And such an accusation, John might have added, is as serious as sinning gets. But we don't want to end this section with such a thought. The main thrust of John's presentation, we need to remember, is intended, not to point out the problems of the schismatics, but to provide hope and joy for the faithful (1 John 1:4; 5:13). With that in mind, the most significant statement in 1 John 1:5-10 is that "if we confess our sins, He is faithful and just, He forgives our sins and cleanses us from all unrighteousness" (verse 9). That promise is for each of us for every day of our lives.

4. God's Answer to the Sin Problem

1 John 2:1, 2

> ¹*My little children, I am writing these things to you so that you will not sin. But if anyone sins, we have an Advocate with the Father, Jesus Christ the righteous; ²and He is the propitiation [atoning sacrifice] for our sins; yet not for ours only but also for those of the whole world.*

What a change! Between 1 John 1:10 and the first verse in chapter 2 the apostle has shifted from thundering about liars to "my little children." But there is a good reason for the transition. John here moved away from discussing the problems of the secessionists and toward the needs of his faithful flock.

That change brings with it words of endearment. "My little children" should be thought of as "my dear children." Yet the words reflect not only his pastoral affection for them but also his age. John has been around a long time. It has been a half century since the Crucifixion, and he is an old man, perhaps the last person alive who actually walked and talked with the earthly Jesus. Yet he hasn't lost touch with His spirit. "He remembered how the Master had dealt with His disciples, and he would deal with his people after the same fashion and be to them what Jesus had been to himself—as gentle and patient" (David Smith, p. 173). John in his "little children" address is modeling the heart of every genuine pastor.

He tells his parishioners that he is "writing these things to you so that you will not sin" (2:1). By "these things" he refers to 1 John 1:6-10, in which he dealt with the issue of owning up to one's sins and confessing them. In chapter 2 the issue of sin is still very much at the forefront of his thinking. And for good reasons. For one thing, sin, which he defines as "law-lessness" (3:4), is destructive to both individual lives and the fellowship of the community. As such, the apostle hates sin. Robert Law observes that "horror, hatred, fear, repudiation of sin pervade the whole Epistle" (Law, p. 128).

Yet confessed sin, John had pointed out, could be forgiven. And if it could be forgiven, some might be tempted to think, why make such a fuss about it. In fact, what is the use of struggling against sin if it is an inevitable part of the human situation?

It is in response to such a line of thought that John unequivocally states that it is God's will for His children not to sin. Now that is a wonderful ideal. But the apostle is also a realist, as we saw in 1 John 1:8, 10, in which he declared that anyone who claimed to never sin was a liar and made God into a liar.

The sad fact is that people do sin. But the good fact is that God in His understanding mercy made provision to cover the human situation. Thus, John writes, if anyone does sin, "we have an Advocate with the Father, Jesus Christ the righteous" (2:1). Before discussing God's solution to the sin problem, it is crucial to note that verse 1 is not talking about dwelling in a state of sinful rebellion or living life as a "sinner." Rather the apostle has in mind single acts of sin, a fact made clear by his Greek verb tense. For John, as we will see in our discussion of chapters 3 and 5, a vast difference exists between acts of sin and living the life of a sinner. The first, he described as a sin not unto death, while the second is impossible for the Christian and is unto death (3:9; 5:16, 17, KJV). Acts of sin were not "unto death" because of God's solution to the sin crisis. But there can be no solution for those who have opted to live a sinful life in rebellion toward God and His law (2:4).

God's solution to the sin problem, as outlined by 1 John 1:6-2:2 has three aspects:

1. Confessed sin is forgiven (1:9).
2. Sinners have an Advocate (2:1).
3. Sinners have an atoning sacrifice (2:2).

We have discussed the forgiveness part of God's solution to the sin problem in our treatment of 1 John 1:9. But we have yet to examine the advocacy and atoning sacrifice aspects and the relationship between the three of them.

When John calls Christ our Advocate he uses the word *paraklētos*, which we transliterate into English as "paraclete." He is the only writer in the New Testament to use the word—here and four times in the Fourth Gospel. But in the Gospel it is the Holy Spirit sent by Christ who is the paraclete (John 14:26; 15:26; 16:7), while in 1 John it is Christ Himself. The most common meaning of *paraklētos* is "one who appears in another's behalf, *mediator, intercessor, helper*" (Bauer, p. 766). People of New Testament times often used the word to signify a witness in someone's favor or an advocate in their defense. Thus the *paraklētos* was one who pled one's case. That is the sense employed in 1 John 2:1.

While only that verse specifically refers to Jesus as our Advocate, several other places in the New Testament present the concept. Paul, for example, puts Jesus forth as the one who "intercedes for us" at "the right hand of God" (Rom. 8:34, RSV). But the fullest treatment of the topic appears in the book of Hebrews, which provides extensive treatment of the priestly ministry of Jesus in the heavenly sanctuary. Especially pertinent is Hebrews 7:25: "He is able to save fully and completely those coming to God through Him, because He continually lives to intercede for them."

> ### The "Unfinished" Work of Christ
> "We must recognize both the finished and unfinished work of Jesus Christ. As our High Priest in sacrifice before God His work is finished. As Advocate in sustaining us before the Father His work is unfinished" (Laurin, p. 52).

The best of the good news is that we have an Intercessor in heaven who shares the throne with God the Father. And as our Intercessor or Advocate He "does not maintain our innocence but confesses our guilt" (G. Barker, p. 313), just as we have previously confessed it. God utilizes Christ's heavenly ministry in forgiving His repentant people. Thus when we confess our sins, Christ represents us before the Father who "forgives our sins and cleanses us from all unrighteousness" (1 John 1:9). For that reason we may as Christians "with confidence draw near to the throne of grace, that we may receive mercy and find grace to help in time of need" (Heb. 4:16, RSV). We can thank God daily that we have an Advocate in heaven.

I need to make three further points before leaving the topic of Christ our Advocate. First, having an advocate does not mean that God is against us or out to get us. That will become clear in the discussion of the atoning sacrifice in the next few paragraphs. The Bible never depicts Jesus as begging for our forgiveness. Rather, it presents him as a victorious conqueror who died and rose again and sits on God's throne as an equal (Heb. 1:3; 7:26). Far from being a beggar, Christ intercedes as a victor who is more than willing to share the fruits of His triumph with those who come to Him seeking His help.

Second, we should note that no conflict exists between the roles of Christ and the Holy Spirit as our Paracletes. In promising the gift of the Spirit, Jesus told His disciples that He would send "another" Paraclete (John 14:16), thereby implying that He Himself is the primary Paraclete. Thus, just as we have an Advocate or Paraclete in heaven, so Jesus has one on earth. "But whereas the Holy Spirit pleads Christ's cause before a hostile world, Christ pleads our cause against our 'accuser' (Rev. 12:10) and *to the Father*, who loves" and is more than willing to forgive His repentant children (Stott, p. 86).

Third, when 1 John 2:1 refers to "Jesus Christ the righteous" it is alluding to His qualification to be our Advocate. His holy life gives Him standing before the universe and with the Father. The same connection appears in Hebrews 7, which qualifies the Intercessor (7:25) in terms of being "holy, innocent, undefiled, separated from sinners" (7:26). In other words, Christ's sinless life makes it possible for Him to be our Advocate in the eyes of the universe.

The final element of God's solution to the sin problem in 1 John 1:6-2:2 is the fact that Jesus is "the propitiation for our sins" (2:2). Now here is a theological word that has caused a great deal of discussion. "Propitiation" is a most unpopular term among large sectors of the theological community. One reason for that hostility is that the basic meaning of the term has to do with turning away wrath (see Richardson, p. 25). In the Greek world in which the New Testament arose, propitiation had the flavor of bribing the gods, demons, or the dead in an attempt to win their favor and get their blessing. Since the gods were "mad," one had to appease them. Thus worshippers offered sacrifices in an attempt to please the supernatural beings, buy back their favor, and avert their wrath (see Kittel, vol. 3, p. 311).

But to superimpose that pagan concept onto the New Testament is to overlook the biblical data on the topic. After all, the Bible does not picture God as being angry with people. While it is true that He hates sin, He loves those who have fallen into it. Thus we read that "*God so loved* the world that *he gave his only Son,* that whoever believes in him should not perish but have eternal life. For *God sent* the Son into the world, not to condemn the world, but that the world might be saved through him" (John 3:16, 17, RSV). We find the same message in 1 John, which declares that because "he loved us" God "sent his Son to be the propitiation for our sins" (4:10, KJV). Or as Ellen White so nicely put it: "The Father loves us, not because of the great propitiation, but He provided the propitiation because He loves us" (E. White, *Steps*, p. 13).

Propitiation is a word related to sacrifice, thus the NIV's translation of the word as "atoning sacrifice." In the context of 1 John, it is "the blood of Jesus" that "cleanses us from all sin" (1:7) and provides forgiveness and cleansing when we confess our sins (1:9). We have an Advocate in heaven (2:1) who takes our confessions to the Father who in His love for sinners is more than willing to forgive His repentant children on the basis of the fact that they have accepted Christ's atoning sacrifice (propitiation). Thus John, like Paul, places Christ's substitutionary sacrifice at the very foundation of the plan of salvation (see Rom. 3:21-26; Gal. 3:10-13).

Jesus is truly the "Lamb of God, who takes away the sin of the world" (John 1:29, RSV) through His death on Calvary. Thus 1 John 2:2 can forcefully proclaim that "He is the propitiation [atoning sacrifice as the Lamb of God] for our sins; yet not for ours only but also for those of the whole world."

The good news is that Jesus died for every person in history, even His enemies (Rom. 5:10). That is, His death made provision for every last person to be saved. But it is up to each individual to accept that gift (Eph. 2:8). "Whoever believes" in Christ and accepts Him as both Propitiation and Advocate has "eternal life" (John 3:16, RSV). That "whoever" includes you and me. There is no better time than right now to line up with John the apostle to accept God's gifts in Christ so that we might truly have "fellowship . . . with the Father and . . . His Son Jesus Christ" (1 John 1:3).

5. Knowing That We Know God

1 John 2:3-6

> *³Now by this we know that we have come to know Him, if we keep His commandments. ⁴The one saying "I have come to know Him," yet is not keeping His commandments, is a liar and the truth is not in that person. ⁵But whoever keeps His word, in that person the love for God has truly reached completeness. By this we know that we are in Him. ⁶The one claiming to live in Him ought to walk like He walked.*

John's first letter begins with a wave of ifs:

- "If we say that we have fellowship with Him yet are walking in the darkness" (1:6).
- "If we walk in the light" (1:7).
- "If we say that we have no sin" (1:8).
- "If we confess our sins" (1:9).
- "If we say that we have not sinned" (1:10).
- "If any one sins" (2:1).
- "If we keep His commandments" (2:3).

Through the repeated use of that short word the apostle sets up two ways of life that he deals with throughout his letter. On one side are those who claim fellowship with God but are disobedient, deny their sin, and walk in darkness. The other side finds those who walk in the light, confess their sins, rely on Jesus as their Advocate, and keep the commandments.

"If" may be a tiny word, but it doesn't lack forcefulness in the apostle's hands. He puts it to mighty use. John uses "if" in a conditional sense that ties actions to deeper meanings. That is, he repeatedly indicates that the actions and claims of individuals have a direct relationship to larger realities. Thus, for example, if we confess our sins, we are forgiven (1:9); if we sin, we have an Advocate who died in our place (2:1, 2).

But what if we claim forgiveness and the blood of Christ yet go on to live in deliberate transgression? It is the possibility of such abuse that John addresses in 1 John 2:3-6. He trumpets the message that combining a life of uncaring or rebellious sin with forgiveness is an impossibility and a delusion. It is one way or the other. No one who walks in darkness has fellowship with God (1:6).

For John, obedience and practical holiness follow forgiveness of sin. "As St Paul makes sanctification the concomitant of justification and works of love the proof of saving faith," George Findlay notes, "so with St John commandment keeping is the test of knowledge of a sin-pardoning God. A penitent backslider, like Peter, will be forgiven; but Peter was not a *calculating* backslider. . . . Deliberate transgression, on the part of one who presumes on God's mercy and discounts the guilt of sin by the value of the Atonement, is an act that shows the man to be ignorant of God" (Findlay, p. 152).

In short, John is no more into "cheap grace" than Paul, or James, or Jesus (see especially, Matt. 7:21-23). Christianity at its heart is living the Christlike life (2:6). There are no halfway Christians who have somehow managed to straddle 1 John's wall of "ifs." Each of us is on one side or the other.

That thought brings us to the topic of what it means "to know" God. Knowing God was just as important in the ancient world as it is to many people in our day. Four major avenues to knowing God existed in John's day. One was knowing God through the intellect. The ancient Greek philosophers approached knowing God as if religion were a series of mental problems. The goal of understanding God through intense mental activity is much like solving an equation in higher mathematics. While such a course may lead to intellectual satisfaction, it may not result in moral action or better relationships.

A second approach to knowing God in the ancient world focused on emotional experience. Thus the mystery religions in the early Roman Empire utilized heightened emotional liturgies that led worshippers to sense a unity with God. William Barclay is on target when he writes that the emotional route to religion was "not so much *knowing* God as *feeling* God" and that it functioned as "a kind of religious drug" (Barclay, p. 50).

A third way to God was through obedience. Certainly some of the Pharisees that Jesus had to deal with were on that track. Obedience became the dominating passion of their religious life. Yet it never led them to God. To the contrary, it diverted them away from Him and into religious self-satisfaction and pride, hypocrisy, and judgmentalism toward those who didn't live up to their standards of behavior. One of the great discoveries of Paul the former Pharisee was that obedience does not lead to God.

That conclusion may seem to be at odds with 1 John 2:3-6 with its statement that "by this we know that we have come to know Him, if we keep His commandments" (verse 3). But such an apparent contradiction leads us to way number four on how to know God.

That fourth avenue was through God's revelation of who He is. That revelation, which is at the heart of all biblical religion, tells people two things: first, that God is holy; and second, that those who worship Him are to be holy also.

Now that conclusion leads to obedience, but not the self-righteous, judgmental variety. After all, since all people sin, they must confess their sins and rely on the sacrifice of the Lamb of God who died for the sins of the world (1 John 1:8-10; John 1:29). Such individuals have no room for pride. And they certainly did not come to know God through obedience. Rather, they experienced Him through the fullness of His self-revelation in Christ (Heb. 1:1-4), the solution to the sin problem.

Both testaments, however, tie that revelation to a love response of obedience from those whom God has saved through Christ. Thus the Bible route to knowing God is primarily through the revelation of His love.

C. H. Dodd makes a helpful point when he writes that "for the Hebrew . . . to know God is neither (primarily) an intellectual exercise nor an ineffable mystical experience. It means rather to acknowledge God in His ways with man, to recognize His claims upon man, to understand His law with the intention of obeying it." Again, "in the Fourth Gospel . . . it is made perfectly plain that to know God is to experience His love in Christ, and to return that love in obedience" (Dodd, pp. 30, 31). John's first letter puts forth that same theology when it claims that knowing God means keeping His commandments and walking like Christ (2:3, 6) in the context of God's forgiveness and His sacrifice and advocacy (2:1, 2).

As a result, *even though Christians come to know God through His revelation in Christ, they can only know that they know Him when they live their lives in harmony with His revealed will.* That important distinction brings us back to the heart of the problem that 1 John 2:3-6 deals with. The apostle aimed his words at individuals who claimed to know God at the level of their intellects but were at the same time demonstrating that they did not know Him in their daily lives. Thus they presented themselves as above sin (1:8, 10), did not keep His commandments (2:3), and were unloving toward fellow church members (2:5).

Such imitation saints still plague the church in the twenty-first century. Some of them can tell us all about the Bible and may even be experts in the biblical languages, others have warm emotional experiences that they claim come from God, while yet others are great at outward obedience. But those are not the tests of true Christianity that John puts forth. After all, most of us have known people who have exceptional Bible knowledge, or warm emotional fuzzies about God that they like to talk about, or are strenuous about observing the letter of the law, but who are meaner than the devil in their daily lives.

For John the true tests of people's Christianity are that it leads them to walk in the loving way of Christ (2:6; 4:8, 11, 20) and to a keeping of His commandments (2:3). Anything that doesn't result in such a life is, from John's perspective, not valid Christianity.

Those tests, however, raise the question of what John means by "His commandments." Given the emphasis on love in both its immediate context (see 2:4) and throughout his letter, it is probable that the apostle is referring primarily to the two great commandments set forth by Christ—loving God supremely and loving other people (Matt. 22:36-40) rather than to the Ten Commandments. That does not mean that 1 John 2:3 does not also imply obedience to the Decalogue. After all, the New Testament explicitly ties the two "great commandments" to the Decalogue (see Rom. 13:8-10). Thus those who live God's law of love will by the very nature of that law be led to obey the moral law. Findlay summarizes John's teaching nicely when he writes "that *love to God* means keeping His commands, goes almost without saying. For indeed, the first and great commandment is, 'Thou shalt love the Lord thy God.' All other commands depend on this" (Findlay, p. 158).

We can thank God for His teaching in 1 John 1:6-2:6. In those verses we find the core of our assurance of salvation. John tells us that we can know that we know God if we are walking in harmony with the life of Christ (2:6) by keeping His commandments (2:3) in the context of a life of confession of sin (1:9) through the heavenly Advocate (2:1) who died for our sins (2:2).

The good news is that we can know that we know God (2:3) and can have full confidence in Him (5:14). Such is the Christian doctrine of assurance that John also clearly set forth in his Gospel (see John 3:36; 5:24).

6. The Acid Test of Christianity

1 John 2:7-11

⁷Behold, I am not writing a new commandment to you, but an old commandment which you have had from the beginning. The old commandment is the word which you have heard. ⁸Yet on the other hand I am writing a new commandment to you, which is true in Him and in you, because the darkness is passing away and the true Light is already shining. ⁹Anyone claiming to be in the Light yet hates his brother is in the darkness until now. ¹⁰Anyone who loves his brother dwells in the Light and in him is no cause for stumbling. ¹¹But anyone who hates his brother is in the darkness and is walking in the darkness, and does not know where he is going, because the darkness has blinded his eyes.

How can you tell if you have something genuine or merely an imitation? Good questions, since the true and the false at times have many outward similarities.

Historically, authorities often used acid to distinguish between true gold and other substances that looked like it. Acid would eat up the imitators but could not destroy the real thing. Through time the phrase "acid test" became generalized in application, Webster notes, to represent "a crucial, final test that proves the value or quality of something."

John 2:7-11 presents us with the acid test of genuine Christianity, the test that separates true Christians from those who may claim the part but who are merely deceptive imitations. Many aspects of Christianity can be successfully faked. But genuine and heartfelt loving care for other people cannot be counterfeited for extensive periods of time, even though one may manage to fool some of the people some of the time for short periods. But times of crisis or tension or opportunities for selfishness and self-centeredness eventually arrive to supply the "acid" that demonstrates the difference between the genuine and it's many imitators.

Note that John begins this section with the word "beloved." It is no accident that he is known as the apostle of love. He not only can speak about the virtue of love, but John also models it. B. F. Westcott puts it nicely when he writes that "St. John while enforcing the commandment of love gives expression to love" (Westcott, p. 52). And here is a lesson we each need to learn to practice. After all, when warning people of their spiritual needs, for example, it is all too easy to become cold and critical or to allow anger into our voices. But one of the high points of John's ministry is that he had learned to speak the truth in love. The apostle had managed to become what he taught. And that is important for all of us in our roles as parents, teachers, pastors, church members, and human beings.

> ### How Old Is the "Old" Commandment?
>
> "'Before the mountains were brought forth'. . . , God was *love*. The commandment is grounded in His changeless being. God could not create, could not conceive, such creatures as ourselves otherwise than as designed to love Him and each other. . . . The commandment, in its absolute basis and beginning, is old as the creation of the race, old as the love and fatherhood of God."
> (G. G. Findlay, p. 181).

David Rensberger sums up the message of 1 John 2:3-11 nicely when he writes that "the idea here is a very straightforward one, that a claim to relationship with God should be verified by a life lived in the way that God desires" (Rensberger, *Epistles*, p. 24). And 1 John never beats around the bush. For him "God is love" (1 John 4:8), and the acid test of genuine Christianity is emulating God's loving character in daily life (2:9-11).

Many readers of 1 John get hung up on the apparent contradiction between the new yet old commandment of 1 John 2:7, 8. The first question that we need to ask about the passage is how old is the "old commandment"? The answer takes us at least as far back as John's Gospel: "A new commandment I give to you, that you love one another; even as I have loved you, that you also love one another. By this all men will know that you are my disciples, if you have love for one another" (John 13:34, 35, RSV; cf. 15:12).

"But," you might be saying to yourself, "Jesus said that this was a 'new commandment.'" Quite true. But decades had passed since Jesus first enunciated His message recorded in the Fourth Gospel and more years since John had first provided that message to the recipients of his letter. So the "new" commandment of Jesus was an "old" commandment for John and his readers. It was something they had heard long ago, when they had first become Christians.

But some had forgotten. Thus the apostle reiterates his earlier teaching with great clarity and force:

- "Anyone claiming to be in the Light yet hates his brother is in the darkness until now" (1 John 2:9).
- "Anyone who loves his brother dwells in the Light and in him is no cause for stumbling" (verse 10).
- "Anyone who hates his brother is in the darkness and is walking in the darkness, and does not know where he is going, because the darkness has blinded his eyes" (verse 11).

Here is the acid test of Christianity for the apostle. If you are a Christian you *will* love others. John repeatedly pounds home that teaching throughout his first two letters. It is impossible to be in the Light yet not care about others from a heart of love.

You may have noted that in the above sentence and in my translation I have consistently capitalized the word "Light." Why? Because in John's writings the first nine verses of the Fourth Gospel repeatedly refer to Jesus as "the true Light" who "enlightens every man" (John 1:9, NASB). Thus the apostle in 1 John 2 is telling his readers that they cannot be in Christ (i.e., be Christians) and at the same time "hate" their brothers (1 John 2:9).

That brings us to the word "hate." The Greek word *miseō* is not equivalent to the English word "hate." To the contrary, it is better reflected by the concept of being "unloving." Thus English meanings for *miseō* run "the entire spectrum from *little love* to *disregard* to *hate*" (Balz, vol. 2, p. 431; cf. Bauer, pp. 652, 653).

As a result, John tells us that those who even disrespect their "brother" are on the opposite side of love and of the Light. And who is "brother" in this passage? We might be tempted to interpret the word in the light of Jesus' teaching to love everybody universally (Matt. 22:36-40) or to love one's enemies (Matt. 5:44). But that is definitely not what he has in mind in 1 John 2. Here he is being much more exclusive. In his letter the "brothers" are believers or fellow Christians (cf. 3 John 5-8). He is speaking to a serious problem in the congregation he is writing to, in which some of the members are disrespecting others who may be more "unsophisticated" than they are. In 1 John 2, Tom Thatcher points out, the expectation is for those who "claim to be Christians to treat other Christians as Jesus commanded" (Thatcher, p. 441).

And if they don't, John thunders in no uncertain terms, they are lost in darkness and don't know where they are heading (1 John 2:9-11) in spite of their claims to superior knowledge and spirituality.

John was obviously speaking to people in the churches he had charge of. But there is a powerful lesson here for every Christian and every congregation in every age. A lack of love, respect, and daily kindness is not something that once upon a time happened in ancient Asia Minor but got corrected once and for all by John's letters. To the contrary, John is dealing with a universal problem that is with us in every age and every place. It is no accident that Jesus told His followers that people would know they were truly His disciples *if* they honestly loved one another (John 13:35). *In the mind of Christ that expressed love for one another is the acid test of our Christianity*. Without it we have nothing, no matter how orthodox our doctrines, how correct our lifestyle, or how theologically sophisticated we might be. Without passing the acid test we are not even in twilight but in total darkness.

In these verses we have something extremely practical. Each of us faces daily choices between being Jesus to our fellow church members in our ongoing relationship with them or of being disrespectful if not downright hateful. Perhaps the greatest tragedy in the latter course is that the person we hurt the most by our wrong attitudes and actions is our own self.

While such individuals may think they are in the Light in their walk with God, John tells them that they have completely misled themselves. Such people are not only "in darkness" but they are darkness and haven't got the slightest personal recognition of where they are going because they are blinded (1 John 2:11). Yet all the while, like those "superior church members" who John is writing to, they may be disillusioned enough to be-lieve that they are really far in advance of others. Such a state is what the Bible refers to as being *lost*. And the real tragedy in 1 John is that the lost are church members. May God grant us eyes to see the true nature of the acid test of Christianity.

7. An Encouraging Pastoral Intermission

1 John 2:12-14

[12]I am writing to you, little children, because your sins have been forgiven through His name. [13]I am writing to you, fathers, because you have known the One who has been from the beginning. I am writing to you, young men, because you have overcome the evil one. I have written to you, children, because you know the Father. [14]I have written to you, fathers, because you know the One who is from the beginning. I have written to you, young men, because you are strong, and the word of God dwells in you, and you have overcome the evil one.

How much repetition can you have in three verses? With three "I am writing" leads and three "I have written" beginnings John seems to be pushing the limit. But he has good reasons for his strategy.

All we have to do is to look at the verses preceding and following John's six repetitions to discover what he seeks to accomplish in verses 12-14. Beginning in verses 3 to 6 the apostle starts to drive home the need to keep God's commandments and to walk like Jesus did. Then in verses 7-11 he uplifts the need for Christians to love their fellow church members. Failures in such realms not only make one "a liar" (verse 4) but indicate blind lostness (verse 11). Those conditions, needless to say, are not a happy outcome for Christians.

Then in verses 15-17 John warns his readers against loving the world and the things of the world, adding the idea that the world will eventually pass away along with those who put it in the wrong place.

Those paragraphs contain important information and warnings that

John's faithful readers needed to understand. He wrote with the secessionists in mind, since they were the ones making false claims and failing in
even attempting to live their lives by God's principles. John certainly
doesn't want his faithful members to follow the disastrous lead of the problematic "Christians" in his area, so he speaks forcefully.

But his audience is the faithful, not the secessionists. Perhaps, he
thinks in his pastoral heart, he will discourage his people with the stong
words in verses 3-11 and 15-17. After all, his purpose is to help them
rather than to depress them. Thus in verses 12-14 he provides what we
might best think of as "an encouraging pastoral intermission" in his uplifting of God's ideals.

Martyn Lloyd-Jones points out that John "was anxious to comfort
these people; he has been holding forth a very strong and stern doctrine
before them . . . and it is as if he said to himself, 'Now I wonder if these
people will be discouraged. Will they feel I am holding the standard so
high that they cannot attain to it? Will it make them feel they are condemned sinners and that there is no hope for them at all? Very well, I will
just stop and give them a word of comfort" (Lloyd-Jones, *Walking*, p. 68).

That brings us to John's interesting use of verb tenses in verses 12-14.
A definite shift in verb tense splits the passage right down the middle, with
three "I am writing" leads followed by three "I have written" beginnings.

Why the change? Some have suggested that it was an attempt to avoid
monotony of expression. But a more fruitful explanation, William Barclay
argues, is that John sought to create in his readers an aura of total encouragement. Thus "the sense would then be that the whole letter, the part
which is already written, the part which he is writing, and the part which
is still to come, is all designed to remind Christians of who and whose they
are, and of what has been done for them." After all, the best defense of the
Christian against sin is for them to remember what God has accomplished
for them through Jesus (Barclay, pp. 60, 59).

And who is the apostle trying to encourage and comfort in 1 John
2:12-14? Commentators have responded in more than one way. But
before moving to the proposed solutions, we should look at the words that
John used to address the readers:

1. "little children" (*teknia*, verse 12)
2. "fathers" (verses 13, 14)

3. "young men" (verses 13, 14)

4. "children" (*paidia*, verse 13)

The first thing that we should note is that the apostle is addressing only three groups, even though he uses two quite different Greek words for children. Some, for obvious reasons, have viewed the three categories as related to chronological age. But that suggestion runs up against two significant problems. For one thing, John uses "children" to address his readers throughout the letter, irrespective of their age (2:1, 12, 28; 3:7, 18; 4:4; 5:21). For a man approaching 100 years of age, everyone else is younger. But more important is the fact that John is their spiritual father and guide, the one who brought many of them into the faith. Beyond that, they were children of their Father in heaven.

Another difficulty with the chronological age interpretation is that the blessings of each group are not the exclusive possession of any one age. Forgiveness, for example, does not belong to only the young. And overcoming the evil one can take place at any stage of life.

A second interpretation of the age groupings suggests they are not physical ages but stages in spiritual development. Thus "the *dear children* are those newborn in Christ. The *young men* are more developed Christians, strong and victorious in spiritual warfare; while the *fathers* possess the depth and stability of ripe Christian experience" (Stott, p. 101).

That solution is quite an attractive solution to the age categories, but so is a third. Some propose that John is addressing the church as a whole, with the words for each group including all Christians. And it is true that every Christian possesses the forgiveness and knowledge of the Father attributed to the children, that all Christians have access to the overcoming strength of the young men, and that all Christians have the ability to know the Father in fuller and fuller ways as they live their daily lives. Thus the blessing of each group is one for all the groups.

The good news is that we don't have to solve the "age problem" in order to get encouragement out of the passage. What John really wanted to pass on to his readers was the nature of the benefits that they have as Christians. And those blessings are truly a comfort that we can daily rejoice in.

The first blessing is forgiveness through the name of Jesus (1 John 2:12). Here we have the heart of the good news. Since every person has sinned (Rom. 3:23) and the wages of sin is eternal death (Rom. 6:23), forgiveness of our sins is the best of the good news. John had earlier set forth the blessing of forgiveness when he declared that "if we confess our sins, He is faithful and just, He forgives our sins and cleanses us from all unrighteousness" (1:9). And John had also raised issues related to Christ's role in forgiveness when he wrote that Jesus "is the propitiation [atoning sacrifice] for our sins" and each Christian's "Advocate with the Father" (2:2, 1).

In John 2:12, 13 the apostle drives home the fact that all Christians have the inestimable blessing of forgiveness even though they haven't been able to meet flawlessly the high standards he is setting forth (see 2:1). God may expect much from His children, but He is willing to forgive much when we come to Him on our knees as little children asking for forgiveness. Of such is the kingdom of heaven (Matt. 18:3, 4).

Just as trusting humility is childhood at its best, so those who are for-

> **The Three Blessings of Every Christian**
>
> 1. Forgiveness of sin
> 2. Strength to overcome
> 3. The ability to know God ever more completely

given trust in the name of Jesus (1 John 2:12). "Some trust in chariots," writes the psalmist, "and some in horses: but we will remember the name of the Lord our God" (Ps. 20:7, KJV).

A second blessing that every Christian possesses is strength to overcome the evil one (1 John 2:13, 14). Here the apostle is emphasizing God's empowering grace. We too often limit it to the forgiveness of our sins. But grace comes in three flavors. The first is *forgiving grace* that brings people under the Fatherhood of God. He is, as we noted above, more than willing to forgive every person who approaches Him asking as a little child would.

And at the very time a person comes to Him, God also gives the gift of *transforming grace* in terms of a new heart and mind. Born from above Christians have changed hearts and desire to serve their Father in heaven (Rom. 12:1, 2; 2 Cor. 5:17; John 3:3-6). And for the accomplishment of that new way of life God gives us *empowering grace* through the Holy Spirit. Through that gift God has given each of His children the spiritual strength and vigor of young adulthood (1 John 2:13, 14).

A third blessing that God bestows on every Christian is a knowledge of Himself. Just as the wisdom of earthly fathers at their best increases with age, so it is that God gives every Christian the desire and ability to grow in both a knowledge of and a relationship to the Father in heaven.

It is these three great gifts that form the focus of John's encouraging pastoral intermission in 1 John 2:12-14. He wants each of his readers to grasp the fact that as they deal with the evil one in their daily walk they can continually be assured of forgiveness, strength, and wisdom.

The good news 2,000 years after John penned his letter is that those gifts are still ours every day. *We are not alone.*

8. We Can't Love Everything

1 John 2:15-17

>*¹⁵Do not love the world nor the things in the world. If anyone loves the world, love for the Father is not in him. ¹⁶For all that is in the world, the lust of the flesh and the lust of the eyes and the boastful pride of life, is not of the Father but is of the world. ¹⁷And the world is passing away, and the lust of it; but the one who does the will of God continues forever.*

No one can serve two masters; for either he will hate the one and love the other, or he will be devoted to the one and despise the other. You cannot serve God and mammon" (Matt. 6:24, RSV).

Jesus' words help us set the stage for our study of 1 John 2:15-17. The stark truth is that we can't love everything. We need to make choices.

Paul Hoon is on target when he writes that "the key to these verses lies in the profound cleavage between the world and the Father, and in the consequent choice every man must make between them. Men cannot live without consciously or unconsciously having to choose some reality to which they give ultimate devotion. They must and will love something. . . . They may offer their ultimate devotion to God, the devil, the world, mammon, the state, a political party, truth, beauty, their own lower desires. But life requires decision and the Christian life demands decision" (Hoon, p. 238).

John, of course, is quite aware of that fact. And in 1 John 2:15 he sets the choice as between loving the world or loving the Father. No one can have it both ways.

Why? Because of what "the world" is. The world in the present context is not the physical world around us, which God deemed "very good"

73

at the end of Creation week (Gen. 1:31, RSV). And we must never forget that "God so loved the world that he gave his only Son" for its redemption (John 3:16, RSV). Thus there are some things about the world as God's creation that Christians should love and cherish.

But "the world" as verse 15 uses the phrase is "the life of human society as organized under the power of evil." It is "pagan society, with its sensuality, superficiality, and pretentiousness, its materialism and its egotism"—the realm dominated by "evil powers which Christ lived and died to destroy" (Dodd, pp. 39, 42, 41). The "whole world," John tells us, "is in the sphere of the evil one" (1 John 5:19).

And it is that godless, evil world that John commands Christians not to love. "Thus he sees the Christian life as one which demands a clear choice between God and the world; that is, in practical terms, the Christian must not compromise with the principles and ways of pagan society" (*ibid.*, p. 41).

But that is not normal! We have a natural desire to fit in, to be one of the crowd. After all, we don't want to witness to Christianity in a way that makes it look odd.

> ## "The World"
>
> "Whatever puts God out of one's thoughts, whatever weakens the power of religion over the soul, whatever hinders one from doing God's will in the ordering of his life, whatever sets itself up to rival the love of God in one's heart—be it even the love of father or mother—this belongs to what St John understands by 'the world'" (Findlay, p. 215).

Yet it is that attitude that the apostle is fighting. To put it bluntly, Christianity is odd and has a different value system from what John calls "the world." And, as a result, Christians must oppose those values, attitudes, and actions that are against the ideals that God has revealed in His Word. Their "love for the Father" (1 John 2:15) dictates the direction of their lives.

In 1 John 2:16 the apostle moves beyond the generality of the world to some specific examples that have been problematic for Christians across time. The first in his "trinity of evil" (Findlay, p. 217) is the "lust of the flesh." Most of us probably interpret that phrase in terms of sexual sins.

While that is a part of it, the biblical use of the term includes much more.

In the New Testament "the flesh" is that aspect of human nature, when separated from God, that provides an entry for the devil. He knows our weaknesses and exactly the temptations that will entice those weaknesses into acts of sin, which are in effect rejections of the Father's ways for responding to "the world."

One possible translation for the "lust of the flesh" is "sinful desire," which "refers to fallen human nature in general; to a disposition of hostility toward God" (Smalley, pp. 65, 84). In the world of both John's day and ours that fallen human nature tends toward making a god out of pleasure, to living a life dominated by the senses, to existing for the gratification of earthly and material desires. The way of the flesh is to neglect the commandments of God, along with His standards and perhaps His very existence.

From the "lust of the flesh" John moves onto the "lust of the eyes" or a "craving for what is seen" (ibid., p. 65). While the "lust of the flesh" represents temptations from within, stemming from a perverted heart (Matt. 15:19), the "lust of the eyes" involves assault from without that obtains entrance through our vision.

Thus it was that Eve found the forbidden fruit to be a "delight to the eyes" (Gen. 3:6. RSV) and David started down a disastrous path with Bathsheba when "he saw from the roof a woman bathing" and noted that "the woman was very beautiful" (2 Sam. 11:2, RSV). The rest is history. James portrays the process nicely when he writes that "each person is tempted when he is lured and enticed by his own desire. Then desire when it has conceived gives birth to sin" (James 1:14, 15, RSV). In David's case the initial temptation arrived through the eye gate to the human soul, by way of the "lust of the eyes" or a "craving for what is seen."

The "lust of the flesh" and the "lust of the eyes" are not unrelated. To the contrary, they mingle together constantly in every person, a fact that "the evil one" (1 John 2:14) is more than happy to utilize as people exist in a media world steeped in materialism, violence, and illicit and unnatural sex. If John were around in the twenty-first century he would probably have a strong word of counsel for Christian approaches to television and the other media. The unfortunate truth is that most Christians have adopted "the world's" standards in that area rather than the Father's.

The third item in John's unholy trinity is "the boastful pride of life" (1 John 2:16), a phrase translated as "life's empty pride" by William Barclay and "pride in one's life style" by Stephen Smalley. Here we have the reference to the pride of possession or even a tendency to exaggerate what one possesses "in order to impress other people" (Rogers, p. 594).

The underlying motivation for such actions is to make ourselves look important. Thus self-worship as opposed to the worship of God lies at the root of "the boastful pride of life." Uplifting the human self and placing it at the center of one's thoughts and actions is at the very core of sin. It is no accident that C. S. Lewis writes that "pride leads to every other vice: it is the complete anti-God state of mind" (C. Lewis, *Mere Christianity,* p. 109). Jesus taught that the antidote to "the boastful pride of life" is humility (Mark 10:44).

Thus in summary, John tells us in no uncertain terms that the core of the way of "the world" resides in the "lust of the flesh," the "lust of the eyes," and the "boastful pride of life." In 1 John 2:15-17 he grounds his command not to love the world on two arguments. The first is that love for the world is incompatible with love for the Father (verses 15 and 16). The second is that the world and everything of it is transient, whereas those who do the will of God have eternity in their future (verse 17).

R. R. Williams pictures John as seeing his readers caught up in the "exciting city of Ephesus. All around them are the allurements of a life of passionate excitement, of captivating theatrical displays, of boasting competition for earthly fame or wealth. He calls on them to see the transient nature of all this, and instead, to concentrate on obedience to God's will, which has the promise of eternal life" (Williams, p. 29).

Not bad advice. It was good for Ephesus in the first century, but it is also excellent counsel for those of us living in San Francisco, Tokyo, New York, or even my little village of Rogue River in the twenty-first century.

"Choose you this day whom ye will serve" (Joshua 24:15, KJV).

9. The Last Hour and the Antichrist

1 John 2:18-21

¹⁸Children, it is the last hour, and as you heard that antichrist is coming, so now many antichrists have come; therefore we know that it is the last hour. ¹⁹They departed from us, but they were not [really] of us; for if they had been of us they would have remained with us; but they departed in order that it might be revealed that they all are not of us. ²⁰But you have an anointing from the Holy One, and you all know. ²¹I am not writing to you because you do not know the Truth, but because you know it, and because no lie is of the truth.

With 1 John 2:18-27 the apostle picks up a line of discussion that dominated verses 3-11—namely how to discriminate between genuine and imitation members of the Christian community. In verses 3-6 he set forth the moral test—that true believers would walk as Jesus did and keep God's commandments. And in verses 7-11 he enunciated a social test, whereby genuine Christians truly love and care for their fellow communicants rather than disrespect them. Now in verses 18-27 John adds a doctrinal test. In the process he first makes a clear distinction between true Christians and the heretics (verses 18-21) and then defines the exact nature of their heresy (verses 22, 23).

The first thing many readers will note is the fact that John believed that he was living in "the last hour" (verse 18). "What," we need to ask, "did he mean, since he made his statement nearly 2,000 years ago?"

The best way to get at the topic is to recognize that first-century Jews divided world history into two parts: the present age, which is evil, and the

77

age to come, during which God would reign. Early Christians correctly believed that Christ's declaration that the kingdom of God had begun with His arrival (Matt. 4:17) signaled the start of the age to come and the beginning of the doom of the evil age. Thus "early Christians . . . regarded the whole period between the first and second advents of Jesus as constituting the last days" (Marshall, p. 148).

> ## Three Great Tests
>
> 1. The moral test—that believers obey God's commandments and walk as Jesus did (1 John 2:3-6).
> 2. The social test—that believers love one another (verses 7-11).
> 3. The doctrinal test—that believers truly believe that Jesus came in the flesh, is the Son of God, and is the Christ (verses 22-27; 1:3, 7; 3:8, 23; 4:2, 9, 10, 11, 15; 5:1).

Of course, no first-century Christian expected the period between Christ's advents to last so long. Here John Stott's insight is helpful when he observes that "the 'last days' will themselves have 'last days,' a period of grievous moral and religious decadence (2 Tim. 3:1ff.; 2 Peter 3:3). Similarly, the 'last times' will have a 'last time' in which ungodly scoffers will arise (Jude 18; cf. 1 Tim. 4:1). Nor is this all. The 'last time' of the 'last times' will have a culminating 'last time' when our eternal inheritance will be revealed (1 Peter 1:5; cf. James 5:3). In the same way, 'the last days' of the 'last days' will themselves have a final 'last day' when Christ raises the dead and judges the world (John 6:39, 40, 44, 54; 11:24; 12:48)" (Stott, p. 113).

If all that is true, then what did John mean when he claimed that the last hour had come? He was obviously not making a chronological statement. Rather he affirmed a widely accepted theological truth that end times had begun with Christ's earthly ministry. Thus while the "last hour" started during the apostle's day, we still await the consummation of hope in the Second Advent.

One evidence for John that the "last hour" had indeed begun was that antichrists had arisen (1 John 2:18). And on what basis did that constitute proof? John's mind undoubtedly went back to the declaration of Jesus on the Mount of Olives that "false Christs and false prophets" would arise before His return who would "lead astray, if possible, even the elect" (Matt. 24:24, RSV). And he was probably familiar with Paul's teaching in 2 Thessalonians 2 that before the end a sacrilegious, lawless power would emerge, seeking to take the place of God.

John's addressees had "heard" about such things because he had earlier taught them to his congregations. And now, he tells them in 1 John 2:18, we know that "it is the last hour" because "many antichrists have come." The apostle was especially sensitive to heresy because of Paul's prophecy to the same Ephesian Christian community decades earlier. "I know," he told them, "that after my departure fierce wolves will come in among you, not sparing the flock; and from among your own selves will arise men speaking perverse things, to draw away the disciples after them" (Acts 20:29, 30, RSV). That time, John announces to his readers, had arrived. Antichrist had come.

That brings us to the meaning of "antichrist," a term that only John uses in the New Testament (1 John 2:18, 22; 4:3; 2 John 7). Antichrist is "formed from *anti*, 'against,' or 'instead of,' and *christos*, 'Christ.' The word may therefore mean one who opposes Christ, or one who claims to take the place of Christ, or one who combines both these functions" (Nichol, vol. 7, p. 643).

While the original antichrist is Satan, John tells us that "many" of the evil one's follower "antichrists" had infiltrated the apostle's congregations (1 John 2:18). While he does not identify them, we can have no doubt that he is referring to those he designates as "false prophets" in 1 John 4:1 and who are seeking to tear apart the church through their false teachings related to keeping God's commandments (1 John 2:3-6), the need to genuinely love other church members (verses 7-11), and, most important in the context of 1 John 2:18-21, their denial of the Father and the Son (verses 22, 23).

In verse 19 John tells us that the antichrists had been members of his Christian community, but that they had withdrawn from it. He then continues on by making the provocative statement that the false teachers, even though they had been members of the church, had not been genuine Christians. And with that thought he has brought us to the distinction between the visible and invisible church. Thus the significance of A. E. Brooke's insight "that external membership is no proof of inward union"

(Brooke, p. 54) and C. H. Dodd's comment that "formal membership is no guarantee that a man belongs to Christ and not to Antichrist" (Dodd, p. 53). Put somewhat differently, it is the life and teachings of people that indicate if they are genuine members of Christ's heavenly congregation or if they merely have church membership or attend weekly services. Jesus said the same thing when He proclaimed "by their fruits ye shall know them" (Matt. 7:20; see verses 15-23). Church membership and participation in religious events have meaning only if they are outward signs of an inner transformation and spiritual orientation. Without that inner change, the exterior has a value of zero.

John sets forth three important truths in 1 John 2:20 and 21. First, the "Holy One" has anointed all Christians. That teaching runs parallel to that of the Fourth Gospel, which declares that Christians are born of both "water and Spirit" (John 3:5, NASB). As English reformer William Tyndale (c. 1494-1536) put it, "Ye are not anointed with oil in your bodies, but with the Spirit of Christ in your souls: which Spirit teacheth you all truth in Christ, and maketh you to judge what is a lie, and what truth, and to know Christ from antichrist" (in Barton, p. 51).

The second important truth in 1 John 2:20, 21 is that, because of their anointing, Christians know the truth. It wasn't only the secessionist Gnostic types who had knowledge, but every Christian. But genuine Christians, the apostle pounds home, have *true truth*, while that of the secessionists is false.

And where did the genuine believers get such truth? From such leaders as Paul and John, who had taught them both when they became Christians and as they developed in their walk with God. Thus they had "heard" from human lips certain truths "from the beginning" of their Christian experience (1 John 3:11; 1:1; 2:7, 13, 14, 24), truths that the Spirit (2:20) simultaneously impressed on their minds.

Therefore "the object of the Apostle in writing was not to communicate fresh knowledge, but to bring into active and decisive use the knowledge which his readers already possessed" (Westcott, p. 74).

Here is an important lesson that each of us needs to keep near the surface in our daily lives. That is, our most important defense as Christians is to remember what we know. It is not new truth we need so much as to bring to consciousness and to put into practice what we have learned in the past. How much more victorious our lives would be if we put into practice those Christian truths that we have already learned.

The third great truth tucked away in verses 20 and 21 is that no lie comes from the truth. The clear teaching of the Bible is that God is the source of truth while the devil "is a liar and the father of lies" (John 8:44, RSV). That reality brings us to 1 John 2:22-27 and what might be thought of as "the master lie."

10. The Master Lie

1 John 2:22-27

²²Who is the liar but the one who denies that Jesus is the Christ? This is the antichrist, the one who denies the Father and the Son. ²³No one who denies the Son has the Father; [but] the one who confesses the Son has the Father also. ²⁴Let what you heard from the beginning dwell in you. If what you heard from the beginning dwells in you, you also will dwell in the Son and in the Father. ²⁵And this is the promise which He promised us: eternal life.

²⁶I have written these things to you concerning those trying to deceive you. ²⁷And the anointing which you received from Him dwells in you, and you have no need that anyone should teach you. But as that anointing teaches you about everything, and is true and is not a lie, even as He taught you, dwell in Him.

With 1 John 2:22 we reach the heart of the doctrinal heresy espoused by the secessionist party. John, so to speak, puts the issue right in our face when he writes "who is the liar but the one who denies that Jesus is the Christ." Those who make that claim are in no uncertain terms the antichrist. Such a denial in the eyes of John is "the lie of all lies," "the master lie," "the lie par excellence" (Barclay, p. 79). Or as The Venerable Bede (c. 673-735) framed it, the "denial of Christ is the supreme lie, a lie so great that it is hard to think of anything which can be compared with it" (in Bray, p. 189).

"What," we need to ask, "does it mean for a person to deny that Jesus is the Christ?" To answer that question we must delve into the theological problem John faced throughout his first letter. For starters, we should note that those who denied that Jesus was the Christ also disavowed that Christ came in the flesh (1 John 4:2). Beyond that, they rejected that Jesus was the Son of God (4:15).

In those denials we find a philosophical tendency that ran throughout the Greek world of the early Christian era. The basic idea was to separate the divine Christ from the human Jesus. Some, for example, promoted the idea that matter was evil while God was good, and that a good God could never take on a body composed of an evil substance. Thus they repudiated the incarnation of Christ. For He didn't really come in the flesh but only appeared to do so (from the Greek *dokein*, which means "seemed"). Thus Jesus was not really the Christ or the Son of God. Rather, they probably taught (as some later Gnostics did) that Jesus lived and died as a man, whom the divine Christ descended upon at His baptism and departed from right before the Crucifixion.

Thus the "sophisticated" secessionists in John's congregations had no problem with Christ's divinity. It was His humanity that troubled them. And in their philosophical "smartness" they had apparently been circulating the idea that even though they had different ideas about Jesus, they agreed with John and others about God.

Not so! thundered the apostle. "No one who denies the Son has the Father" (1 John 2:23). Why? Because at least twice God declared from heaven that "this is my beloved Son" (at His baptism, Matt. 3:17, RSV, and at the Transfiguration, Matt. 17:5). Thus to deny that Jesus is the incarnate Son of God is to disavow the very words of God Himself.

We should note that John calls the one who denies that Jesus is the Christ "the liar" (1 John 2:22). The central antichrist claim finds its roots in the temptation of Jesus, when the devil repeatedly challenged Him with the words, "If you are the Son of God" (Matt. 4:3, 5, RSV). Thus those denying the divinity of Jesus are linked up with the original liar (John 8:44) as they repeat the master lie. As a result, the antichrists of John's day (and ours) join the ranks of those who can be labeled "the liar."

Jesus, we need to remember, also made claims to divinity when He proclaimed "I and the Father are one" (John 10:30, RSV; cf. 17:21, 22). To reject the divinity of Jesus is to lay the foundation for repudiating the validity of His teachings. "If Jesus was wrong about who He was,"

R.E.O. White points out, "He is wrong about everything" and "all who have followed Him have been misled, the whole Christian vision is a perilous mirage, all Christian enterprise is built on lies" (R. White, p. 68).

Consequently, with the denial "that Jesus is the Christ" one wipes out the entire Christian message. Little wonder that John calls those who make that claim "the liar." And that lie as it circulated among the sophisticated Greek population of the late first century is the reason that the apostle proclaimed that Jesus "the Word was God" in the opening verse of his Gospel (John 1:1, RSV; cf. verse 14). He realized the centrality of that claim to Christianity.

"No one who denies the Son has the Father; [but] the one who confesses the Son has the Father also" (1 John 2:23). What John first stated negatively, he now puts positively: those who confess the Son also have fellowship with God the Father because, as we noted above, the two are united (John 10:30). Jesus made it very plain that we know the Father through the Son (John 1:18; 12:44, 45; 14:6-9) and that only the Son represents us and reconciles us to the Father (1 John 2:1, 2).

Thus "to deny Jesus is to lose all knowledge of God, for He alone can bring that knowledge of God. To deny Jesus is to be separated from God, for on our reaction to Jesus our relationship to God depends" (Barclay, p. 80).

First John 2:22, 23 set forth the distinctive difference between true and false believers. Now verses 24-27 will highlight two safeguards for believers. One is to remember to hold to that which "you heard from the beginning" (verse 24). The first thing we need to ask about his statement is the meaning of "the beginning." Here the apostle is referring to what the believers had been taught regarding the message of the gospel as they first heard it at their conversion. "The beginning" in their case is the teachings about Christ and the gospel as set forth by Paul, John, and the other apostolic witnesses instrumental in bringing them into the faith. To return to "the beginning" in this context is to go back before heresies regarding the nature of Jesus Christ had entered their Christian community and caused the division and dissension that John is struggling with. By doing so they could find safe doctrinal understanding.

That counsel was true for the individuals John was writing to, but we also find a message here for those of us reading 1 John 2,000 years later. All too often we are just as prone as John's parishioners to go off after the latest speculative ideas in theology. It is all too easy to emulate the Athenians in Paul's day, who "spent their time in nothing except telling or hearing something new" (Acts 17:21, RSV). And it is nothing new for Christians to tire of "sound teaching, but having itching ears . . . for . . . teachers to suit their own passions" (2 Tim. 4:3, ESV).

John's inspired advice for every age is that our only protection is to go back to "the beginning." And for us that beginning is found in the apostolic writings of the New Testament. Christian theology is not a speculative sport tied to philosophic curiosity. To the contrary, valid Christian understanding must of necessity be rooted and grounded in the revealed Word of God in the Bible. Christians are not at liberty to forsake that Word for human reasonings and church traditions. To do so is to confuse the Word of God with the words of people, which is one definition of that spiritual confusion that the Bible refers to as Babylon (Rev. 14:8). As Ellen White so nicely put it, "the Bible is the only rule of faith and doctrine" (see Knight, *Angry Saints*, pp. 109-111). It is that book and that book alone that is the source of that "eternal life" that John is so fond of upholding before his readers (1 John 2:25; John 5:24; 6:47).

A second safeguard for believers that John highlights is "the anointing which you received from Him" (1 John 2:26, 27). The apostle first mentioned that anointing in verse 20, in which we found that it was a gift of "the Holy One." Not only did John's parishioners receive the teachings of the apostles at the time of their conversion, but also the gift of the Holy Spirit (John 3:5), who would guide them "into all the truth," (John 16:13, RSV).

Here are the two great gifts that God has given His people down through the ages to protect them from error. And they are meant to go together. Reliance upon the written Word without the enlivening and informing input of the Spirit can lead to strange interpretations and dead theology, while the separation of the subjective experience of the Spirit from the objective Word of God has led some to excesses of all sorts.

John Stott is onto something important when he writes that "both the apostolic teaching and the heavenly teacher are necessary for continuance in the truth. And both are to be personally and inwardly grasped. This is the biblical balance which is too seldom preserved. Some honour the Word and neglect the Spirit who alone can interpret it; others honour the Spirit but neglect the Word out of which he teaches. The only safeguard against lies is to have remaining [dwelling] within us both the Word that we 'heard from the beginning' and the 'anointing' that we 'received' from him" (Stott, pp. 119, 120).

Part III

God Is Righteous

1 John 2:28-4:6

11. Being Ready for Jesus to Come

1 John 2:28, 29

²⁸And now little children, dwell in Him, so that when He appears we may have confidence and not be ashamed before Him at His coming. ²⁹If you know that He is righteous, you also know that everyone who continues to do righteousness has been born of Him.

With 1 John 2:28 and 29 we come to a transition in the flow of the letter. The phrase "He is righteous" reminds us of "God is light" of 1 John 1:5 and "God is love" of 1 John 4:8. Who God is is one of the great ongoing motifs of John's first letter. But in John's hands who God is is always related to who God's followers should be. Therefore, if God is light, His true followers must "walk in the light" (1:7), and if God is love, then Christians must love one another (4:11). In the same way, if God is righteous, then everyone "born of Him" will also continue "to do righteousness" (2:29).

Thus being like God is central to John's theology. And his emphasis and the way he sets it forth in his first letter are based upon the characters of those seeking to divide and destroy the Christian integrity of his congregations. The secessionists were walking in spiritual darkness (1:6), were not obedient to God's commandments (2:3, 4), and were unloving to other church members (2:9; 4:20).

In the section running from 1 John 2:28 to 1 John 4:6 the apostle will return in his spiral-like approach to the three tests of genuine Christianity that he has already discussed in 1 John 2:3-27. By way of recapitulation, those tests were

1. the moral test of obedience (2:3-6).

2. the social test of loving others in the community (2:7-11).

3. the doctrinal test of accepting that Jesus is the Christ (2:18-27).

First John 2:28-4:6 circles once again through the same territory. Thus we find

1. the moral test—living the righteous life (2:28-3:10).

2. the social test—living God's love (3:11-18).

3. the doctrinal test on the nature of Christ (4:1-6).

The apostle John is relentless in pounding his themes home. But the second cycle of his three tests of genuine Christianity is not a mere repetition of the first round. To the contrary, he elaborates on the meaning of each test and thoroughly applies the implications of each to Christian living.

The passage running from 1 John 2:28 to 4:6 not only discusses the same three tests, but it does so in the same order. Thus we are not surprised to find the moral test coming first. Here we discover that the proof of genuine Christianity is not merely believing the right doctrines, but also living the transformed life in the everyday world. Just as a Christian must walk in the light and keep God's commandments as Jesus did at His first appearing (2:3-6), so it is that true believers will continue "to do righteousness" at His second (2:29). "Unrighteous conduct is unthinkable," John Stott points out, "in the Christian who has grasped the purpose of the two appearings of Christ" (Stott, pp. 120, 121).

That idea brings us to the word *parousia*, which I translated as "appears." The ancient world employed the word "for the visit of a King or Emperor" (Brooke, p. 66). The Bible picked up that usage and applied it to the visit of the "King of Kings" at the Second Advent. The idea in 1 John 2:28 is that the King is coming and His subjects need to be ready. Thus they must continue to "dwell" in Him or, to say it more plainly, to live their lives within the principles of His kingdom.

Marianne Thompson suggests that "the command ('abide in Christ') functions . . . in two ways. On the one hand, it exhorts readers to continued faithfulness to God as God is made known in Christ. Yet, on the other hand, it is a promise. For it promises to those who continue in their commitment to God that nothing will bring them to shame at the judgment" (Thompson, p. 86).

That thought brings us to the two possible responses to Christ's coming that 1 John 2:28 sets forth. The apostle is quite clear that people will be either confident or ashamed at His return. There are no other ways, no hints at being kind of confident or being partially ashamed. John is certain here, just as he is in Revelation 22:11, in which he records the words of Jesus that there would arrive a time near the end of earthly history when every individual will have made a decision to remain "filthy" or "holy" forever. Jesus set forth the same stark contrast in His parables of the sheep and the goats in Matthew 25:31-46. The Bible consistently teaches the "doctrine of the two conditions" at the return of Christ. Every person will be either confident or ashamed. In 1 John 2:28-3:10 the apostle uses those alternatives to inspire his readers toward the one possessing the moral life capable of meeting the coming King with absolute confidence.

"Confidence" is a powerful word. *Parrēsian* represents the absence of fear when speaking. Our English Bibles usually translate it as "confidence," "assurance," "courage," or "boldness." First John uses *parrēsian* four times. Twice in relation to the Second Advent—here and in 4:17 ("that we may have assurance in the day of Judgment")—and twice to refer to that bold confidence that Christians can have when they approach God in prayer (5:14; 3:21). The book of Hebrews employs the term in a similar way when it asserts that Christians can "come boldly" before "the throne of grace" (Heb. 4:16, KJV). Needless to say, it is a wonderful thing to be able to stand before the King in boldness when He returns.

> ### The End-time Alternatives
> "The little phrase 'before him' [at the end of verse 28] suggests a scene in which believers personally appear before Christ, as people coming into the presence of a king, and react to him as ones who either know him or have reason to fear for their lives" (Johnson, p. 66).

The opposite to such confident boldness is "ashamed." That word "carries the idea of shrinking back or being separated from God through guilt or shame" (Akin, pp. 129, 130). It brings to mind the words of Jesus in Mark 8:38: "For whoever is ashamed of me and of my words in this adulterous and sinful generation, of him will the Son of man also be ashamed, when he comes in the glory of his Father with the holy angels" (RSV).

The distance between the two alternatives that John sets forth is staggering. When Jesus returns people will either be ready to meet him with bold confidence or will "shrink away from Him in shame" (1 John 2:28, NASB).

The apostle utilizes the end-time alternatives of confidence and shame in verse 28 to lead into verse 29, in which he proclaims that if we know that God is righteous, we should practice that righteousness in our daily lives.

The key words in 1 John 2:29 that not only explain the righteous living of that verse but also open the way to further treatment of the topic in 1 John 3:1-10 are "born of Him." Although being born again or born of God has been hinted at earlier in 1 John, this is the first use of the word *gennaō* in the letter. But it won't be the last. John employs it again in 3:9 (two times); 4:7; 5:1 (three times), 4, 18 (two times). Each of the other nine uses means "born of God," which is the obvious meaning in 1 John 2:29.

Being "born of God" is an important theological concept in 1 John. So it was also in the Fourth Gospel. Thus in John 1:12, 13 we read: "to all who received him, who believed in his name, he gave power to become children of God; who were born, not of the blood nor of the will of the flesh nor of the will of man, but of God" (RSV). Then again, in John 3 we find Jesus telling Nicodemus that people must be "born again" or "born from above" by the Holy Spirit (verses 3, 5). In summary, John saw entrance into the Christian life as a supernatural event "effected by God through his Spirit in conjunction with faith in Jesus Christ on the part of those concerned" (Kruse, p. 114).

From John's perspective, the only way in which a person can "dwell in Him" (1 John 2:28) is to be "born of Him" (verse 29). The fruit of that born-again experience, he asserts, is a life in which a believer "continues to do righteousness." Such righteous living is the evidence that a person has been born of God (verse 29). Without it, any profession of Christianity is a lie (1 John 2:4). And such people, as John pointed out in verse 28, will have plenty to be ashamed of when Jesus comes again.

The apostle has no doubt about it: since God "is righteous," He expects those individuals who have become a part of His family to be like Him. Lip service and big claims have no weight with God. "The profession of a man's lips will always be proved or disproved by the practice of his life" (Barclay, p. 85).

With that thought we have the apostle's challenge to the secessionists seeking to divide his congregations and his warning to those who might be tempted to follow them. And that is still an important challenge and warning to those living today. Christianity is a life-changing experience that will set every believer on the pathway to emulating God's character.

12. Being Like God

1 John 3:1-3

¹See what sort of love the Father has given to us, that we should be called children of God, and such we are. Therefore the world does not know us, because it did not know Him. ²Beloved, we are now children of God, and it has not yet been revealed what we will be. We know that when He appears we will be like Him, because we will see Him as He is. ³And everyone having this hope in Him purifies himself, even as He is pure.

"See what sort of love the Father has given us, that we should be called children of God." That is the wonder of wonders for John. The Greek word I translated as "what sort" "always implies astonishment, and generally admiration" (Plummer, *Epistles,* p. 71).

The Message paraphrase of 1 John 3:1, 2 captures the awe John felt as He contemplated God's great gift: "What marvelous love the Father has extended to us! Just look at it—we're called children of God! That's who we really are. But that's also why the world doesn't recognize us or take us seriously, because it has no idea who he is or what he's up to.

"But friends, that's exactly who we are: children of God. And that's only the beginning. Who knows how we'll end up! What we know is that when Christ is openly revealed, we'll see him—and in seeing him, become like him. All of us who look forward to his Coming stay ready, with the glistening purity of Jesus' life as a model for our own."

The real wonder is that we are not merely "called children of God," but that "we are" God's children. Our daughterhood and sonship is a reality.

John points out several things about that reality in verse 1. One is that it is a gift. The Bible is plain that all humans enter the world as creatures of God, since He is Creator, but that only those who are born of the Spirit are God's children (see John 1:12, 13). In biblical terms, the gift comes in the form of our being adopted into God's covenant family (Gal. 4:5).

That adoption did not happen as a result of any preexisting virtue, John tells us, but because of God's love. Here is a second element in the adoption process that we need to keep at the forefront of our minds. The wonder of salvation is that God loved us in spite of who we are, in spite of our rebellion and slowness, in spite of the fact that we are "dirty goods." Paul caught this same idea when he wrote that God "destined us in love to be his sons through Jesus Christ, according to the purpose of his will" (Eph. 1:5, RSV). In other words, it was God's love that inspired the gift of His grace that enabled us to become His children.

The apostle is telling us that it is God's love that led to the gift of what John Newton has so aptly called "Amazing Grace." And we need to remember that all grace is amazing, given the nature of its recipients.

First John 3:1 closes with the thought that being a Christian so changes people's lives that those who live a life not centered in God (i.e., living in "the world") cannot even understand them. Why? Because they have been born into God's family and now live by a new set of principles and values that the apostle will spend much of chapters 3 and 4 explaining.

Although 1 John 3:1 is a text of great wonder, it does raise practical questions of importance. For example, if the secular world does perchance understand us as individuals, is it because we are not really different? Is it because we laugh at the same jokes, enjoy the same entertainments, and have the same priorities? Everybody reading verse 1 needs to ask themselves such questions if they are taking the Bible seriously. If Christianity hasn't made a difference in how I act and think from the society around me, then I don't have the real thing, but only a deceptive imitation. That is exactly the point that John is making about those in his congregations who had departed the Christian path.

First John 3:2 reiterates the fact that "we are *now* children of God." It does not say will be but "are now." Picking up on that idea, Martyn Lloyd-Jones writes that "perhaps the greatest weakness of all in the Christian church" is "that we fail to realise what we are, or who we are. We spend our time in arguing about the implications of the Christian truth or the application of this, that and the other. But the central thing is to realise what the Christian *is*" (Lloyd-Jones, *Children*, p. 23).

Having made that identity statement, verse 2 begins to shift in the direction of how who we are will affect our lives, a topic that will consume him for the rest of chapter 3.

Here the apostle has hit upon a connection of great importance, because even in the earthly sphere we link identity and conduct. Many has been the parent ready with the advice to his or her children to remember who they are when they go out in public.

We too often fail to recognize that the New Testament repeatedly emphasizes the fact that good conduct and correct living is based upon our position. Take the pattern we find in Paul's letters to the Galatians and Ephesians for example. In the first half of each letter comes the exposition of their Christian standing with God because they have been saved, then in the second half occurs the imperative to live the Christian life. That is invariably the New Testament pattern. Put in theological terms, first conversion, new birth, adoption, and justification take place, then progressive sanctification or growth in grace.

John is in harmony with the rest of the New Testament in his view of the relationship between identity and good living. For him *conduct does not determine relationship. Rather relationship determines conduct.* Thus the central fact is that Christians are children of God and, as such, will act the part rather than imitating the evil one.

Having established the identity aspect, John moves on in verse 2 to point out that "it has not yet been revealed what we will be." Here we find a bit of what we might term "apostolic agnosticism." Even God's prophets and apostles don't know everything. They only have some knowledge of what God has chosen to reveal to them. And the precise nature of existence in glory is not one of those things.

But just because the apostle John doesn't have the final word on the nature of humanity in the future does not mean that he knows nothing about what is to come. We do "know," he asserts, "that when He appears we will be like Him, because we will see Him as He is" (1 John 3:2).

One thing the apostle knows with certainty is that Christ will appear. Here we have a connection to 1 John 2:28, in which John tells us that His appearance takes place at His second advent or *parousia*. With the rest of the New Testament authors, John looks forward to Christ's coming as the culmination of hope.

A second thing that John knows for sure is "that when He appears we will be like Him, because we will see Him as He is." We can approach that passage from different perspectives. The first is that when He appears "we will see him as he is" and become like Him. Tom Thatcher challenges that understanding when he writes that "believers will not be like Jesus because they will see him; rather, believers will see Jesus because they have been like him. As God's children, true Christians are already 'like him,' and Christ's appearing will only confirm this established fact" (Thatcher, p. 459).

A reading of the context in the rest of 1 John 3 indicates that the latter interpretation is the correct one. True Christians, John argues, will be "like Him" in that they do not live in a state of sin (verses 4-10) and they express love in their daily actions (verses 11-18).

Reflecting the God who is love (1 John 4:8) brings to fulfillment the purposes He had in the creation of humans in Genesis, in which the Creator made people in His "likeness" and "image" (Gen. 1:26). But the Genesis 3 fall fractured that image, and humans became *unlike* their Maker. Biblical history records the process by which God has sought to renew His image in fallen people (see Col. 3:10), and 1 John 3:2 provides us with a glimpse of God's accomplishment. F. F. Bruce points out that "the consummation of God's purpose in man coincides with the advent of Christ in glory: then those who 'have borne the image of the man of dust' will 'bear the image of the man of heaven' (1 Cor. 15:49)" (Bruce, p. 87).

> ## Being Like Jesus
>
> "Believers will see Jesus because they have been like him. As God's children, true Christians are already 'like him'" (Thatcher, p. 459).

In summary, everyone having the hope of Christ's return will through God's grace live a pure life here on earth (1 John 3:3) and approximate the fullness of God's image here on earth. But when He appears in the clouds of heaven to bestow His final gifts on them (1 Cor. 15:51-54) they will reflect that image in totality. At that time Christians will be even more "like Him" than they are in the present age.

13. The Lawless Life

1 John 3:4

> *'Everyone who continues to practice sin also practices lawlessness; and sin is lawlessness.*

Here is a verse freighted with theological baggage. Most readers are probably more familiar with the King James translation, which reads: "Whoever committeth sin transgresseth also the law: for sin is the transgression of the law." That is an unfortunate translation because it leaves the impression that the "sin" that John is talking about is "the contravention of this or that specific law rather than a general lawless attitude towards God" (Bruce, p. 89). Sin, as John uses the word here, includes specific acts of transgression, but it signifies much more.

But before we examine the meaning of the text, it is important to note whom John is warning his readers against. We must always remember that he has certain people in mind, even though what he has to say is still applicable to those of us living 2,000 years later.

John's target in verse 4 and up through verse 10 is the secessionists from his congregation who claimed to know God but disobeyed His commandments (1 John 2:4). Such people were "liars" (verse 4) and were "walking in darkness" (1:6). The apostle meets such misguided "teachers" with his forceful statement in 1 John 3:4 that "everyone who continues to practice sin also practices lawlessness" because "sin" by definition "is lawlessness."

John's first word is central to his argument in verses 4 through 10. The passage is loaded with such phrases as "everyone who," "anyone who," "he who," and "no one who." Listen to him:

- Everyone who sins is lawless (verse 4).
- No one dwelling in Him sins (verse 6).
- No one who sins knows Him (verse 6).
- Let no one deceive you; those who do right are righteous (verse 7).
- The one who sins is of the devil (verse 8).
- No one who sins is born of God (verse 9).
- Anyone who doesn't do right is not of God (verse 10).

John has no doubt concerning what he is talking about. Christian morality has no exceptions. All Christians will avoid sin and lawlessness. The moral implications of the gospel are for everyone.

Now let's turn to the verse itself: "Everyone who continues to practice sin also practices lawlessness." That teaching is the polar opposite of the previous verse in the letter, which stated that "everyone having this hope in Him purifies himself, even as He is pure" (1 John 3:3). At the other end of the spectrum from those who practice purity are those infected with lawlessness. John here makes vivid the contrast between true Christians and the secessionists, who were seeking to win over his parishioners.

The two key theological words in 1 John 3:4 are "sin" and "lawlessness." The Greek word translated as sin is *amartia* which literally means "not to hit" or "to miss," such as missing a goal or target. By extension, it came to have the figurative meaning of "to fall short morally" or "to do wrong" (Bromiley, p. 48). My translation of the verb as "continues to practice" represents the force of the Greek verb tense. John is not speaking about someone who commits a wrong act from time to time, but a person who lives *a life of continual sinning*.

But sin in verse 4 is not merely a wrong action or a series of wrong actions. While *amartia* can refer to sin as a specific deed, it can also indicate "a state of being sinful," as in "sinfulness," or as "a destructive evil power" in people's lives (Bauer, pp. 50, 51).

The crucial thing to note is that SIN at the deepest level is more than an action or series of actions (sins). Perhaps we can best understand the nature of SIN as a state of being sinful by looking at the first sin in Genesis 3. The essential question is, "Did Eve sin when she took the fruit or before she took it?" The answer will help us come to grips with the nature of both SIN as a state of being and the sins that result from that condition.

A reading of Genesis 3 leads to the conclusion that something happened in Eve's mind and heart before she acted to take the fruit. In essence, she first rebelled against God and His authority, and then and only then did she commit the acts of taking and eating. That is, SIN in her mind and heart led her to choose sinful actions or sins. Such a conclusion is quite in harmony with that of Jesus when He noted that "out of the heart come evil thoughts, murder, adultery, fornication, theft, false witness, slander" (Matt. 15:19, RSV).

Thus SIN is more than mere wrong actions. In its essence it is living a life of rebellion against the God of the universe (Isa. 1:2, 4; Hosea 7:13). SIN, therefore, is a moral choice against God. As a result, Herbert Douglass can write that "sin is a created being's clenched fist in the face of his Creator; sin is the creature . . . deposing [God] as the Lord of his life" (Douglass, p. 53) and Emil Brunner can claim that sin "is like the son who strikes his father's face in anger, . . . it is the bold self-assertion of the son's will above that of the father" (Brunner, p. 462).

In the overall context of the letter "sin" in 1 John 3:4 is living in a continuing state of sinfulness in harmony with the principles of "the evil one" (1 John 2:14). Out of that sinful state flows a series of sinful actions or sins.

That conclusion agrees with the second important theological word in 1 John 3:4—"lawlessness," which the passage equates with the living of a sinful life. We should note that the word "law" (*nomos*) is not in verse 4. In fact, it does not appear anywhere in 1 John. Rather the apostle uses "lawlessness." The English "lawlessness" is from the Greek *anomia*, which literally means "without law." While it is true that lawlessness is generally understood to be the violation of the law of God (see R. Brown, p. 398; Lenski, p. 455), the problem in 1 John 3:4 is much more serious than that. "It is" rather "a willful rejection and an active disobedience against God's moral standard, which is a characteristic of the child of the devil" (Akin, p. 140).

Thus to live a life of *anomia* is to behave as if the law did not exist. Such a life, of course, would lead to the regular breaking of the law, but that is not John's focus. While the people he is writing about do not keep

God's commandments (2:4), the apostle's charge against them in 1 John 3:4 is much deeper and broader than their actions. That is, they live in total disregard of His laws as if they didn't even exist. They live a life of lawlessness.

With that understanding in mind, it is not surprising that John's opponents don't keep God's commandments (1 John 2:4) or feel any need to confess their sins (1:9). After all, since they are without law, or lawless, they don't even admit that they are sinners (1:8, 10). Thus they see no need of the Advocate (2:1) or the atoning sacrifice or propitiation of Jesus (2:2). As a result, from the perspective of John, the secessionists are not just mixed up, they are totally off the Christian map. That leads to his forceful warning to the faithful members of his congregations to avoid such "false prophets" (4:1).

God's commandments were important for John. And obedience to them was one indication that people knew God (5:2, 3; 3:3, 4). The condition of lawlessness was an anti-God state of mind leading to a life that he described as sin.

The apostle has now set forth the alternatives open to his parishioners and to us. Either we will be purifying ourselves, "even as He is pure" (3:3), or we can live in a state of lawlessness. The choice is open to each of us as to whether we want to follow in the footsteps of the evil one (2:14) or become a member of the family of God (2:28, 24).

14. Biblical Sinlessness

1 John 3:5–10

⁵And you know that He appeared that He might take away sins, and in Him is no sin. ⁶No one dwelling in Him keeps on sinning; no one who keeps on sinning has seen Him or has known Him. ⁷Children, let no one deceive you; the one who continues to practice righteousness is righteous, even as He is righteous. ⁸The one who continues to practice sin is of the devil, because the devil has sinned from the beginning. For this reason the Son of God was revealed, that He might destroy the works of the devil. ⁹No one having been born of God practices sin, because His seed dwells in him, and he is not able to sin because he has been born of God. ¹⁰In this are revealed the children of God and the children of the devil. Anyone not continuing to practice righteousness is not of God, nor is the one who does not love his brother.

We encounter several central ideas in 1 John 3:5-10. One is that Christ came to "take away sins" (verse 5). It is difficult to read that verse without recalling John the Baptist's declaration, "Behold, the Lamb of God, who takes away the sin of the world!" (John 1:29, RSV). Another passage presenting the same idea is Hebrews 9:26, in which we read that "he has appeared once for all at the end of the age to put away sin by the sacrifice of himself" (RSV).

The statements by John the Baptist and the book of Hebrews both make it plain that the way that Jesus takes away sin is through His sacrificial death on our behalf. That same teaching appears in 1 John 2:2, which claims that Jesus is the "propitiation" or "atoning sacrifice" (NIV) "for our sins" and "for those of the whole world."

102

That the substitutionary sacrifice of Christ as the Lamb of God who died in our place is behind 1 John 3:5's teaching that Christ "appeared that He might take away sins" is also implied by the fact that that same verse describes Him as absolutely sinless. Thus like the sacrificial animals of the Old Testament He was without "blemish" and thus qualified to be the sacrificial "Lamb of God."

Closely related to Christ's appearing to "take away sins" (verse 5) is the teaching of verse 8 that "the Son of God was revealed" in order that "he might destroy the works of the devil." Calvin Kruse makes the insightful point that "through his atoning death Jesus dealt with the problem of human sin and in so doing destroyed the work of the devil" (Kruse, p. 123).

A second important teaching in 1 John 3:5-10 is that the devil and those associated with him (the secessionists that John is combating) teach that behavior doesn't matter. "Let no one deceive you," John writes regarding the pedagogical efforts of the secessionists, that behavior doesn't matter. After all, he adds, "the one who continues to practice righteousness is righteous" and is therefore like God (verse 7). Again, "no one having been born of God practices sin" (verse 9). And John concludes the passage with the thought that behavior reveals who are the children of God and who are those of the devil. Those who practice righteousness as a way of life and love their fellow church members are of God (verse 10). The conclusion of the matter is that *behavior does matter*, in spite of the deceptive teachings of the "false prophets" troubling John's congregations.

The proclamation that behavior does matter brings us to a topic in 1 John 3:5-10 that has troubled people down through the ages. That is, in that passage the apostle seems to be teaching some sort of sinless perfectionism. After all, doesn't he say in verse 6 that "no one dwelling in Him keeps on sinning" and in verse 9 that Christians are "not able to sin" or "cannot sin" (RSV)? And doesn't the apostle plainly tell us in 1 John 5:18 that whoever is "born of God does not sin," but that "God keeps him" and the evil one cannot "touch him" (RSV)?

In the light of those verses we need to admit that John explicitly teaches that we may be sinless in this life. But, we must hasten to ask, what does he mean?

That question is especially pertinent in the light of other verses in

1 John that seem to teach just the opposite perspective. For example, John also wrote that "if we say that we have no sin, we deceive ourselves" (1:8); "if we confess our sins, He is faithful and just, He forgives our sins and cleanses us from all unrighteousness" (1:9); "if we say that we have not sinned, we make Him a liar" (1:10); and "I am writing these things to you so that you will not sin. But if anyone sins, we have an Advocate with the Father, Jesus Christ the righteous" (2:1).

How can the same author declare that Christians cannot sin but that if they claim that they haven't sinned they are liars? It is clear that John is either terribly confused or he is operating with a definition of sin that is more complex than generally acknowledged by those who glibly quote him as saying that "sin is the transgression of the law" (3:4, KJV) and give that verse an interpretation based purely on outward behavior.

The fact that John has a complex definition of sin in mind is evident not only from the passages quoted above, but also from 1 John 5:16, 17, in which he notes that some sin is "not unto death," while other sin is "unto death" (KJV).

The fault line between that sin which cannot be found in the believer (3:9 and "sin unto death," 5:16) and those open to mediation by Christ (1:9; 2:1 or are "not unto death," 5:17) runs through a person's attitude or condition. Here it is important to note that in all the passages in 1 John demanding sinlessness, the Greek verbs are in the present tense, thereby denoting people who live in a state of continual or habitual sinning or lawlessness. On the other hand, in 1 John 2:1, in which the apostle tells us that if we sin we have an Advocate, the verb is in the aorist tense, indicating a definite action in a point of time. Thus the action is not ongoing and therefore not a way of life.

First John depicts the contrast between those who have an attitude of rebellion toward God and live a lawless life of SIN or lawlessness as a way of life, and those who commit sins or acts of sin that they repent of as they turn to the Advocate for forgiveness and cleansing (1 John 2:1, 2; 1:9). The first category indicates those who have sinned "unto death," while the sin of those in the second category is "not unto death." Sins "unto death" are equivalent to the unpardonable sin of Matthew 12:31, 32. When people are in a state of rebellion, lawlessness, or SIN, and continuously reject the pleading of the Holy Spirit to repent of their sinful acts, they have placed themselves in a position to deny or ignore God's saving grace. Such rebellious hardness is the sin "unto death." It is impossible for a person to be a Christian and live in a state of SIN at the same time (1 John 3:9).

Those with SIN "unto death" live in a state of "lawlessness (3:4) and rebellion to God, while those in tune with the Advocate have been "born of God," dwell "in Him," and have become a part of the family of God through adoption (1 John 3:9, 6, 1).

Because Christians have been born from above and have had their minds transformed, they do not have a rebellious attitude toward God. Rather, they "walk in the light" (1:7) in the same way that Jesus walked (2:6).

By his repeated use of the word "walk" in chapters 1 and 2, it is clear that John is speaking of two ways of life that harmonize with his verb tenses in chapter 3. We can walk or journey with either God or the devil. One way is that of SIN, a lawless relationship to God that leads to a life of sinning and ends in death. The other is a faith relationship, with its born-of-God attitude toward sin and its use of the Advocate for cleansing (1:9; 2:1, 2) and the Holy Spirit for empowerment. John defines those in the second group as being sinless, even though they still commit acts of sin for which they need forgiveness.

Two Ways of Walking and Two Walking Partners

1. "Everyone who continues to practice sin also practices lawlessness" (verse 4).
2. "No one dwelling in Him keeps on sinning" (verse 6).
3. "No one who keeps on sinning has seen Him" (verse 6).
4. "The one who continues to practice sin is of the devil" (verse 8).
5. "Anyone not continuing to practice righteousness is of God" (verse 10).

VERSUS

1. "The one who continues to practice righteousness is righteous" (verse 7).
2. "No one having been born of God practices sin" (verse 9).
3. "He is not able to sin because he has been born of God" (verse 9).

Thus sinlessness in the present life is not only a possibility but a promise and demand. The Christian, John tells us, "cannot sin" (RSV) or is "not able to sin because he has been born of God" (3:9). And those who have been born of God's Spirit (John 3:5) are new creatures (2 Cor. 5:17), who have a new heart and mind and thus a new way of thinking that leads to a new way of living. On the other hand, those not born of God are "the children of the devil" (1 John 3:10), continue "to practice sin" (verse 8), and live in a lawless state of rebellious independence from God (verse 4).

The apostle John couldn't have made the alternatives plainer. The choice of pathways and walking partners, of course, is up to each of us.

15. The Core of Godliness

1 John 3:11, 12

[11]For this is the message which you heard from the beginning, that we love one another, [12]not being like Cain, who was of the evil one and slaughtered his brother. And for what reason did he slaughter him? Because his deeds were evil and those of his brother righteous.

The word "for" might be a little one, but it is important in verse 11, since it reflects back to verse 10 with its teaching that those who do not do right and do not love their brother are not of God.

First John 3:11-18 picks up on the word "love" and expands upon its implications for Christian living. It is not the first time 1 John has treated this important topic. In 1 John 2:7-11 the apostle introduced the new but old command to love one's fellow church members. To do so, he told his readers, is to dwell in light. Not to do so is to exist in darkness. Now in 3:11-18 he "fills in his preliminary sketch," but "he uses no colours but black and white" (Stott, p. 143) as he continues the stark contrast of verse 10 between the children of God and those of the devil.

"The message" that John tells his readers that they had "heard from the beginning" is that Christians need to "love one another." They may have heard that teaching from the beginning, but some of them must have been struggling with it because John will repeat it five more times in his first two letters:

1. "This is his commandment, that we should believe in the name of his Son Jesus Christ and love one another" (1 John 3:23, RSV).
2. "Let us love one another; for love is of God, and he who loves is born of God and knows God" (1 John 4:7. RSV).

3. "If God so loved us, we also ought to love one another" (1 John 4:11, RSV).
4. "If we love one another, God abides in us" (1 John 4:12, RSV).
5. "I ask that we love one another" (2 John 5, NIV).

The sheer repetition of the need to love one another points to one of the problems that John faced in his congregations, but even more important it indicates the absolute centrality of the topic to the Christian message. The paramount significance of the message to love one another is grounded in the very nature of God. If "God is love" (1 John 4:8), then it is imperative that His children have that same core characteristic at the center of their being.

The Centrality of Love to Christian Living

"Joy is love exalted; peace is love in repose; long-suffering is love enduring; gentleness is love in society; goodness is love in action; faith is love on the battlefield; meekness is love in school; and temperance is love in training" (Dwight L. Moody, in Barton, p. 71).

"The beginning" in 1 John 3:11 has two possible meanings. First, it could be referring back to Genesis 1 and 2 and the origin of the human race. Or, second, it could point back to the time when those in John's congregation first heard the Christian message. The first meaning in this particular passage has some credence, since the illustration of Cain in verse 12 indicates the problem of loving others goes back to the time of the Genesis Fall. While that is true, it is the second meaning that best fits the overall context in 1 John.

Again and again when John refers to the beginning he has in mind the time when his readers first heard the gospel message. And the teaching that the true test of discipleship is love for others in the community (John 13:34, 35) and that Christ's followers ought to love one another just as He loves them (John 15:12) permeates that apostolic message. In fact, it was Christ's "command" for them to love one another (verse 17). That ethical imperative stood at the very foundation of the Christianity that John and the other apostles had taught their converts from "the beginning" of their Christian experience.

The repeated appeal to go back to "the beginning" has one more significant overtone that we need to examine before we move on. It is that Christians need to always validate their teachings and those of their church by returning to the apostolic teachings presented at the birth and early development of Christianity. The passage of time all too often has a corrosive effect on Christian understandings. As it moves on error tends to creep in. Thus the appeal of John for his readers to go back to what Christians heard in "the beginning" has very definite meaning for our day. We constantly need to return to "the beginning" of the Christian message to renew our understanding of its essential nature both doctrinally and ethically.

That thought brings us to 1 John 3:12 and the illustration of Cain, whom the apostle uses as the prime example of a person who did not love his brother. The Cain illustration is of interest for several reasons. One is that "this is the only undisputed direct reference to the [Old Testament] in the Johannine Epistles" (Beale, p. 1066).

More significant is the fact that Cain "slaughtered his brother." The Greek word I translated as "slaughtered" is not a gentle one. It signifies "to slay, slaughter, butcher, by cutting the throat" (Wuest, vol. 2, sec. 3, p. 151). John bypassed the usual Greek word meaning "to kill" and employed a more graphic one, indicating a "violent killing" (Rogers, p. 596).

And why did Cain perform such an atrocity? Because, John tells us, he belonged to "the evil one" (1 John 3:12), who was a "murderer from the beginning" (John 8:44, RSV). "The story of Cain," I. Howard Marshall points out, "shows what failure to love one's brother can lead to—sheer murder—and thus stresses that all hatred is embryonic murder" (Marshall, pp. 189, 190).

With that thought John expands upon the teaching of Jesus. In Matthew 5:21, 22 He proclaimed that angry and unloving thoughts toward others have a direct relationship to the commandment against murder. Thus John warns his readers that unloving attitudes not only place one on the side of the devil, but that they are much more serious than some might claim.

The apostle has begun to answer the question of why Cain did evil by telling his readers that he was acting like his spiritual parent, but John has more to say on the topic as he plunges into the motivational depths of Cain's action. He goes on to say that he slaughtered Abel because "his deeds were evil" while "those of his brother righteous." Jealousy directed his actions. And that jealousy was not over money or beauty or talent but because Abel was determined to do right. "In essence, Cain murdered his brother Abel because the wicked person hates righteousness." It was his "inner nature" that "brought forth the outward action" (Akin, p. 155).

But, we must ask in closing our study of verses 11 and 12, why did John even bring up the Cain story? His underlying purpose seems to be that "the attitudes of the two first brothers become the archetypes of the two families in this world—the children of God and the children of the world" or the evil one (Roberts, p. 88).

For John there existed only two spiritual families on earth. One centers on an unloving attitude that leads to jealousy and evil actions, while the other finds its genesis in a love for others that overflows into caring and sacrificial actions for and toward other people. The first orientation reflects that of the evil one, while the second has its roots in the character of God, which is love (1 John 4:8). There is no doubt in John's mind. The very core of godliness is that love that emulates the character of the Father. To John, as for Jesus, true religion is first and foremost a matter of the heart. Once in the heart it can then flow out in everyday living.

16. Godliness in Action

1 John 3:13-18

¹³Do not be surprised, brothers, if the world hates you. ¹⁴We know that we have passed out of death into life because we love the brothers. He who does not love dwells in death. ¹⁵Anyone hating his brother is a murderer, and you know that no murderer has eternal life dwelling in him. ¹⁶By this we know love, because He laid down His life for us; and we ought to lay down our lives for the brothers. ¹⁷Now whoever has this world's possessions and sees his brother having need yet closes his inner affections against him, how does the love of God dwell in him? ¹⁸Little children, let us not love in word or in tongue but in deed and reality.

The reference to Cain's hatred toward his brother in verse 12 leads the apostle into an additional aspect of the struggle between good and evil: Satan-inspired hatred in verse 13 and God-inspired love in verses 14-18.

The sad truth is that the war between goodness and evil reflected in Cain and Abel will be with us until the Second Advent. Apparently the hostile attitude from not only the larger non-Christian world around them, but also from the secessionists (1 John 3:15), had shocked some in John's faithful congregation.

"Do not be surprised," the apostle tells them. Just as Cain hated Abel because of his goodness, so the world will hate you. After all, as William Barclay notes, "the good man is a walking rebuke to the evil man, even if he never speaks a word to him. . . . The life of a good man always passes a silent judgment on the life of an evil man" (Barclay, p. 101).

It is interesting that the apostle employs the word "brothers" only in this passage in 1 John. That usage is not an accident. Not only does the term reflect on the unity of the Christian community, but here it is a continuation of the Cain and Abel relationship of verse 12. Just as Cain reacted against his brother, so the children of Cain (and by extension the devil, verse 10) will respond in similar ways against those following Abel and God. Love and Hate are two characteristic paths of those who emulate different leaders from what had once been a family of "brothers." "Just as love is the defining characteristic of the child of God, so hatred is the natural response of the world toward righteousness" (Akin, p. 156).

One other reason that the world's hatred should not startle faithful Christians is that such warnings were a part of the gospel message they had heard "from the beginning" (1 John 3:11). Thus we find Jesus telling His disciples in the Fourth Gospel that the world would hate them just as it had first hated Him (John 15:18; 16:1-4). But a major difference existed between the Gospel's warning and the situation of John's readers. Jesus was speaking of the animosity of non-Christians, whereas 1 John deals with hatred from those who had once belonged to the family of believers. Those of us who live in the twenty-first century can find an important lesson here. We also must not let the animosity of those who give up the faith surprise and devastate us. It is important to learn insights from biblical history as we seek to navigate the perils of life while at the same time keeping our faith and sanity in tact.

In 1 John 3:14-18 the apostle shifts from an exposition of the hatred of those following the evil one and toward the kind of love God's children need to exhibit. John emphasizes in verses 14 and 15 the fact that a life of love proves that individuals have advanced from death to life and in verses 16-18 he stresses the essence of love as self-sacrifice.

"We know," John write, "that we have passed out of death into life because we love the brothers" (verse 14). Here we find an important point about the order of salvation. That is, we do not earn eternal life because we are loving. Rather, loving is evidence that a person has moved from life to death. Here we find an echo of the apostle's new birth idea found in his Gospel (see John 1:12, 13; 3:5, 7). Because of that transforming experience, Christians are children of God (1 John 3:1) transported from the realm of darkness, hate, and death to that of light, love, and life. And, John tells us, the very fact that we love from our hearts our fellow believers (even those difficult to get along with or those whom we find personally obnoxious) is proof that we have made the transition. Thus loving is not the means of obtaining "eternal life" (1 John 3:15) but the assurance of already possessing it.

In the teaching that Christians already possess eternal life we find another echo of the Fourth Gospel, in which the apostle teaches that "he who believes in the Son has eternal life" (John 3:36, RSV) and "has passed from death to life (John 5:24, RSV). Having eternal life, of course, does not mean that believers don't die or already possess immortality. To the contrary, they do die, but God will resurrect them at the Second Advent and give them immortality at that time (1 Cor. 15:51-54). Currently having eternal life reflects on the truth that believers are among that group that are assured of being granted immortality in the future. But beyond that, it speaks to the quality of life that a Christian lives on this earth. More specifically, Christians from the time of their conversion begin to live the life of heaven characterized by godliness or being like the God who is love

> "Love is the very essence of life: without it there may be physical existence, but not life" (C. J. Barker, p. 56).

(1 John 4:8). Love, in John's thought, is both the essence of Christian living and the proof that a person has indeed passed from death into life.

Proof in 1 John 3:14, 15, we should note, is a two-way street. Not only does lovingness indicate those who have eternal life, but lack of love or the possession of hatred demonstrates total lostness. And in John's equation of hate with murder, as we noted earlier, we find an allusion to the Sermon on the Mount and Jesus' teaching on the full implications of a person's thoughts (see Matt. 5:21, 22, 27, 28).

But the good news for the secessionists and other haters/murderers is that they do not need to remain in the death of lostness. Forgiveness is always available (even to murderers) for those who confess their sins and repent (1 John 1:9). Even the worst of sinners can pass from the realm of death to that of eternal life.

In 1 John 3:16 to 18 the letter moves on from what love proves to what it is. And in his discussion John leaves his readers with no doubts about the core of love being self-sacrifice—the kind of self-sacrifice that

Christ exhibited in giving His life for the salvation of others. It is that quality of love, the apostle urges, that must characterize the lives of true Christians. Here again we find teachings repeated from the Fourth Gospel: "This is my commandment," Jesus told His disciples, "that you love one another as I have loved you. Greater love has no man than this, that a man lay down his life for his friends" (John 15:12, 13, RSV).

In that passage and in 1 John 3:16 we find Jesus as the ultimate example of loving others in the life of service that was at the center of His agenda (Matt. 20:27). But, one student of John's letter points out, "laying down one's life for sisters and brothers seems by definition to be a once-in-a-lifetime heroism at best. Perhaps for that reason the elder offers a matter-of-fact example of what he has in mind" in verse 17 (Black, p. 419), in which he urges his readers to share their possessions with those who have earthly needs.

That transition from the ultimate act of love to daily living reminds me of Romans 12:1, 2, in which Paul tells his readers that transformed existence means becoming a "living sacrifice." I have often thought that it would be easier just to die for a cause once and get it over with than to have to die daily as a prerequisite to living the Christian life in an ongoing manner. But it is that continuing life of sacrifice and service that John highlights when he sets forth the practical lesson that sharing what we have in this life with those who are less fortunate is the essence of love.

First John 3:16 demands that we get real. Most of us will never be called upon to sacrifice our physical life for another person. But, we can share what we have. And here, C. H. Dodd indicates, is the "same principle of action, though at a lower level of intensity" (Dodd, p. 86). Love that leads to service for others, John is telling us, is essentially the same whether it be giving up one's life all at once or continually living the life of service, sacrifice, and "self" denial.

Thus, the apostle commands us, "let us not love in word or in tongue but in deed and reality" (1 John 3:18). In today's idiom he would say "put your money where your mouth is." Christianity is not a theory about love. It is love in action—godliness put into practice.

17. The Reassurance of God

1 John 3:19-24

¹⁹By this we will know that we are of the truth, and reassure our heart before Him, ²⁰if our heart condemns us, because God is greater than our heart and He knows all things. ²¹Beloved, if our heart does not condemn us, we have confidence before God; ²²and whatever we ask we receive from Him, because we keep His commandments and we practice the things pleasing to Him. ²³And this is His commandment, that we believe in the name of His Son Jesus Christ, and practice loving one another, just as He commanded us. ²⁴And the one keeping His commandments dwells in Him and He in him. And by this we know that He dwells in us, by the Spirit whom He gave to us.

It's easy to feel lost, even if a person is saved!

That is especially true for those of us blessed (or cursed) with an overly sensitive nature. "Historically, and in our own practical experience," D. Moody Smith observes, "it is not the careless Christian, but more often the carefully conscientious one, who is plagued with a sense of guilt and inadequacy" (D. M. Smith, p. 97). That observation is akin to the one that claims that the closer we get to Christ the more we will be aware of our sinfulness (see E. White, *Steps*, p. 64).

Although the Greek *kardia* literally means "heart," the rendering of the word as "conscience" by the *Revised English Bible* captures the meaning of the passage for our day. It is a condemning conscience that is at issue in 1 John 3:20. And one of the functions of the human conscience is to convict of sin as the Holy Spirit continues to operate in our lives (John 16:8). When we do wrong, the Spirit, utilizing the ideal of the law, declares us to be sinners (Rom. 3:20; 4:15; 5:20; 7:7-10).

Now it is a fact that the human conscience is not an altogether trust-worthy guide to guilt. Sometimes the conscience's accusations are true, which should lead to confession (1 John 1:9) through the Advocate (2:1), but at other times they are false. As a result, "unnecessary self-condemnation has marred many a Christian's experience. Many," for example, "depend on their own moral judgments to determine their spiritual condition, and fail to realize that their feelings are unsatisfactory criteria for deciding the state of their spiritual health" (Nichol, p. 656).

The apostle targets in 1 John 3:19-21 those needing comfort and reassurance of their spiritual status. Whereas the motif of reassurance has been in the background since the mention of the antichrist in 1 John 2:18, here it comes to the foreground just before the apostle again brings up the topic of the antichrist in 1 John 4:1-3.

> ## A Point to Ponder
>
> "John would have said that a so-called heretic, whose heart was overflowing with love, and whose life was beautiful with service, is far nearer Christ than someone who is impeccably orthodox, yet coldly correct, and remote from the needs of men" (Barclay, p. 102).
> What do you think? Why?

Verses 19-21 put forth reassurance in two flavors. First, we can "know that we are of the truth" and reassure our own "heart before Him" (verse 19). And just how can we do that? By applying the test of love that John has been explaining in chapter 3: "We know," John wrote in verse 14, "that we have passed out of death into life because we love the brothers." When we feel God's love surge into our lives in the face of the needs of others or even when we have to deal with difficult sisters and brothers in the church, then we can be sure that we possess the real thing. At such times we may be quite aware of our own short comings, but if God's love is our ruling motive we can have confidence that we are on the right path.

Of course, self-reassurance is only possible, John implies, if we "know" the truth about both ourselves and God. That is where the pinch comes in. No human knows fully. Thus there is always room for nagging doubt. After all, we sometimes do good things for very bad reasons. And then again, we humans are excellent at deceiving ourselves about our true condition. Most of us need more than just self-affirmation.

That is where verse 20 comes in: if our heart still continues its condemnation, God has supplied us with a second level of reassurance, because He "is greater than our heart and He knows all things." Foundational to this verse is the truth that even though our knowledge is faulty, God knows everything about us.

Our realization of God's omniscience may have two quite different effects upon our minds. On the one hand, it might strike terror into our hearts since He knows absolutely everything about us. Or, on the other hand, it can bring comfort to our hearts because He can understand what shapes and drives us.

Both meanings are possible from a reading of the isolated words of 1 John 3:20, but in their context only the second option is a possibility. That context is one of reassurance (verse 19) and having "confidence before God" (verse 21).

Thus the implication of verse 20 is that "we can, therefore, appeal from our conscience to God, who is greater and more knowledgeable. Indeed, he knows everything, including our secret motives and deepest resolves, and, it is implied, will be more merciful towards us than our own heart." Therefore, "his omniscience should relieve, not terrify us (cf. Ps. 103:14; Jn. 21:17)" (Stott, p. 150).

First John 3:21 finds the apostle addressing his readers as "beloved," a term in its context that undoubtedly expresses his personal concern for those of his readers who have struggled with a condemning heart. He uses it to indicate that the God of love holds them in His own heart. And because God loves them they can come confidently into His presence. The word translated as "confidence" signifies "*free and fearless confidence, cheerful courage,* boldness, assurance" (Thayer, p. 491). In short, John is telling his readers that Christians have nothing to fear as they enter the divine presence (cf. Heb. 4:16).

They cannot only come before Him in "cheerful courage," but whatever they ask, He will give them (1 John 3:22). That promise, we should note, goes to those following God's commands and practicing "the things pleasing to Him." Thus the promise is not a blank check for anyone to ask anything of God. The conditions set forth in verse 23 imply that such people would only request blessings in harmony with God's will, a thought in line with 1 John 5:14, which reads: "This is the confidence which we have in him, that if we ask anything according to his will he hears us" (RSV).

And just what is the commandment that is pleasing to God in verse 23? The word "commandment" in that verse is singular, but John goes on to enunciate two of its aspects. First, Christians are commanded to "believe in the name of His Son." Belief in 1 John, as we have repeatedly noted, is fraught with a great deal of theological meaning. In other places we find that it includes acknowledging that Jesus is the Christ (2:22; 5:1) and that Christ had come in the flesh (4:2).

Coupled to the need to believe in the Son is a second aspect of God's command—that Christians "practice loving one another." We find an interesting theological point tucked away in the verb tenses of the two aspects of the singular commandment of verse 23. "Believe" is in the Greek aeorist tense, which implies a decisive act at some point, while the word "love" is in a tense signifying continuous action. Thus when people become Christians they accept belief in the Son, but after doing so they habitually "practice loving one another." Those two elements of God's commandment are not only both tests, but they are linked to the Christian experiences that theologians have labeled as justification and sanctification.

One more aspect of the two parts of the singular commandment of verse 23 needs highlighting. The unity of the command sets forth the truth that Christian life in its fullness depends upon both correct theology and right conduct. As William Barclay so aptly puts it: "There can be no such thing as a Christian theology without a Christian ethic; and equally there can be no such thing as a Christian ethic without a Christian theology. The one depends on the other. Our belief is not real belief unless it issues in action; and our action has neither sanction nor dynamic unless it is based on belief" (Barclay, pp. 104, 105).

John closes the final paragraph of chapter 3 with an allusion to the allegory of John 15 regarding the vine and the branches. The we in Him and He in us wording expresses the spiritual unity of believers with God. The apostle presents that spiritual unity in terms of a relationship to Christ in the Fourth Gospel, while here in verse 24 it is with God. But for John that is no problem. He quotes Jesus regarding the spiritual unity of Himself with the Father and His desire for that same unity to be between believers and "us," meaning the Father and the Son (John 17:21). The condition that the apostle sets forth in verse 24 for that mutual indwelling is ongoing obedience to God's will. Or as he said it in his first chapter, believers will "walk in the light" (1:7). Such individuals have the Holy "Spirit whom He gave to us" (3:24). Thus John ends chapter 3 with the Spirit, the same member of the Godhead who becomes the focal point in the opening verses of chapter 4.

18. Testing the Prophets

1 John 4:1-3

¹Beloved, do not believe every spirit, but test the spirits to determine if they are from God, because many false prophets have gone out into the world. ²By this we know the Spirit of God: every spirit that confesses Jesus Christ has come in the flesh is from God, ³and every spirit which does not confess Jesus is not from God; and this is the spirit of the antichrist, of which you have heard that it is coming and now already is in the world.

Many false prophets have gone out into the world." John was dealing with religious leaders who claimed to have a word directly from God, but actually had one from the devil. Thus the apostle's admonition "to test the spirits" to determine which were from God.

The sad fact is that not all religion is good religion, not everything or everyone who claims to be of God is the real thing. George Findlay observes that "to identify the supernatural [with] the Divine is a perilous mistake. It seems that in this world there is no truth without its counterfeit, nor good wheat of God unmixed with tares. Christ is mimicked by Antichrist; the Spirit of God is mocked by lying spirits, and the prophets of truth are counter-worked by 'many false prophets' which 'have gone out into the world'" (Findlay, p. 327).

The problem of false prophets is not unique to John's day.

The Bible first treats the topic in Deuteronomy 13:1-5, in which a "prophet" arises who can perform miraculous signs and wonders and has a message directing the people to follow "other gods." The Lord's command to Israel was that they should "not listen to the words of that prophet" because of his false teaching (cf. Deut. 18:22).

One of the important things to note in that passage is that the false prophets that Moses dealt with had supernatural power. They could perform supernatural signs and miracles. Unfortunately they did so through the aid of an evil power.

The problem of false prophets claiming to have a divine word for God's people continued throughout the Old Testament period. Thus in Elijah's time prophets of Baal and Asherah challenged him (1 Kings 18:1-22). And the book of Jeremiah finds God saying, "Do not listen to the words of the prophets who prophesy to you, filling you with vain hopes; they speak visions of their own minds, not from the mouth of the Lord" (Jer. 23:16, RSV).

The New Testament depicts Jesus warning His followers that "many false prophets will arise and lead many astray" (Matt. 24:11, RSV) and "false Christs and false prophets" would show "great signs and wonders" that would be so convincing that it would tempt "even the elect" to go "astray" (verse 24, RSV). Such "Christian" prophets would prophecy and cast out demons and do many mighty works in Christ's name, but they would not do God's will (Matt. 7:22, 21). Jesus, therefore, advised His followers to "beware of false prophets, who come to you in sheep's clothing but inwardly are ravenous wolves. You will know them by their fruits" (verses 15, 16, RSV).

Paul also had to combat false prophets. Picking up on Jesus' warning, he prophesied to the church in Ephesus that "I know that after my departure fierce wolves will come in among you, not sparing the flock; and from among your own selves will arise men speaking perverse things, to draw away the disciples after them" (Acts 20:29, 30, RSV).

That time had arrived. John who had charge of the church in Ephesus was indeed dealing with "perverse" teachers who had emerged from the midst of his flock and were actively seeking to make converts to their false teachings. That problem is the focal point of his letters as he seeks to warn those still faithful to the church.

But how do you innoculate people against religious teachers who seem to be sincere and may even have supernatural powers? Paul faced that issue in 1 Thessalonians. "Do not quench the Spirit," he penned, "do not despise prophesying, but test everything; hold fast what is good" (5:19-21, RSV).

The reason that Christians can't just flatly reject all who make prophetic claims is that God can still use prophets whenever He chooses to do so. Thus, Gene Green writes, "the apostle's counsel is that the reaction of the church should be more balanced than simply rejecting prophetic utterances: *Test everything. Hold on to the good*" (Green, p. 264).

The Greek word translated as "test" means "to prove, test, verify, examine prior to approval, judge, evaluate, discern" (Spicq, vol. 1, p. 353) or "to make a critical examination of [something] to determine genuineness" (Bauer, p. 255). First John 4:1 and 1 Thiessalonians 5:21 both use the same word for test..

Paul does not explain how the Thessalonians were to verify the validity of prophets, but in 1 Corinthians 12:3 he said that "no one speaking by the Spirit of God ever says 'Jesus be cursed!' and no one can say 'Jesus is Lord' except by the Holy Spirit" (RSV). Thus he applied the theological truth test.

In summary, in the teachings of Jesus and Paul we find that the two tests of those who had a true Christian spirit were the moral test (see Matt. 7:15-23) and the truth test (see 1 Cor. 12:3; 14:29). Both of them also appear in the *Didache* or *The Teaching of the Twelve Apostles*, penned just a few years after John's death. That important early Christian document advises that "if the teacher himself goes astray and teaches a different teaching" they should "not listen to him" (*Didache* 11:2). Thus we find the doctrinal test. But even "if any prophet teaches the truth, yet does not practice what he teaches, he is a false prophet" (11:10). Both the doctrinal and the moral tests were important to the author of the *Didache*, just as they were in the New Testament.

That thought brings us back to 1 John 4:1 with its command to "test the spirits to determine if they are from God." The apostle has already established the moral test in 1 John 1:6, 7 and 2:3-11, in which he noted that those who walked in darkness and did not obey God's commandments were false, and the truth test in 1 John 2:18-28, in which he claimed that anyone "who denies that Jesus is the Christ" is a liar (verse 22).

First John 4:2, 3 revisits the truth test. "By this," John proclaimed, "we know the Spirit of God: every spirit that confesses Jesus Christ has come in the flesh is from God, and every spirit which does not confess Jesus is not from God" but is "the spirit of the antichrist."

To John the denial of the incarnation of Christ was the ultimate heresy. His Gospel opens with the claim that Jesus "the Word was God" and that "the Word became flesh and dwelt among us" (John 1:1, 14, RSV). There was no more important topic to the apostle. To deny that reality was to undermine the entire message of salvation. Without the incarnation, the life and death of Jesus are meaningless fictions. And if those are meaningless, then so is Jesus' life as an example for Christians to follow, His sacrifical atonement for sin (1 John 2:2), His role as Advocate in heaven (1 John 2:1; Heb. 7:25), and any possible forgiveness that might come from His work (1 John 1:9). John realized that to deny the foundational New Testament truth that the second member of the Godhead had become flesh was to destroy the entire theology and ethic of the New Testament.

Thus his forceful attack on the antichrist. To John, their teachings denying that Jesus was not the Christ (2:22), that Christ had not become incarnate in Jesus (4:2), and that Jesus was not the Son of God (2:23; 3:23) were equivalent to the false prophets of Moses' day telling the people to follow "other gods" (Deut. 13:1-5). Such people, he has already told his readers in 1 John 2:22, are the antichrist.

We should note two things about the antichrist beyond the fact of false teaching in 1 John 4:1-3 before we move on to verses 4-6. First, verse 1 states that those false prophets inspired by the spirit of the antichrist "have gone out into the world." That phrase signifies that they had once been members of the flock but had now departed into the non-Christian "world" (cf. 2:19). The reality that they had once been members of John's flock indicates that they were well known to the remaining faithful members, a fact that might have not only given them access to the members but also made their arguments more acceptable, since they came from a friend who had grown in "light and knowledge."

The second item is that the prophesied antichrist (see Acts 20:29, 30) already operated in their midst. And that is the reason that John has written his first letter—to warn the faithful against the false teachings that undermine both Christian theology and the ethical living that flows out from it.

In these few short verses we have a problem that has existed since at least the time of Moses: friends telling friends about the "new light" that

they have discovered. And what is John's answer? To go back to the beginning and use it as a standard to test *all* new light. And what is the truth
in "the beginning" that is so crucial in exposing heresy? Nothing less than
the apostle's witness to the fact that Jesus Christ came in the flesh. That is
the basic platform on which all other Christian teaching is built. To be
wrong about Jesus is to be wrong about everything.

19. A Lesson in Genuine Christianity

1 John 4:4-6

4You are of God, little children, and you have overcome them [i.e., the spirits of antichrist], because greater is He who is in you than he who is in the world. 5They are of the world, therefore they speak of the world and the world listens to them. 6We are of God; he who knows God listens to us; he who is not of God does not listen to us. By this we know the spirit of truth and the spirit of error.

Little children" or "dear children" is the direct form of address that John uses to introduce a point he especially wants to impress upon his readers. Thus the apostle employs the word to tell them that it is God's will that they do not sin, but if they do, they then have an Advocate (2:1); to inform them that their sins are forgiven (2:12); to let them know how important it is to do right (3:7); and so on. Altogether *teknia*, or "little children," appears seven times in 1 John (2:1, 12, 28; 3:7, 18; 4:4; 5:21). In 1 John 4:4 the apostle uses the word not only to let the faithful know that they have been victorious over the secessionists plaguing their community, but to increase "their consciousness of being a community separate from the world" (Grayston, p. 122).

It is all too easy for Christians to forget how truly distinct they are as a people. That is especially the case for those who live in a so-called Christian society whose citizens mouth the name of Christ and who claim to be living a "Christian life" but who deny the person and biblically revealed work of Christ along with the radical ethics of service that He taught. It is not the name of Christ or Christianity that makes people

Christians, John reminds his readers repeatedly in his first letter, but those who accept the incarnate Christ and what He has done and is doing to save them (4:1-6; 2:1, 2), and those who partake of God's love and love fellow believers from their heart (2:10, 11; 3:14). Such people, he never tires of reminding his readers, are the community of the saved.

And in 1 John 4:4 the community of the saved is also the community of the overcomers or the victorious. In its immediate context verse 4 reflects on the fact that the deceivers who have been troubling the community have withdrawn from the fellowship of the church. Thus there are times when "outright schism is truly victory" (Hoon, p. 277). That truth is not always clear to those of us who live in an era when many define true Christianity as accepting everything, anything, and everyone into fellowship in the name of love, no matter how they behave or what they believe. That is exactly the concept of Christianity that John opposes. He and his faithful members are in a death grapple with that definition. Thus he proclaims something definitely needed in our day. What we call postmodernism in the early twenty-first century is a replay of the syncretistic temptation of the first century that sought to unite Christianity to Greek philosophical insights. It is against such a move that John is writing. Victory in such a situation is maintaining a Christian community true to the apostolic witness on Christian truth and ethical living.

> ### True Christianity
>
> We live in an era when many define Christianity as accepting everything, anything, and everyone into fellowship in the name of love, no matter how they behave or what they believe. That is exactly the concept of Christianity that John opposes. He and his faithful members are in a death grapple with that definition.

Verse 4 is not the first time that John has referred to his faithful readers "overcoming." In 2:14 he points to their overcoming the evil one. But in that context it was a moral victory, whereas in 4:4 it is intellectual—the false teachers had not succeeded in deceiving them on the incarnate Christ. Thus as in chapter 2 they were forced to depart (2:19), leaving the church members victorious in the struggle between truth and error.

But the victory or overcoming of the faithful did not happen because they were "more learned, more skilled in philosophical debate, than the false teachers" (Bruce, p. 105), but because "greater is He who is in you than he who is in the world" (1 John 4:4). Here we find an important element in John's understanding of the dynamics of Christian living. Christians are not only "of God" or "from God," but they are indwelt by God (4:12, 13, 15), which is effected by the Holy Spirit (4:13). In other words, the Spirit of God who indwells and empowers believers is more powerful than the spirit of the antichrist that influences the secessionists (4:4).

That does not mean that the spirit of the antichrist is weak or powerless, however. To the contrary, the spiritual power that John calls the "ruler of this world" (John 12:31; 14:30; 16:11, RSV) and whom Paul refers to as "the prince of the power of the air, the spirit that is now at work in the sons of disobedience" (Eph. 2:2, RSV) and "the world rulers of this present darkness" (Eph. 6:12, RSV) is strong enough to dominate the affairs of the planet. Only the greater power of God can defeat it (Rev. 12:7-9).

John's point is clear. Christians are only victorious when they remain connected to their source of power. In his teaching of the centrality of the Spirit in Christian living, the apostle reasserts the teaching of his Gospel, in which he declared that people could enter the kingdom of God only by being born of the Spirit (John 3:5-8; cf. 1 John 2:20) and that the Spirit would instruct them in everything (John 14:26) and guide them into the truth (John 16:13).

Thus in 1 John 4, as in 2:18-27, both protection against falsehood and overcoming victory depend upon the indwelling of the Spirit and the standard of doctrine that they had heard from "the beginning" (2:24) in the apostolic witness to the truth. From John's perspective, it requires *both* the objective truths found in the apostolic teachings (recorded for us in the New Testament) and the guidance of the Holy Spirit to have overcoming victory in the battle against the forces of evil.

"No stream rises above its source" (Lenski, p. 490). That saying best characterizes 1 John 4:5 with its concept that those of the world speak of the world. Calvin Kruse helps us understand the verse in its context when he writes that "by rejecting the message heard from the beginning" the secessionists "have to all intents and purposes thrown their lot in with the world. When they speak, 'they speak from the viewpoint of the world' (*ek tou kosmou*), because their teaching about the person of Christ is shaped, not by the original gospel message, but by worldly (albeit religious and philosophical) categories. And 'the world listens to them,' because their teaching is shaped by worldly categories and is therefore acceptable to those of the world" (Kruse, p. 149).

Another way of putting the idea is that "evangelism" prospers better in the pagan world when those who claim to be Christians present a message expressing its own values and agenda. Rudolf Schnackenburg suggests that the statement "the world listens to them" is evidence that the message of the secessionists had met with considerable success in the pagan world (Schnackenburg, p. 204). Other students of 1 John are not convinced on that interpretation, but there is no doubt that people find it easier to listen to and accept that which is closest to what they already believe. That principle is true in both the realm of philosophy and ethics. Thus in a postmodern society a "truthless Christianity" that downplays the importance of revealed doctrine and the ethical imperatives of God's law is more attractive and acceptable than a religion with the intellectual and moral substance that John outlines.

> **Reformer John Calvin on the Spirit and the Word**
>
> "When . . . false spirits pretend the name of God, we must inquire from the Scriptures whether things are so. Provided a devout attention be exercised, accompanied with humility and meekness, the spirit of discernment will be given us, who, as a faithful interpreter, will open to us the meaning of what is said in Scripture" (Calvin, pp. 237, 238).

Opposite the easy and worldly "gospel" of the secessionists is John's claim that "we are of God; he who knows God listens to us; he who is not of God does not listen to us" (1 John 4:6). That statement, John Stott claims, sounds like "the height of arrogance" (Stott, p. 161). And so it would be, he argues, if an individual Christian said it. After all, it is a pretty heady remark to assert that whoever knows God agrees with me and those who don't know God disagree with me.

But John is not writing as an individual. He has a message from God that the other apostles and writers of the New Testament share with him. His statement in 1 John 4:5, 6 "is consistent with John's repeated emphasis that safety from error is to be found in loyalty to that which his readers 'had' or 'heard' 'from the beginning' (2:7, 24; 3:11; 2 Jn. 5; cf. 2 Jn. 9)" (*ibid.*).

On the other hand, those who refuse the teachings of the apostles and opt for human philosophies and the doctrinal formations built upon them pass judgment on both themselves and their message. Such is the teaching of the "apostle of love." Being loving in 1 John does not mean accepting those doctrines and ethical practices that happen to be in vogue in the larger world or even the church, but judging such teachings and practices by the apostolic witness of the New Testament and following God's will as set forth in it. That is not a popular message in a world that sees everything in shades of gray. John is kind of a black and white sort of guy when it comes to the original source for doctrine and ethics. Every teaching and practice finds its origin in either the "spirit of truth" or the "spirit of error" (1 John 4:6). Unfortunately, that is a spiritual insight of the first magnitude that is in danger of being lost in the twenty-first century.

ETLOJJ-5

Part IV

God Is Love

1 John 4:7-5:12

20. God Is Love

1 John 4:7, 8

⁷Beloved, let us love one another, because love is from God, and everyone who loves has been born of God and knows God. ⁸The one who does not love does not know God, because God is love.

John has framed his first letter around three great affirmations about God:

1. "God is light" (1:5).
2. God "is righteous" (2:29).
3. "God is love" (4:8).

In the apostle's skillful pastoral hands those three affirmations about the divine one do not stand by themselves. Rather, they are intrinsically related to what we might call the three great tests of Christianity in a person's life (see Law, pp. 21-24):

1. the test of truth, especially that those who are from God believe that Christ came in the flesh (4:1-6).
2. the test of righteousness, that those who are from God confess their sins (1:9), walk in the light (2:6), and keep God's commandments (2:4).
3. the test of love, that those who are from God love their fellow church members (2:10, 11; 3:14; 4:7).

In short, the imperative all through 1 John is that Christians are to be like God. Or as Clement of Alexandria (c. 150-c. 215) put it, the real Christian "practices being God" (in Barclay, p. 115). While such a claim might shock us on first reading, it is exactly what John is teaching his readers. Each and every Christian is to be, or, better yet, "must be," like God in truth, righteousness, and love.

In practical experience that being like is equivalent to imitating Christ, whose incarnation put the divine attributes on display in flesh and blood. The New Testament, as we might expect, is full of teachings on the necessity of following Christ's example. Thus Peter wrote that Christ left His followers an "example" so that others could "follow in his steps" (1 Peter 2:21, RSV). Again, the disciple penned, "as he who called you is holy, be holy yourselves in all your conduct; since it is written, 'You shall be holy, for I am holy'" (1 Peter 1:15, 16, RSV). Jesus encouraged the attitude of imitation when He referred to Himself as "the way" (John 14:6). And Christians, John tells us, are those who "walk like He walked" (1 John 2:6). Thus Paul could urge the Corinthians to have "the mind of Christ" (1 Cor. 2:16, RSV) and commend the Thessalonians for being "imitators . . . of the Lord" (1 Thess. 1:6, RSV).

Along that same line, theologian G. C. Berkouwer ties the imitation of Christ to progressive sanctification. "The imitation of Christ," he writes, "is not merely a form of sanctification, one among several, but a description of its essence" (Berkouwer, p. 135). With those ideas in mind Clement's dictum that the real Christian "practices being God" doesn't sound all that radical. In fact, it is exactly the position that John advocates to his readers.

After applying John's tests to both the dissidents and themselves, his readers know that they are the ones who know God, have fellowship with Him, and have eternal life. Thus the apostle's criteria not only expose the secessionists but at the same time confirm their own faith and status. As a result, John's overall presentation agrees with his first letter's one explicit statement of purpose: "I write these things to you who believe in the name of the Son of God, so that you may know that you have eternal life" (1 John 5:13, NIV). First John 4:7 says it a bit differently when it applies the love test, but its implications are the same: "Everyone who loves has been born of God and knows God."

That thought brings us to the descriptor of God that dominates the third major section of 1 John and is evident throughout the letter: "God is love" (verse 8). W. E. Vine points out that His love is not "merely a quality which He possesses." Rather, "it is His essential nature, and it is for this special reason that one who does not exercise love has not been born of God and does not know Him" (Vine, p. 80).

"God is love." Really? Many seem to have the idea that the Old Testament God is one of retribution and judgment while the New Testament exhibits Jesus as love supreme.

That interpretation, to put it mildly, drives a wedge between the Father and the Son that just isn't there. The devil down through history has always sought to create that impression between the first two members of the Godhead. In fact, that is one of the core problems John addresses in his first letter (see, e.g., 4:2, 15; 2:21-23).

The fact is that the essence of God's character is revealed throughout the Bible. Thus Moses can say of the God of Exodus that "thou hast led in thy steadfast love the people whom thou hast redeemed" (Ex. 15:13, RSV). And even though God's judgments fall on those who rebel against Him, He shows "steadfast love" to those who love Him and respond to Him in faith (Ex. 20:6, RSV). Likewise, the Lord proclaimed to Moses that He was "merciful and gracious, slow to anger, and abounding in steadfast love and faithfulness, keeping steadfast love for thousands, forgiving iniquity and transgression and sin" (Ex. 34:6, 7, RSV).

The Old Testament repeatedly affirms God's love. And we find that love reflected in the genesis of the New Testament in the God who "so loved the world that he gave his only son" (John 3:16, RSV). The action of Christ on the cross is the fullest expression of that love, even though His daily life was also a demonstration of God's love in action.

The devotional classic *Steps to Christ* reflects the centrality of God's love in both the Bible and the creation. "Nature and revelation alike testify of God's love. Our Father in heaven is the source of life, of wisdom, of joy. Look at the wonderful and beautiful things of nature. Think of their marvelous adaptation to the needs and happiness, not only of man, but of all living creatures. The sunshine and the rain, that gladden and refresh the earth, the hills and seas and plains, all speak to us of the Creator's love." Even the effects of sin have not been able to eradicate the signs of God's love. After all, "there are flowers upon the thistles, and the thorns are covered with roses" (E. White, *Steps*, pp. 9, 10).

135

God is love! And that central fact of His character shows up in every corner of the Bible and across the vast universe He has created.

The fact of God's love brings us humans face to face with the great dividing line between the two families of human beings and to what we called "The Acid Test of Christianity" in our discussion of 1 John 2:7-11. The two great families of earth, according to John, define themselves through their response to God's love.

On the one hand, "everyone who loves has been born of God and knows God" (1 John 4:7).

On the other hand, "the one who does not love does not know God" (verse 8).

> ### Agapē in John
>
> "If Paul's word for describing the way men turn to God is *pistes* [faith], John's is *agapē* [self-sacrificing love]. . . . In John, mutual love is grounded even more clearly than in Paul in the love of God (Jn. 13:34; 1 Jn. 4:21). Love is a sign and a proof of faith (1 Jn. 3:10; 4:7 ff.). Love of one's brother derives from God's love; and without love for one's brother, there can be no relationship with God" (C. Brown, vol. 2, p. 544).

In the taxonomy or classification of human beings there are no other types. One lives by either the principle of self-sacrifice or that of selfishness. Every person is predominantly in the camp of Christ or in that of the devil. And it is each person's response to the love of God that separates them. Thus it is that Christ on the Mount of Olives centered the findings of the final judgment on "one point"—whether they had let God's love live through them as they met their fellow beings in need (see Matt. 25:31-46; E. White, *Desire*, p. 637).

Augustine of Hippo (354-430) had it right when he wrote, "If God is love, it follows that the more companions and partners in the faith whom we see being born, in addition to ourselves, the more effusive will be the love in which we rejoice, since it is the possession of this love which is being set before us" (in Bray, p. 213).

"God is love!"

You bet He is. And that's the reason that His followers have no choice in the matter. Of course, we can reject both Him and who He is. But if we accept Him we have no choice but to express His love in our every action and to drop to our knees when we fail to do so.

God is love defines the essence of His character. Love in imitative action prescribes the essence of the character of His followers. Those followers have no choice but to "practice being God" every day of their lives. That practice is what being a Christian is all about.

21. God's Love Revealed

1 John 4:9-12

⁹By this the love of God was revealed among us, that God sent His one and only Son into the world that we might live through Him. ¹⁰In this is love, not that we loved God, but that He loved us and sent His Son as a propitiation [atoning sacrifice] for our sins. ¹¹Beloved, if God so loved us, we ought also to love one another. ¹²No one has ever seen God. If we love one another, God dwells in us and His love is completed among us.

As we noted in our discussion of 1 John 4:7, 8, God's love has been evident in the world from Creation onward. But the fullest revelation of that love we find in His sending of "His one and only Son into the world that we might live through Him" (verse 9). God not only sent Jesus, but did so with the purpose of His being a "propitiation" or "atoning sacrifice for our sins" (verse 10, NIV).

Verses 9 and 10 are rich in insights that enable us to glimpse in a fuller way the claim that "God is love" in verse 8. The first thing that we should note is that God didn't send Jesus because of any goodness or worthiness on our part. It was "not that we loved God," but rather because He loved us (verse 10). Humans, in fact, were in rebellion against God. Or as Romans 5 puts it, "Christ died for the ungodly" (verse 6, RSV), God showed "his love for us in that while we were yet sinners Christ died for us" (verse 8, RSV). We were "enemies" of God when He sent His Son (verse 10). Thus it was not good people that Christ came to save (verse 7) but ungodly sinners and enemies. That says something about the quality of divine love.

A second thing of great importance that the apostle tells us in 1 John

4:9, 10 is that Jesus was sent that "we might live through Him" (verse 9), that He came to die "for our sins" (verse 10). The problem here, as we noted in our discussion of 1 John 2:1, 2, is that all humans are sinners (Rom. 3:23) and the wages of sin is death (Rom. 6:23). Thus all humans stand justly condemned. In ourselves we have no hope. And that fact reveals the majesty of God. He "sent the Son as Savior of the world" (1 John 4:14).

Here we find the central core of Jesus' mission expressed throughout the New Testament. Thus Matthew writes of the birth of Christ that "you shall call his name Jesus, for he will save his people from their sins" (Matt. 1:21, RSV). And Jesus tells Zachaeus that "the Son of man came to seek and to save the lost" (Luke 19:10, RSV).

The wonder of wonders is that God sent the Son because of human need. He sacrificed of Himself that we might have life. That is what *agapē* (love) is all about. Truly His gift is a demonstration of the claim that "God is love" (1 John 4:8).

A third thing that John declares to his readers in verses 9 and 10 is that God took the initiative in the plan of salvation. He "sent" His Son. Here we find proactive love. He never dispatched Jesus because people asked for help, but rather because they were so blind that they didn't even know that they needed help. They were like Adam in the Garden. He knew he was in trouble, but didn't know what to do about it (Gen. 3:7, 8). God searched Adam out and offered him hope (verses 9-15). The divine initiative in salvation is at the center of God's revealed activity. Thus Jesus came "to seek and to save" the lost (Luke 19:10) and told parables about the divine effort to locate those who are lost (Luke 15).

God never waits for sinners to come to Him. He is on a search and rescue mission. And that is the best part of the good news of the gospel. The Lord always takes the lead in salvation. The human part is one of response, and even that can take place only because God has already sent His Holy Spirit into the hearts of men and women so that they might even have a desire to recognize their need of help and then accept the gift that God offers through Jesus.

A fourth important insight that John has for us in verses 9 and 10 is hidden in the word "sent" itself. Here we have a glimpse of the preexistence of the Son, although the evidence in this verse by itself doesn't prove

His preexistence. After all, Jesus "sent" His disciples into the world, and they most certainly did not have a preexistence.

But at this point we find in the thinking of John the fact that Jesus was different from the disciples in the sense that He claimed that "I came from the Father and entered the world" (John 16:28, NIV). In addition, several references in the Fourth Gospel state that Jesus had come down from heaven (see John 3:13; 6:33, 41, 42, 50, 51). And then we have the powerful opening verses of John's Gospel that find Jesus as an active agent at the time of Creation (John 1:1-3). There is no doubt that John believed in the preexistence of Christ. And it is with that understanding that he uses the word "sent" in 1 John 4:9. God not only sent, but He sent one preexistent person of the Godhead (see John 1:14).

That thought brings me to a fifth important insight tucked away in 1 John 4:9, 10. The word that I have translated "one and only" (*monogenēs*) is pregnant with meaning. The King James Version renders both verse 9 and John 3:16 by the rather confusing English expression "only begotten." For years I wondered about the meaning of "only begotten." If Jesus was the only Son that was "begotten," were there more, and if there were more, might they have originated in some other manner than being "begotten"? At any rate, even though I could quote John 3:16 from the King James version by heart, that part of the verse left me somewhat mystified.

Fortunately, the meaning of *monogenēs* becomes clear as we study its use in other passages. Altogether the New Testament employs the word nine times. *Monogenēs* appears four times outside of the Fourth Gospel and 1 John.

1. In Luke 7:12 it describes the one and only son of the widow of Nain.
2. In Luke 8:42 it describes the one and only daughter of Jairus.
3. Luke 9:38 uses it of the one and only son of the man who came to Jesus seeking help with his demon possessed son.
4. Hebrews 11:17 utilizes the word to describe Isaac as the one and only son of Abraham.

"In each of these cases," Colin Kruse writes, "the expression is used to add poignancy to a story by highlighting that it was the person's 'one and only' child who was in dire need, threatened, or had died. The stress is not on the fact that the person was begotten of the father or mother concerned, but on the fact that the father or mother had only one child, and that child was the one who was so sadly affected" (Kruse, pp. 158, 159).

The Fourth Gospel uses *monogenēs* four times (John 1:14, 18; 3:16, 18). In each case, as in its other New Testament appearances, the word highlights the uniqueness of Jesus as God's one and only Son rather than the idea that He was "begotten" by the Father. First John 4:9 employs *monogenēs* in the same way as its other eight appearances in the New Testament. Thus God sent "His one and only Son into the world" to become an "atoning sacrifice" for our sins (1 John 4:9, 10). As a result, in its present context "one and only Son" serves to heighten the value of God's gift.

> **Only Begotten?**
> A better translation of *monogenēs* is "one and only." Nowhere does the Bible employ the word for parenting a child.

A sixth important teaching of 1 John 4:9, 10 is that Jesus was sent to be a "propitiation" or "atoning sacrifice for our sins." Since the section dealing with 1 John 2:1, 2 dealt extensively with that topic, we will not discuss it here other than to point out that it is the substitutionary sacrifice of Jesus on the cross that qualifies Him to be Savior (1 John 4:14) and provides us with life (verse 9).

First John 4:11 places the obligation of human love in the context of God's priceless gift of love. Since God loved us so much, "we ought also to love one another."

That idea brings us to the absolutely astounding thoughts of verse 12. The verse starts out with the truth that "no one has ever seen God," an idea repeated several times in the Fourth Gospel (e.g., 1:18; 5:37; 6:46).

Thus while the first part of 1 John 4:12 adds no revolutionary ideas, the second part not only reiterates John's oft-repeated command for Christians to love one another but moves beyond the frontiers of his teaching up to this point to claim that when Christians love one another they not only demonstrate that God dwells in them but that they "complete" or "perfect" the circle of His love. Thus the flow of thought in

1 John 4:7-12 is that God's love originates in Himself (4:7, 8), was revealed in the gift of His Son (verses 9, 10), and is made complete in His people (verse 12). Accordingly, "God's love *for* us is perfected only when it is reproduced *in* us or . . . 'among us' in . . . Christian fellowship" (Stott, p. 167). David Rensberger puts it in a different way when he writes that "*Christian love is the ongoing revelation of God*" (Rensberger, *1 John*, p. 119).

22. The Grounds of Christian Assurance

1 John 4:13–17

[13]By this we know that we dwell in Him and He in us, because He has given us of His Spirit. [14]And we have witnessed and we testify that the Father sent the Son as Savior of the world. [15]Whoever confesses that Jesus is the Son of God, God dwells in him and he in God. [16]And we have come to know and believe the love which God has for us. God is love, and the one who dwells in this love dwells in God, and God dwells in him. [17]By this, love is completed with us, so that we may have assurance in the day of judgment, because as He is, so also are we in this world.

How can we know that God dwells in us? We have faced that topic several times in 1 John already (2:5; 3:24) and the apostle will tell us in 1 John 5:13 that the very reason that he even wrote his letter was that his readers could be assured of their standing with God and thus their possession of eternal life. C. H. Dodd labels 1 John 4:13–18 "the high-water mark of the thought of the epistle" (Dodd, p. 118). And so it is. John is now ready to tie together some of the strands of thought that he has been developing in his first four chapters.

"By this we *know* that we dwell in Him." The key word for 1 John's doctrine of assurance, we saw in the introduction to the letter, is "know." Thus true believers have confidence or assurance because:

- they "know" they are in Him because they keep His commandments (2:3, 5).
- they "know" that they have passed from death to life because they love fellow believers (3:14).

- they "know" that they dwell in Him because He has given them His Spirit (4:13).
- they "know" that they are the children of God because they love and obey Him (5:2).
- they "know" that they are born of God because they do not live in a state of sin (5:18).

Another key word that the apostle employs repeatedly throughout his letter is *menō*, which I have generally translated as "dwell," but which can also be rendered as "abide," "remain," or "continue." *Menō* is an important word for John. Of the New Testament's 118 uses, 69 occur in John's writings, including 40 in the Fourth Gospel and 23 in his first letter.

Menō appears five times in 1 John 4:13-17, in which John reminds his readers three times that they dwell in God and He in them (verses 13, 15, 16). We should note, however, that each of the mentions of reciprocal indwellings has evidence attached to it. Thus

1. "we dwell in Him and He in us, *because* He has given us of His Spirit" (verse 13).
2. "God dwells in him and he in God," *because* they confess "that Jesus is the Son of God" (verse 15).
3. the believer dwells "in God, and God dwells in him," *because* each believer "dwells in this love" (verse 16).

In John's argument the second and third "becauses" flow out of the first. In other words, the gift of the Holy Spirit underlies the apostle's presentation. Thus it is only because we have the Holy Spirit that we can acknowledge that Jesus Christ has come in the flesh (4:1-3). Likewise, it is the Spirit that enables us to love (3:23, 24; 4:12, 13). "In our fallen and unredeemed state," John Stott points out, "we are both blind (unable to believe) and selfish (unable to love). It is only by the grace of the Holy Spirit, who is the Spirit of truth and whose firstfruit is love (Gal. 5:22), that we ever come to believe in Christ and to love others" (Stott, p. 168). Thus it is the gift of the Spirit that is foundational to John's understanding of assurance and to every other aspect of a believer's intellectual understanding of the faith and ethical activity. Said somewhat differently, it is the gift of the Holy Spirit that "brings all other blessings in its train" (E. White, *Desire*, p. 672).

Before moving away from the apostle's emphasis on the Spirit in 1 John

4:13-17, it is important to clarify the sequence of events in his argument. Some Christians seem to think that the gift of the Spirit depends upon their having correct beliefs and a good life. But that is not what John is saying. For him a loving life and sound theology is evidence that one already has the Spirit, whose function is to guide believers into truth (John 16:13) and convict them of sin (verse 8). As a result, Martyn Lloyd-Jones asserts, "a correct belief is proof of the possession of the Holy Spirit. . . . A correct belief is impossible apart from the Holy Spirit" (Lloyd-Jones, *Love*, p. 119).

While 1 John 4:13 highlights the gift of the Spirit, verse 14 does the same for the Son, whom God "sent . . . as Savior of the world." Here we find an informative description of the interaction of the three members of the Godhead. The Father sends the Spirit into our hearts while dispatching the Son to earth to become an "atoning sacrifice" (verse 10) on our behalf. While the Holy Spirit impresses our hearts and minds, transforms our lives, and "testifies with our spirit that we are God's children" (Rom. 8:16, NIV), the Son died to save those who believe in and accept His "atoning sacrifice" from "the day of judgment" that will come on all the earth (1 John 4:17). And to help us with our struggles to believe, God provided us with the apostolic witness to Christ in the Bible. As John puts it, "we have witnessed and we testify that the Father sent the Son as Savior of the world" (verse 14). Note the apostle's emphasis. Jesus wasn't merely a nice man who did good things and fed the poor. While he did those things, the apostolic witness of both John and the rest of the New Testament to Jesus is that He died as a "propitiation" or "atoning sacrifice" to save us from our sins (verse 10; 2:2). Thus He is the "Savior of the world" (4:14).

First John 4:17 raises several important points. The first is a replay of the idea posited in verse 12 that God's love is perfected or completed in Christians. "The confession of Jesus as Lord and the mutual abiding between God and the believer allow for God's love to have its full expression. It is in his close union with God (referring to the mutual relationship) that a believer's love is made complete or perfected" (Akin, p. 185).

And it is a transformed heart and mind that leads to a loving life that gives believers assurance or confidence in "the day of judgment" (verse 17). In the context of 1 John 4, assurance comes from the fact that believers have the Holy Spirit (verse 13), confess that "Jesus is the Son of God" and

"Savior of the world" (verses 14, 15), and live God's love (verses 15, 16).

In that triology of evidence John has not fallen into the pit of "merely believe and be saved." All the way through 1 John the apostle relates salvation to how people live their lives (e.g., 2:3-11; 3:4-24; 5:2, 3). While belief is obviously important to John, he also moves to the practical level of everyday life "showing that the Christian can be assured of his salvation in that God has brought about fundamental changes in his life," including both righteous living (2:3-6) and loving relationships with other believers (4:20; Boice, p. 9). Thus we cannot divide justification and sanctification in 1 John—"they are always together" (Lloyd-Jones, *Love*, p. 190).

First John 4:14 and 15 also link the importance of Jesus' person with that of His mission. It is only through Christ becoming incarnate in Jesus of Nazareth that He could be our "atoning sacrifice" (2:2; 4:10) and thus our "Savior." And because He is our Savior who died in our place, one can approach Him as our advocate in heaven (1 John 2:1), confess our sins, and receive forgiveness and cleansing (1:9).

In that logical sequence we find the problem that has bothered John so much throughout his letter. Namely, those who deny that Jesus is God incarnate have no Savior. Thus the apostle's repeated emphasis on confessing that Jesus is the Christ (5:1), that He came in the flesh (4:2), and that He is the Son of God (1:3; 7; 2:23; 3:8, 23; 4:9, 10, 11, 15). John clearly recognized that to repudiate the incarnation undermined the significance of both Christ's life and death. Thus those who rejected His humanity saw no need to follow the ethics and values of the earthly Jesus and also were destitute of a Savior. With those connections in mind, the reasons for John's emphasis on the centrality of the incarnation is understandable. Without the divine becoming human Christianity is merely a fiction.

John's discussion of "assurance in the day of judgment" raises issues related to the second advent of Jesus and the separation between those who will be saved and those who won't. His point in verse 17 is that those who live the transformed life of God's love will have nothing to fear on judgment day. And why? "Because as He is, so also are we in this world."

Now we encounter a passage that has confused some people, especially those who take it out of context. By isolating the text and superimposing foreign thoughts on it, some have developed support for a doctrine of sinless perfection from 1 John 4:17.

But the context provides a different interpretation. From verse 7 on John has been speaking of the need for Christians to be like God in loving one another, just like He has loved them. Then in verse 16 the apostle tells us that those who dwell in love dwell in God. And then in the first part of verse 17 he asserts the fact that the circle of God's love is completed or perfected by Christians living out His love. And it is at that point that John winds up his argument by claiming that Christians have no need to fear the judgment because they are "as He is" in "this world." And how is He? Loving! "God is love" (1 John 4:8, 16). And how will believers be? The same. "In so far as we are living this life of love, we are conforming to the pattern of Christ's own character and life." He is our Judge, and those who are living as He is have nothing to fear (G. Lewis, p. 109).

23. Fearless Living

1 John 4:18-21

¹⁸There is no fear in love, but perfect love drives out fear, because fear has to do with punishment, and the one who fears is not perfected in love. ¹⁹We love because He first loved us. ²⁰If anyone says, "I love God," and hates his brother, he is a liar. For the one who does not love his brother, whom he has seen, is not able to love God, whom he has not seen. ²¹And this commandment we have from Him, that the one who loves God should love his brother also.

Perhaps the most interesting thing about 1 John 4:18 is that it assumes that fear of divine punishment is a normal human state. Doesn't John know that such fear is out of style? That because God is love, He wouldn't ever do anything to terrify His creatures?

Here we have one of the lost emphases of the Bible. It is Jesus Himself who tells us not to "fear those who kill the body but cannot kill the soul; rather fear him who can destroy both body and soul in hell" (Matt. 10:28, RSV). Perhaps some of us moderns need to inform Jesus that He had it all wrong. After all, no one had more to say about judgment and hell in the New Testament than Jesus. For example, of His five recorded "sermons" in Matthew, three of them each feature three scenes of judgment and hell (Matt. 7:19, 23, 27; 10:28, 32, 39; 25:12, 30, 46), one of them two scenes (13:30, 42, 49, 50), while the fifth has one such episode (18:34, 35).

We moderns and postmoderns have a choice. Either we can conclude that Jesus was filled with relics of primitive superstition or that He knew more than we do about the dynamics of the universe.

In 1 John 4:17, 18 we find the same "outdated" concept. John assumes that informed people will have a healthy fear of "punishment" on the "day of judgment." Without that assumption, his teachings that faithful believers can have "assurance in the day of judgment" and "perfect love drives out fear" of punishment are nothing but nonsense.

The concept that a day of reckoning will come and that people ought to fear the consequences of their life when confronted with a holy God may not be popular in our day, but that doesn't make it untrue.

God, as the Bible pictures Him, cannot and will not forever stand idly by while His creation suffers. His reaction is judgment on that sin that is destroying His people. Scripture portrays Him taking action to put an end to the mess that we call world history. At that time, John tells us in Revelation 6:16, 17, there will indeed be fear of God on the earth, even among those who don't believe in the teaching. At the "day of judgment" (cf. 1 John 4:17; 2:28) there will be those who call "to the mountains and rocks, 'Fall on us and hide us from the face of him who is seated on the throne, and from the wrath of the Lamb; for the great day of their wrath has come, and who can stand before it?'" (RSV).

Whether we like it or not, we do have something to fear in the anger of a holy God who has seen too much suffering, death, war, and famine and decides that enough is enough. But that's not the kind of God most of us want. What we desire, C. S. Lewis suggests, is "not so much a Father in Heaven as a grandfather in heaven—a senile benevolence" who tells people that they can do whatever they like as long as they are enjoying themselves (C. Lewis, *Pain*, p. 40).

But God knows that the present world order is sick, and He will eventually have to create a new heaven and earth in which "he will wipe away every tear . . . , and death shall be no more, neither shall there be mourning nor crying nor pain any more, for the former things have passed away" (Rev. 21:4).

It is significant that the word "fear" stands at the head of the last series of messages that Christ tells us in Revelation must be preached before the end of the world: "Fear God and give him glory, for the hour of his judgment has come" (Rev. 14:7, RSV).

I have spent a bit of time in exploring what to John seemed to be a very natural assumption (that people should fear punishment from God at the end of time) because most of us have abandoned the idea and because John (and the rest of the New Testament writers) thought it was so vital.

Only in the light of its importance can we begin to make sense out of John's teaching that "perfect love drives out fear" (1 John 4:18). The word that John uses for fear (*phobeō*, from which we get the English "phobia") can have one of two meanings. First, it can signify "to be in an apprehensive state, *be afraid*" or it can mean "to have a profound measure of respect for, *(have) reverence, respect*" (Bauer, pp. 1060, 1061). The context decides the meaning in each use. And without doubt the context in verse 18 dictates the meaning of fear as being afraid.

> Fearless living is the lot of every Christian because Christians by definition embody the loving character of God.

Thus the good news of 1 John 4:18 is that Christians have no need to be afraid of divine punishment at the end of time. Why? Because "perfect love drives out fear." And what does "perfect love" mean? It consists of being "as He is" in terms of love according to verses 16 and 17.

Jesus put it a bit differently when He defined the essence of the law as loving God with all of our being and loving our neighbor as our own self (Matt. 22:36-40) and when He taught that being perfect like the Father (Matt. 5:48) centered in loving all people, including one's enemies, and letting that love flow out into daily activities toward others (verses 43-47), but John has captured His meaning.

Fearless living is the lot of every Christian, John tells us, because Christians by definition embody the loving character of God. That same fearlessness in the face of judgment the apostle also repeatedly expresses in his Apocalypse, which consistently pictures God's final judgment as a time of hope and encouragement for them (see Rev. 6:10; 11:18; 18:20; 19:2: cf. Dan. 7:22, 26, 27).

And what does John tell us about that "perfect love" that makes Christians fearless? Two things in verses 19-21.

First, that "we love because He first loved us" (verse 19). While fear is (or should be) the natural condition of humans before they meet God as Savior in Christ (verses 14, 10), true love is not. In fact, people are born selfish. Our fallen nature centers on me and mine. It is only because God loves us and transforms our hearts and lives that we can truly love God and other people. Natural "love" might focus on others for what they can give us, but converted, godlike love centers on what we can give to God and others. That shift of focus is included in what John calls being "born again" or "born from above" (John 3:3) and what Paul

refers to as "transformed" living through the "renewal of" the "mind" (Rom. 12:2) and becoming a "new creation" "in Christ" (2 Cor. 5:17).

The godlike love of the Christian, John tells us in 1 John 4:19, emerges through a person's recognition and acceptance of God's love. Christians have nothing to fear in a diety who so loved the world that He "sent His one and only Son into the world that we might live through Him" (1 John 4:9; cf. John 3:16).

If the first great fact of fearless living is that Christians have nothing to dread because they have accepted and been inspired by God's love to them, the second is that they have

> ## A Thought on 1 John 4:20
>
> "There . . . is a great principle in Scripture which we neglect at our cost: *Doctrine and application always go together.* Indeed it is possible . . . for people . . . to be very well versed in the Bible, and yet it does not profit them in the end because they never apply it. They analyse it as if they were analysing a Shakespearean play . . . , but Scripture never does that. There must always be an application" (Lloyd-Jones, *Love,* p. 180).

nothing to be terrified about because they daily are living the godlike life (1 John 4:16, 17) in loving other people. John drives that fact home in verses 20 and 21, in which he lets his readers know in no uncertain terms that Christian love is not merely a sentiment, but an activity—a topic he has treated already in 1 John 2:7-11 and 3:11-24. The apostle's spiral style in terms of repeating his teachings keeps pounding home the truths he wants to impress on his readers. Thus his dictum that those who proclaim their love to God while hating their brothers and sisters not only cuts the ground away from the secessionists who are disrupting his churches, but hits each of us full in the face.

"How is it with me?" I am forced to ask myself in the light of John's clear teaching. Self-evaluation of my own thoughts, motives, and actions in relationship to other people is John's command to me. "How," I must ask myself, "can I love others more fully?" as I move forward in a life of truly (rather than deceptively or hypocritically) fearless living.

24. The Life of Victory

1 John 5:1-5

¹Everyone believing that Jesus is the Christ has been born of God, and everyone loving the parent also loves the child born of Him. ²By this we know that we love the children of God, when we love God and observe His commandments. ³For this is the love of God, that we keep His commandments, and His commandments are not a heavy burden. ⁴For whatever has been born of God overcomes the world; and this is the victory that overcomes the world—our faith. ⁵Who is the one who overcomes the world? No one except the one who believes that Jesus is the Son of God.

Here is a strange fact—"No New Testament writer makes such frequent use of the metaphors of combat and victory as this gentle Apostle John. None of them seem to have conceived so habitually of the Christian life as being a conflict, and in none of their writings does the clear note of victory in the use of that word 'overcometh' ring out so consistently as it does in the very Apostle of Love" (MacLaren, p. 1).

Victory and overcoming is the central concept in 1 John 5:1-5. But intertwined with it we find a replay of the three tests of genuine Christianity that have been so prominent throughout the letter. The tests of belief or truth, love, and obedience have shown up repeatedly in the first four chapters.

First John 5:1-5 resurrects John's three tests in an intertwined triumphant finale, with faith and belief appearing in verses 1, 4, and 5; love in verses 1, 2, and 3; and the necessity to obey in verses 2 and 3. What we need to understand is that those three threads form a unit in John's thinking, with all of them combined being the full test of a genuine Christianity that overcomes the world. Two out of the three won't do. All three are required—for everyone always. And the tragedy is that the secessionists that he is warning his readers about lack all three.

The apostle's logic as it unfolds in the tightly packed verses of 1 John 5:1-5 is that

1. those who believe Jesus is the Christ must of necessity love the Father and His children (verses 1, 2a).
2. one cannot love the Father without obeying His commandments and overcoming (verses 2b-4a).
3. one cannot overcome the world without belief in Jesus as the Son of God (4b-5).

The sequence begins and ends with faith and belief in the incarnate Christ. That understanding is crucial. Without that central affirmation and reality all else is lost. And without the incarnate Christ there can be no plan of salvation. Thus John's repeated attack on those who deny the foundational truth that frames his discussion in 1 John 5:1-5. It is within that framework of belief that he treats the necessity of love and obedience. Outside of it, they have no meaning.

But undergirding John's entire discussion in these verses (and in the entire letter as well as the Fourth Gospel) is the absolute necessity of the new birth (1 John 5:1, 4; cf. 2:29; 3:9; 4:7; 5:18; John 1:12, 13; 3:3-7). The new birth is the transforming event from which faith, love, and obedience flow. Of course, an element of God-imparted faith does lead up to the new birth experience, but that event is only the prelude of ever-deepening faith and understandings that spring up naturally in the Christian life as love and obedience, or what we might think of as the life of faith.

John's Three Tests

Obedience	Love	Belief
2:3-6	2:7-11	2:18-27
2:28-3:10	3:11-18	4:1-6
	4:7-12	4:13-15
	4:16-21	

With that general survey of the rich theological implications of 1 John 5:1-5 in place, we now need to turn to the individual insights of those verses. First, everyone born of God loves God (5:1). That fact seems to be self-evident. Church members unanimously through the ages have agreed that believers should love God. That is not the difficulty. But problems arise with the implications that flow out of loving God.

That brings us to a second point: that everyone who loves God must also love other Christians (5:1b). Now, here is a problem for some. It is one thing to love God, but quite another to love those who have hurt our feelings, have insulted us, or are uncouth if not just plain disgusting. But here John is just as uncompromising as Jesus (see Matt. 5:44; Mark 12:28-31). It is impossible to truly love the Parent without loving the other children that He also loves. Here we as Christians need to pray to God that He will give us not only transforming grace, but also empowering grace to love those members of

> ### The Life of Victory
>
> The incarnate Jesus Christ is the key to victory for every Christian. And the life of victory is a faith-based one that issues forth into the daily practice of loving others and keeping God's commandments.

"our family" that we don't even like or whom we find obnoxious, and also forgiving grace when we fall short of His ideal.

A third important issue arises in verse 3, in which we read that obedience to His commandments is also an evidence of our love for God.

Within the New Testament framework that means that we not only obey the two great commands to love God supremely and our neighbors as ourselves (Matt. 22:36-40), but that we follow the apostle Paul's lead when he demonstrates that the two "great" commands to love flow into the keeping of the Ten Commandments as specific ways in which Christians show their love both to God and to other people. Paul makes that connection clear when he writes that "love is the fulfilling of the law" (Rom. 13:10) and that "he who loves his neighbor has fulfilled the law. The commandments, 'You shall not commit adultery, You shall not kill, You shall not steal, You shall not covet,' and any other commandment, are summed up in this sentence, 'You shall love your neighbor as yourself'" (Rom. 13:8, 9, RSV).

A fourth observation that we should note in 1 John 5:1-5 is that for born-again Christians the observance of God's commandments is not a "heavy burden" or "irksome" (verse 4). Here we find an interesting distinction, since some of us really do find loving the unlovable, paying tithe, and keeping God's Sabbath holy to be not only a burden but a distraction from "our life." And therein is the problem. We are more interested in living "our life" than letting God live out His life in us. But when we really understand what He has done for us through Christ as Savior our hearts and minds will then fill with gratitude to Him and living the life of love will become a privilege rather than a duty. But undergirding that transformation of attitudes is the new birth experience (1 John 5:1) so central to John's teaching and so absolutely foundational to overcoming and victory.

A fifth aspect of John's presentation in verses 1-5 is his emphasis on victory and overcoming. Four times in 1 John 5:4, 5 we find words related to the Greek *nikē*, which I have translated as "victory" and "overcome" and a word that has been adopted in modern language as the verbal symbol for the running shoes of those who win. We find an important thought in John's repeated use of *nikē*. Namely, that Christians are victors through what God has accomplished for them in Christ and through what He is currently doing for them in their transformed lives. The good news is that Christians are victors, not losers.

The last thing to note in 1 John 5:1-5 is that victory is built upon faith (verse 4). And that faith, in John's teaching, is not some abstract belief. To the contrary, it is directly and specifically founded upon a clear understanding that "Jesus is the Son of God" (verse 5). That incarnational understanding, John never tires of telling his readers, is the Truth of truths in the Christian pantheon of doctrines. Throughout his letter he has made it abundantly clear that Christ, the Son of God who became the earthly man Jesus who died as a "propitiation" or "atoning sacrifice" (4:10; 2:2) for sinful people, is bedrock Truth. Without that Truth there is no advocate in heaven to minister for us in our sinful condition (2:1) and no forgiveness of sin (1:9). In short, the incarnate Jesus Christ is the key to victory for every Christian. And the life of victory is a faith-based existence that issues forth into the daily practice of loving others and keeping God's commandments.

25. Testimonies of Importance

1 John 5:6-12

[6]This is the One who came by water and blood, Jesus Christ; not by water only but by water and by blood. And the Spirit is the one providing testimony because the Spirit is the truth. [7]For there are three who provide testimony: [8]the Spirit and the water and the blood, and the three are in agreement. [9]If we receive the testimony of men, the testimony of God is greater; for this is the testimony of God that He has testified concerning His Son. [10]The one who believes in the Son of God has the testimony in himself; the one who does not believe God has made Him a liar, because he has not believed in the testimony which God has testified concerning His Son. [11]And this is the testimony, that God gave eternal life to us, and this life is in His Son. [12]The one who has the Son has life; the one who does not have the Son of God does not have life.

As you were reading verses 6-12 you probably thought that they were not the easiest in 1 John to understand. If so, you were correct. Alfred Plummer remarks that the statement of the water and the blood "is the most perplexing passage in the Epistle and one of the most perplexing" in the New Testament (Plummer, *Epistles,* p. 113).

In the next few pages we will unpack the meaning of verses 6-12 step by step. The first stage in our journey is to examine what John means when he says that Jesus "came by water and blood" and not by water only (verse 6). Part of our difficulty in understanding the apostle's meaning is that we don't have all the facts. Especially pertinent is that we do not know the full nature of the exact heresy against which John was defending his people. That lack makes it impossible for us to grasp his full implications, although they were undoubtedly clear to the first readers of his letter.

But even with our lack of essential background information we can still approximate the implications of verse 6. The first thing to note is that water and blood are closely connected to Jesus.

In regard to water, John's Gospel uses the expression "by water" three times, each of them related to the baptism of Jesus (John 1:26, 31, 33). And coupled with that event is the fact that the apostle testified that he saw "the Spirit descend as a dove from heaven" and remain on Him (John 1:32, RSV). Thus it is probable that the water of verse 6 refers to Jesus' baptism, at which time the Spirit provided testimony (1 John 5:6b).

"By blood" probably alludes to Jesus' death as an "atoning sacrifice" on the cross (2:2; 4:10). The fact that the only other reference to Jesus' blood in 1 John outside of 5:6-8 is 1:7, in which John tells us that "the blood of Jesus His Son cleanses us from all sin," reinforces that interpretation.

A combining of the two symbols suggests that coming by water points to the beginning of Christ's ministry and coming by blood indicates His sacrificial death at its end. The problem highlighted in verse 6 is that the secessionists from John's congregations accepted the witness of the water but not the blood. That is, they in some way denied the importance and even the reality of Jesus' atoning sacrifice. Given the problem related to Jesus' being the Christ and the Son of God that John has been fighting throughout his letter, their teaching probably held that it was only Jesus as a human being that died on the cross rather than the divine Son of God. If so, John has been teaching, then the cross has no value and Christianity is a fiction.

That thought brings us to the threefold witness of 1 John 5:7, 8, in which the Spirit, the water, and the blood unite in their testimony that "Jesus is the Son of God" (verse 5), the final assertion of John's previous paragraph and the one that led into the discussion of the threefold witness in verses 6-10.

The agreement of the three witnesses in 1 John 5:6-8 leads to the importance of their unified testimony. The validity of that threefold testimony rests upon the Old Testament idea of what constitutes an adequate witness. Deuteronomy 19:15 tells us that "a single witness" is not sufficient, but that only "on the evidence of two witnesses, or of three witnesses, shall a charge be sustained" (RSV). Thus, William Barclay points out, "a triple human witness is enough to establish any fact. How much more must a triple divine witness, the witness of the Spirit, the water, and the blood, be regarded as convincing" (Barclay, p. 132).

What Happened to the Trinity in 1 John 5:7?

Some readers of this commentary will be familiar with the King James Version's presentation of 1 John 5:7, which reads: "For there are three that bear record in heaven, the Father, the Word, and the Holy Ghost: and these three are one."

As a result, such readers may be wondering where it went in all modern translations. The short answer is that that Trinitarian statement isn't in what John wrote. The long answer can be outlined as follows:

1. It is absent from *all* Greek manuscripts copied before the fourteenth century.
2. None of the early Church Fathers quote it, even though it would have been helpful in some of their controversies.
3. It does not appear in the original version of the Latin Vulgate (late fourth century).
4. The Trinitarian statement most likely began as a marginal note that worked its way into the text of the Latin version of the Bible during the Middle Ages.
5. The first Greek text of the New Testament, published by Erasmus in 1516, did not contain the statement because he knew it was not in any Greek manuscript that he was aware of.
6. But when some who were familiar with the Latin version of the Bible challenged him on its absence, Erasmus promised that if anyone could show him the words in a Greek manuscript he would print them in his next edition.
7. That is where he made his mistake. Given a late Greek manuscript (fourteenth century) influenced as it was copied by the Latin additions, he kept his misguided promise. Thus against his better judgment Erasmus included the Trinitarian statement in his 1522 edition of the Greek text of the New Testament.
8. From there it made its way into the King James Version.

That, in short, is the history of a scribal commentary on the passage that eventually crept into the text of the Bible. *But no modern translations include the Trinitarian statement, which all authorities agree was never a part of the original text of Scripture.*

The good news is that nothing is lost since other New Testament passages contain the doctrine of the Trinity.

But even more important than the threefold affirmation of the incarnation of God in Jesus (1 John 5:8) is the testimony of the Father in verses 9 and 10. God had stated more than once in the gospels that Jesus was His "beloved Son" (Matt. 3:17; 17:5) and any rejection of that declaration was nothing less, John argues, than an attack on God's honesty. Thus J. L. Houlden notes that "the writer is so convinced that God's witness to himself in the life and death of Jesus is authentic that failure to believe the orthodox faith is tantamount to accusing God of lying" (Houlden, p. 132), a charge earlier leveled at the dissidents when they denied that they were sinners in the face of God's word to the contrary (1 John 1:10).

Needless to say, calling God a liar is not what we might think of as a minor sin. That thought sets us up for 1 John 5:11 and 12 and the apostle's discussion of the "sin leading to death" in verses 16 and 17.

With verse 11 John forgets the unbeliever and speaks to the blessings granted to those who receive the testimony of God and the three witnesses of verses 6-10. The nature of God's testimony also transitions in verse 11. Up to this point John has emphasized the person and work of Jesus, but here He speaks about the benefit made available to those who believe in Him. That blessing, put simply, is "eternal life" which "is in His Son" (verse 11). And those who do not accept the Son in the sense of the incarnate Christ in Jesus (2:22) who died as an atoning sacrifice on the cross (4:10) do not have eternal life (5:12).

With the phrase "eternal life" John has come full circle from the beginning of his letter at which time he wrote of that "eternal life which was with the Father" (1:2). The eternal life in 1 John is none other than Jesus who is God incarnate. Thus when believers accept Jesus they receive eternal life, an existence begun on this earth but with infinite possibilities.

The letter proper comes to an end in verse 12. John utilizes verses 13-21 to set forth his conclusions and final remarks. But in the last words of the body of the letter John leaves his readers with the sobering thought that anyone "who does not have the Son of God does not have life." His logic is not difficult to unpack. "If having the Son involves believing in him, and if believing in him involves accepting the message that was proclaimed at the beginning by the eyewitnesses, then, as far as the author is concerned, the secessionists do not have eternal life because they do not 'have the Son' in this sense" (Kruse, p. 183).

Part V

Parting Thoughts

1 John 5:13-21

26. Assurance Versus Condemnation

1 John 5:13-17

[13]These things I have written to you who believe in the name of the Son of God, that you may know that you have eternal life. [14]And this is the confidence which we have before Him, that if we ask anything according to His will He hears us. [15]And if we know that He hears us in whatever we ask, we know that we have the requests which we have asked from Him. [16]If anyone sees his brother sinning a sin not leading to death, he shall ask and He will give him life for the ones who are not sinning unto death. There is a sin leading to death; I do not say that you should ask for that. [17]All unrighteousness is sin, yet there is sin that does not lead to death.

John has the interesting habit of stating the purpose of his writing near the end of documents rather than at the beginning. Thus toward the conclusion of the Fourth Gospel he tells his readers that these things "are written that you may believe that Jesus is the Christ, the Son of God, and that believing you may have life in his name" (John 20:31, RSV). In a similar fashion, as the apostle looks back over his first letter, he adds, "these things I have written to you who believe in the name of the Son of God, that you may know that you have eternal life" (1 John 5:13).

While John's pattern in stating his purpose near the end may have been the same in both documents, the two statements have very different content. He composed the Gospel so that its readers might come to a belief in Jesus and so have life. But the letter he penned to those who were already believers, but ones whose faith had been shaken by internal conflict in their congregations. They had become unsettled about their standing before

163

God and needed to regain confidence in their position before Him. Thus John went to great lengths to provide them with tests or standards in the realms of doctrine, obedience, and loving concern by which they could evaluate both themselves and those seeking to divide the church. He wanted his readers to know that they may have assurance of eternal life.

John's statement of assurance, we should note, is not a general statement about having faith. To the contrary, it is very specific that people may have confidence of eternal life only if they "believe in the name of the Son of God" (verse 13). That name, of course, is Jesus. Here John again affirms his statement in verse 12 that those who have the Son have life, while those who don't have Him do not have life. As we have seen throughout the epistle, John realized that without the incarnation of God in Jesus there could be no salvation or gospel. Thus everything in Christianity rests upon who Jesus is.

The letter shifts quite naturally from John's reaffirmation of assurance in verse 13 to confidence in prayer in verses 14 and 15. Christians, he asserts, cannot only have confidence in their eternal life if they believe in the Son of God, but they can also come boldly before Him in prayer.

The word translated as "confidence" has appeared three times earlier in 1 John. In 2:28 it refers to the confidence that believers can have at the Second Advent and in 4:17 it speaks of the same confidence in the day of judgment. But such confidence is not merely for the future. It is also a present reality for believers as they bring their prayers to God. They can have assurance that whatever they ask of God He will grant. That same thought appears in 1 John 3:22, in which the apostle set forth the condition that they could ask confidently *if* they kept God's commandments. In 1 John 5:14 we also find a condition—that we must ask according to God's will. That is no new thought. The Lord's Prayer contains the words "Thy will be done" (Matt. 6:10, RSV). And Jesus modeled that prayer for His followers in His struggle in Gethsemane when three times He prayed "Thy will be done" (Matt. 26:39, 42, 44) in the face of the fact that His personal will and desires were quite different from what He needed to accomplish on the cross.

Here is an absolutely crucial point about prayer in general and in 1 John 5:14 especially. "Prayer is not a device for inducing God to change His mind" (Morris, "1 John," p. 1269). The Lord's Prayer is "Thy will be done," not "Thy will be changed." Thus prayer is not a means of imposing our will on God, but, as Christ's Gethsemane example indicates, to subordinate our will to His.

First John 5:16 shifts the scene from prayer in general to intercessory prayer for others. Here John reverts to another of the themes that he has pounded home throughout his letter. Namely, that one of the tests of true Christians is that they love their brothers and sisters in the church (2:9-11; 3:14-16; 4:11). Verse 16 applies that love to prayer. Based on the premise that we are each other's keepers, John highlights our responsibility to others. When we see them struggling, he asserts, we need to pray for them. It is significant that when the apostle speaks of prayer, its focus is on others. All too often we treat prayer as if it were for our self-centered needs. While they may be important, prayer must never degenerate into an engine of selfishness.

But verse 16 enters into an interesting realm when it tells us that we can't pray for everyone and expect results. That is an especially shocking statement in the light of Jesus' teachings that we should love our enemies and pray for those who persecute us (Matt. 5:44).

In order to get at John's meaning we need to examine what he has to say about sin in verses 16 and 17. He is very explicit that there exist sins that lead to death and others that do not. While he does not define those sins in chapter 5, his earlier remarks on sin help us understand his intention here.

Chapters 1 and 2, for example, tell John's readers that it is not God's will that they commit acts of sin (2:1). But if they do, John asserts, they have an advocate who died for their sins, which will be forgiven if confessed (2:1, 2; 1:9). It is obvious that such sins are not in the leading to death category in John 5. They are forgiven through Christ. Those who have the Son have life because they have come to Him in penitence (5:12, 13).

On the other hand, we find that SIN that 1 John 3:4 defines as "lawlessness" or living a life without regard to law or obedience. No born again Christian can live such a life because each has a new heart, mind, and relationship to God (3:6). It is impossible for one born of God to live in ongoing rebelliousness and sin (3:9). Thus whereas 1 John 1:8-2:2 pictures sin as wrong acts that are repented of, the SIN described in chapter 3 is a rebellious lawlessness that is outside the realm of both Christianity and the forgiveness it brings with it. After all, when people continue in a state of ongoing SIN or lawlessness in which they refuse to repent, there is no hope of forgiveness. That is the type of SIN that leads to death.

And here we need to make an important point. Namely, that those people who reject the reality of the incarnate Christ are the same ones who have SIN leading to death. It is the theme that John has been hammering home for five chapters, concluding with 5:12 and 13: "The one who has the Son has life; the one who does not have the Son of God does not have life." Only those who "believe in the name of the Son of God" have "eternal life."

The most important point in 1 John is that those who reject the fact that Jesus is the Son of God—the Christ who came in the flesh (1 John 5:1; 4:2, 15)—have spurned any hope of forgiveness and life. They are living in a state of SIN that leads directly toward death. In other words, they have committed the unpardonable sin of not responding in confession when the Holy Spirit convicts their hearts (John 16:8). They have that life characterized by rebelliousness and deliberateness that the book of Hebrews tells us is beyond hope because God can do nothing for people who reject the Spirit's proddings and turn their backs on the sacrifice of Christ, thus having "spurned the Son of God" and "outraged the Spirit of grace" (Heb. 10:26-29, RSV). "It is impossible to restore" such individuals "to repentance" because they have refused the only source of help (Heb. 6:4-6, RSV).

There is, John is proclaiming, a SIN that leads nowhere but to death and is, in his definition, death itself. In the context of his letter, those pos-

> **The Conditions of Prayer**
>
> Prayer must be:
> 1. rooted in faith (Mark 11:24).
> 2. asked in the name of Jesus (John 14:14).
> 3. offered by those who abide in Christ (John 15:7).
> 4. requested by those who have forgiven those who have offended them (Mark 11:25).
> 5. accompanied by obedience (1 John 3:22).
> 6. not be asked to gratify one's passions (James 4:3).
> 7. according to God's will (1 John 4:15).

sessing that sin are the secessionists who have denied the incarnate Christ and the forgiveness, obedience, and love that flow out of His life, death, and ministry. God cannot answer prayer on behalf of those who live in such rebellious ways (1 John 5:16), even though He can respond to prayer for those whose sins do not lead to death (verse 17).

Such are the conclusions of the apostle John. They provide food for thought in our day. Choices for life or death, assurance or condemnation, are up to us individually.

27. Final Affirmations and an Exhortation

1 John 5:18-21

¹⁸We know that no one who has been born of God practices sin, but the One [the Son] who was born of God keeps him, and the evil one does not touch him.

¹⁹We know that we are of God and that the whole world lies in the sphere of the evil one.

²⁰And we know that the Son of God has come and has given us understanding so that we may know the true One, and we are in the true One, in His Son Jesus Christ. This is the true God and eternal life.

²¹Little children, keep yourselves from idols.

What a way to end a letter!

Three great affirmations in a letter of affirmations. Three explosive "we knows" in a letter full of "we knows."

Or is it a letter? After all, it has no salutations at the beginning and no personal remarks or signature line at its ending. It reads more like a sermon from one end to the other.

The good news is that it doesn't make any difference whether 1 John is a letter, sermon, or tract. The important thing is that it comes from the author's heart and speaks to the hearts of the readers, whether they lived in the first century or the twenty-first.

John's closing remarks consist of three affirmations and a word of counsel that look like a PS. Each of the affirmations begins with a "we know," once again highlighting the firmness of John's convictions. Let's look at them one by one.

Affirmation 1: "We know that no one who has been born of God practices sin" (1 John 5:18). Here we have an echo of 1 John 3:6, 9. In both places the apostle uses a verb tense indicating that no Christian can practice sin as a way of life or live in a state of lawlessness. That doesn't mean that a Christian never falls or commits acts of sin. To the contrary, John tells us, anyone who claims that extreme position is both a liar and makes God into a liar (1 John 1:8, 10). What he means in the overall context of his writing is that while believers may commit sins that do "not lead to death" (5:17), they do not "dwell in the arena that is characterized by sinning, for that realm lies in the grip of the evil one (v. 18)" (Thompson, p. 146). Said differently, Christians do not live in the "world" that John has so much to say about—that sphere of life dominated by godless principles.

And why don't Christians end up as lawless sinners in the world? Because, he declares, the "One who was born of God [i.e., Christ] keeps him and the evil one does not touch him" (1 John 5:18b). Here is the secret of spiritual power. Believers are safe because they maintain a connection to God through Christ—one that is everything for a healthy Christian. It is Jesus who shields His followers from the devil and empowers them through the Holy Spirit. B. F. Westcott points out that even though the evil one is powerful, each Christian "has a watchful Protector stronger than his adversary" (Westcott, p. 193). Of that, John writes, we may be certain.

Affirmation 2: "We know that we are of God and that the whole world lies in the sphere of the evil one" (1 John 5:19). The apostle's second affirmation concerns the home base of believers and is closely related to affirmation 1. For him there exist only two realms: one defined as God's sphere and the other as the province of the evil one. John associates the first realm with life and the second with death. Christians have hope because they have passed from the sphere of the world to that of God, from the arena of death to that of life. Of that, John tells us, we may be certain.

Affirmation 3: "We know that the Son of God has come and has given us understanding so that we may know the true One, and we are in the true One, in His Son Jesus Christ." Here we are back to the first paragraph of 1 John, in which the apostle notifies his readers that he is going to tell them about Jesus and the eternal life revealed in Him so that their "joy" might be "filled up" (1 John 1:1-4).

The third affirmation aims at the heart of the secessionists' theology. They had denied the Son, who is the center of God's redemptive plan. To know and be connected to the Son, John has asserted repeatedly, is to possess eternal life (cf. 1 John 5:12, 13).

John's third affirmation closes with an interesting phrase: "This is the true God and eternal life" (verse 20). The natural question is who is the verse talking about—the Father or the Son? Opinions divide, with some scholars pointing out that Jesus Christ is the nearest antecedent, and others arguing that the two references to the "true one" earlier in the verse indicate that this third use of "true" must of necessity be to the Father. Yet others, such as Leon Morris, point out that the Father and the Son are so close and so intertwined in 1 John that "there is little difference" regarding which of them is the correct antecedent in the third affirmation (Morris, "1 John," p. 1270). After all, John has not the slightest doubt about the full divinity of Jesus (see John 1:1; cf. Heb. 1:8). And in the Father and the Son humans can have eternal life.

First John's final words are an exhortation to avoid idols (1 John 5:21). At first sight that counsel appears to be an afterthought somewhat disconnected from the three affirmations.

But that reading is far from the truth. John's topic in the affirmations was the true God in whom people can have eternal life. In that context it is quite natural to raise the issue of false gods. And that is just what an idol is. An idol is a counterfeit god. And beyond that, idols are anything people allow to take the place of God.

Counseling Christians in Ephesus (the target region for 1 John) to keep themselves from idols was needed advice, since that city housed the great Temple of Diana, one of the wonders of the ancient world. Ephesus was a center of pagan worship, with its idols, astrology, sorcerers, exorcisms, and other temptations of the spiritual realm. Such an environment made it difficult for Christians to stay on track. Thus John's firm counsel to stay away from idols and to worship the true God.

While the forms of idolatry have changed during the past 2,000 years, its dynamics are just as powerful as ever. Visible physical idols that people bow down to might be out of vogue with most of us, but such powerful gods as materialism and power have taken their place for some. Others find themselves tempted by the siren calls of the New Age movement, the

Eastern religions, or even the overwhelming desire to save the world from hunger and injustice through human engineering. While some of the above activities and entities have more good about them than others, all of them become ways of avoiding the fact that the incarnate Christ holds the only sufficient answer to the ills of a terminally sick world. At its bottom, each activity and every religious effort outside of Christ is an alternative altar at which modern people can worship.

The truth is that no generation can neglect the wisdom of the apostle John, who never tired of proclaiming that the only road to eternal life is the one that unites individuals to Jesus Christ, the Son of God.

Exploring
Second John

Introduction to the
Second Letter of John

With only 245 Greek words, 2 John is the second shortest book in the New Testament. Some have called it a "postcard epistle" (Akin, p. 217).

Unlike 1 John, which has more of the format of a sermon or tract, 2 John is definitely a letter. The first verse tells us that its author is "the elder" and that its recipients are the "chosen lady" and "her children."

A great deal of discussion has dealt with the identity of the elder, largely because of a postbiblical tradition of an "elder John" quite distinct from John the apostle who also lived in Ephesus in the first century. But the overwhelming evidence in the book itself is that the author of 2 John is the same person who wrote the first letter and the Gospel of John—namely, John the disciple of Christ and the son of Zebedee.

The identity of the "chosen lady and her children" has also been a point of debate, but it seems to be a description of the church and its members. That interpretation lines up with John's reference to the church as a woman in such places as Revelation 12:6, 13, 14. Thus the apostle John is writing to a church whose members he and fellow believers love in the truth (2 John 1).

Especially pertinent to a shared authorship between 1 John and 2 John is the fact that 86 percent of the words in the second letter also appear in the first. Beyond that, stylistically both letters build their arguments around key words repeated several times for emphasis. In the light of that pattern in the first letter, it is significant that the 13 verses of the second use "truth" five times, "love" four times, "commandment" four times, "walk" three times, and "children" three times.

Beyond a shared vocabulary and a repetitive use of words style, we find the unified authorship of First and Second John also indicated by similar themes. Thus the elder:

1. deals with the same historical situation as 1 John. For example, he writes of those "deceivers" who "have gone out into the world" who "will not acknowledge the coming of Jesus Christ in the flesh" (2 John 7, RSV; cf. verse 9; 1 John 4:2; 2:19, 22, 23).
2. labels the false teachers as antichrists (2 John 7; cf. 1 John 2:18, 22).
3. emphasizes the love commandment—not as a new commandment, but one which his readers had had from "the beginning" (2 John 4-6; cf. 1 John 2:7; 3:11, 23; 4:7).
4. finds joy in seeing his children walking in the truth (2 John 4; cf. 1 John 1:6, 7).

The problem that 2 John faces is that certain "deceivers" who deny that Jesus Christ came in the flesh have "gone out into the world" (verse 7). The elder's primary purpose in 2 John is "to forewarn his readers against the infiltration of this error" so that they might be on their guard, and "to stress in no uncertain terms the serious character of the false teaching" (Guthrie, p. 890). He makes it quite clear that their doctrine is not from God and that they are, in fact, antichrists or in opposition to Christ.

A secondary purpose of the author is to warn his readers not to extend hospitality to such false teachers and thereby provide them with a base from which to extend their disruptive ideas (2 John 10). To provide them such a base would make his readers sharers in their "evil deeds" (verse 11).

Although we find no specific indications in the text of 2 John, it is very probable that its author composed it soon after 1 John, which may have been a circular letter to the various congregations in the Ephesus region. If that is the case, 2 John functions as a follow-up letter to one of those congregations. The secessionists were on the move and the elder wanted to specifically emphasize the danger to that particular group of believers. The supplementary nature of 2 John explains the brevity of its treatment of the heresies being spread abroad. Since his readers already had the main exposition, all they needed was a secondary wake-up jolt and a specific warning not to provide aid and assistance to the heretics.

Introduction to the Second Letter of John

During the time of crisis facing them, John felt it imperative that the members of the congregation maintain unity by not only excluding the secessionists from their fellowship, but also by showing love to one another (verses 4-6). That can be seen as a third purpose for the writing of 2 John. In issuing that command, the apostle emphasizes that they have had it from "the beginning" (verse 6), an allusion to their knowledge of both the first letter and the message of the Fourth Gospel with its emphasis on loving one another which believers had been taught from "the beginning" of their Christian experience.

Outside of the issue of hospitality, 2 John provides no new major themes of its own. It rather repeats in a greatly abbreviated manner several of the ideas found in 1 John.

The format of 2 John is quite simple. It is a short letter that consists of a salutation (verses 1-3), a body of counsels and warnings (verses 4-11), and some concluding remarks (verses 12, 13). We can outline it as follows:

I. Greetings (1-3)
II. Counsel and warnings (4-11)
    A. Counsel to love one another (4-6)
    B. Warning against those teaching false ideas about Christ (7-10)
    C. Warning against providing aid and support to the deceivers (10, 11)
III. Closing remarks (12, 13)

List of Works Cited
(see introduction to 1 John)

Part I

Greetings

2 John 1-3

1. Saying Hello With a Blessing

2 John 1-3

¹The elder to the chosen lady and to her children, whom I love in truth, and not only I, but also all those who know the truth, ²because of the truth dwelling in us, and it will be with us forever. ³Grace, mercy, and peace will be with us from God the Father and from Jesus Christ, the Son of the Father, in truth and love.

Second John 1-3 contains both an address (verses 1, 2) and a greeting (verse 3). In line with Greek letter writing custom, the author begins by identifying himself. But the interesting thing is that rather than using his name, as we find in Paul's letters, he merely calls himself "the elder."

The term can indicate one of several things. First, it can indicate that "he was a venerated old man in the community" (Smalley, p. 317). That meaning is undoubtedly true in this case, but the import moves beyond that idea. A second possible significance is that elders were officials in local congregations. Thus Paul and Barnabas "appointed elders . . . in every church" (Acts 14:23, RSV). We find the same usage of the word in 1 Timothy 3:1-5 and Titus 1:6-8. That is not the meaning we find in 2 John and 3 John, since the evidence suggests that he was more than a local pastor. Stephen Smalley correctly suggests that "the influence which he seems to have exercised implies that his position was similar to that of a modern 'bishop' [or conference president] or 'superintendent' . . . , and that he had responsibility" for several churches in the area (Smalley, p. 317).

The fact that the writer identifies himself by using a definite article— "*the* elder"—implies that his readers would clearly understand who was writing to them. As noted in the introduction, "the elder" undoubtedly refers in 2 John and 3 John to the apostle John, who wrote the Fourth Gospel and 1 John.

The "chosen lady" also has elicited a great deal of discussion. It could certainly have been an individual. Those who have followed that route have speculated much regarding who she might be. Favorite candidates are Mary the mother of Jesus and Martha of Bethany. Some argue for Martha because the word for "lady" in Aramaic (the common language of first-century Palestine) was "Martha," while others sponsor Mary since Jesus left her in the care of John, and her traditional area of residence in her later years was Asia Minor. But all such theories are nothing but speculation.

Looking at the text itself, it is probable that the designation "lady" refers to a local church and its members (her "children"). Evidence for that conclusion runs along two lines. First, 2 John shifts effortlessly back and forth between the second person singular and the second person plural throughout the letter, a usage that "seems to betray the fact that the author is thinking of a community rather than an individual" (Stott, p. 204). By way of contrast, 3 John, which is definitely written to an individual, consistently employs the second person singular throughout.

A second line of evidence indicating that the "chosen lady" of 2 John is a church is the fact that the Bible often refers to God's people or the church as a woman. Thus we find Israel in the Old Testament described as a "daughter of Zion" (Isa. 52:2, RSV); married (Isa. 62:4); a mother (Isa. 54:1, 2); and a widow (Isa. 54:4). Meanwhile, the New Testament pictures the church betrothed to Christ as a bride to her husband (2 Cor. 11:2; cf. Eph. 5:25; Rev. 21:9). And the book of Revelation, also authored by John, several times depicts the church as a woman (see Rev. 12:6, 14, 17).

The concluding verse of 2 John with its "the children of your chosen sister greet you" also fits better the idea that the "chosen lady" is a church. In that case 2 John 13 would be a greeting from the local congregation and its members where John is located to another local congregation and its members.

An important aspect of 2 John 1-3 involves how love and truth are interrelated. Those three verses use "truth" four times and "love" twice, both times connected with truth. William Barclay argues that a crucial lesson here is that "it is only in the truth of Christianity that we can love as we ought" (Barclay, p. 162). He goes on to lay out the implications of that association. First, that Christian truth indicates the way we ought to love. *Agapē*, the word for Christian love, he points out, does not represent fickle love that ebbs and flows with one's passions, but an attitude toward others that desires their highest good in spite of how they may have treated us. That love, however, is not a sentimental emotion that shuts its eyes to the faults and failings of others or avoids the difficulties of life. To the contrary, Christian love holds people responsible to "the truth" (both doctrinally and ethically) even if they must be challenged at times. Thus Christian *agapē* is what some have called "tough love." It always wants the highest good for others, even if that may mean painful growth in the wake of confrontation and correction.

> "Our love grows soft if it is not strengthened by truth, and our truth hard if it is not softened by love" (Stott, p. 207).

Christian truth also tells us the reason why believers *must* love their fellow church members and even their enemies. The imperative for that love grows out of the fact that God first loved us (1 John 4:11). Because of that divine initiative "we also ought to love one another" (RSV). The stark fact is that a Christian cannot accept God's love without passing it on to others. The truth of divine love "lays on men the inescapable obligation of human love. Because God loves us, we must love others with the same generous and sacrificial love" (Barclay, p. 163).

Loving others "in truth" (2 John 1) or "the truth" (verses 1, 2) also suggests that it is truth that binds church members together in a mutual love. The fact that they share the same understanding of the important things of life and hold to the same beliefs regarding the nature of the good life and standards of right and wrong provides Christians with a firm basis for a community of love, even though within that community, given human nature, there will always be tensions and "problematic people."

The twin realities of truth and love are foundational to each other in their mutual dynamics. John Stott pictures truth and love in the Christian community as having a symbiotic relationship. Thus, he writes, "the fellowship of the local church is created by truth and exhibited in love. Each qualifies the other. On the one hand, our love is not to be so blind as to ignore the views and conduct of others. Truth should make our love discriminating. John sees nothing inconsistent in adding to his command to love one another (5) a clear instruction about the refusal of fellowship to false teachers, who are deceivers and antichrists (7-11). Our love for others is not to undermine our loyalty to the truth. On the other hand, we must never champion truth in a harsh or bitter spirit. Those who are 'walking in the truth' (4) need to be exhorted to 'love one another' (5). So the Christian fellowship should be marked equally by love and truth, and we are to avoid extremism which pursues either at the expense of the other. Our love grows soft if it is not strengthened by truth, and our truth hard if it is not softened by love" (Stott, p. 207).

Before leaving 2 John 1-3 we should note something unique in the greeting of verse 3, in which the apostle writes that "grace, mercy, and peace *will* be with us." Other New Testament letters always frame such remarks in prayer language. Thus Peter pens, "May grace and peace be multiplied to you" (1 Peter 1:2, RSV; cf. Jude 2). But 2 John gives the blessings in the greeting as a statement of fact, in which John assures his readers that they already possess those priceless gifts.

A final thought on verse 3 is that 2 John also utilizes creativity in its claim that the blessings of grace, mercy, and peace are from "God the Father and from Jesus Christ." While that phrase is quite similar to Paul's usage, John adds "the Son of the Father." By that stroke of the pen the elder emphasizes his special theological concern that Jesus the human being is not only the divine Christ, but also the Son of the Father, a concept that repeatedly shaped the discussion of 1 John (see 3:23; 4:2, 15; 5:1) and one that will dominate the discussion running from 2 John 7-11. The elder writes as a shepherd of his flock of believers, and, like a true pastor, the needs of his people are never far from his thoughts.

Part II

Counsel and Warnings

2 John 4-13

2. Heretics on the Prowl

2 John 4-9

[4]I was exceedingly glad that I found some of your children walking in truth, just as we received a commandment from the Father to do. [5]And now I ask you, lady, not as though I write a new commandment to you, but the one we have had from the beginning, that we should love one another. [6]And this is love, that we should walk according to His commandments. This is the commandment, just as you heard from the beginning, that we should walk in it. [7]For many deceivers have gone out into the world, those not confessing Jesus Christ coming in the flesh. That one is the deceiver and the antichrist. [8]Watch out for yourselves, that you do not lose what we have worked for, but that you may receive a full reward. [9]Everyone who runs ahead and does not dwell in the teaching of Christ does not have God. The one who dwells in the teaching has both the Father and the Son.

The good news is that there are things and people that make John's heart "exceedingly glad." How joyful he is that "some" of them are "walking in truth" (verse 4). But the word "some" also implies that the church is divided—that some but not all are living in the truth while others are following the path of evil. And so "some" are, as we will see in verses 7-11.

The apostle will get to the second half of the "some" soon enough, but first he, in good pastoral fashion, wants to encourage and reinforce those who are doing right. Just as Paul did in eight of his 13 letters, John begins with a word of thanksgiving. "He wishes to continue the warm affection established with his readers in the opening three verses, thereby preparing them for the harsh warnings that will follow" (Akin, p. 224).

After his emphasis on truth in 2 John 1-3, it is quite logical for him to

commend church members for living by it in verse 4. "Walking," a favorite expression of New Testament writers "to describe the whole of a
person's experience and behavior" (see, e.g. Mark 7:5; John 8:12; 12:35;
Romans 6:4), "means to live in accordance with God's revelation in the
gospel and by the standards contained in it. It is the same as living 'in the
light' (1 Jn. 1:7)" (Marshall, p. 66). John himself has utilized walking sym-
bolism from the beginning of his first letter, in which he claimed that "if
we say that we have fellowship with Him yet are walking in the darkness,
we lie and are not practicing the truth" (1 John 1:6; cf. 2:6, 11; 3 John 3).

Those "walking in the light" are following the commandment of the
Father (2 John 4). Succeeding verses suggest that it is probable that here
John has in mind his teaching in 1 John 3:23, which reads that "this is His
commandment, that we believe in the name of His Son Jesus Christ, and
practice loving one another, just as He commanded us."

John's purpose is not to provide the faithful with new information
about the faith but to reemphasize that which they already knew and to reinforce them in their faithfulness. He will save his "new" information for
their relationship with the deceivers who would take advantage of their
hospitality (see 2 John 10, 11).

But before he gets to the deceivers in verse 7 and his warnings against
aiding them in verse 10, he will in typical Johannine style drive home the
need for Christian love by repetition in verses 5 and 6. His repetition forms
a chiasm that begins and ends with the word "command" while featuring
"love" at its center. The finished argument looks like this:

    A. "I write a new commandment to you" (5a)

      B "that we should love one another" (5b)

      B[1] "this is love" (6a)

    A[1] "that we should walk according to His commandments" (6a)

Perhaps not everyone is equally excited with the amount of repetition
that John employs. But we all have to admit that when he is finished we
all know exactly what is important. And mutual love for each other in the
Christian community is crucial since it strengthens its social fabric and is
thus a "safeguard" or buttress "against error" (Westcott, p. 228).

With 2 John 7 the elder comes to the primary purpose of his letter. He
needs to warn the faithful concerning the "many deceivers" who "have
gone out into the world." They are not new to John's first readers nor to

us. The same false believers we met repeatedly in 1 John, they were characterized by their lack of love (1 John 4:20) and obedience (1 John 2:4) and by their aggressive teaching that the divine Christ could not possibly have become the human Jesus (see 1 John 2:22, 23; 4:1-3). Thus they are the very people John characterized as being antichrists in 1 John 2:22.

Here in 2 John the author provides us with a special insight that helps us understand who the deceivers were and the forcefulness of their appeal. Verse 9 describes them as those who "run ahead." The Greek word *proagō* means "to take or lead from one position to another by taking charge" or "to move ahead or in front of" (Bauer, p. 864). Thus "the secessionists may think of themselves as 'progressives,' 'modern,' or philosophically and theologically 'up-to-date'" (Johnson, p. 157).

In this particular context their "advanced" intellectual concepts fit right in with Greek philosophy, which found both the incarnation of God in human flesh and the substitutionary death of Christ to be foolishness in the extreme (see 1 Cor. 1:23).

As we have seen elsewhere, their thinking has its roots in the Greek view of matter and spirit. From that perspective spirit was good and the material aspects of existence (including flesh) were evil. Thus the divine Christ, the Son of God, would never appear in flesh. One result of that teaching would be a heresy eventually called Docetism (from the Greek *dokein*, which means "seemed"). Docetism taught that Christ didn't really become flesh, but only appeared to do so. While such a teaching was serious enough in itself, it also led to a downplaying of Jesus' ethical and doctrinal teachings and an undermining of His atoning sacrifice on the cross.

> John realized that to deny the historicity of the incarnation is to destroy the Christian faith.

The deceivers whom John warns the faithful about were not only caught up in docetic ideas, but they believed that their views were superior to those of the apostle who was not only old-fashioned but backward in his theology, while they were on the cutting edge of the latest ideas. Thus they believed that in their concept of Christ they had "run ahead" of the bulk of the church in their understanding (2 John 9). As a consequence, they desired to teach the church their advanced knowledge and sought to expose John's rather "primitive" followers to their new truth.

Here we come face to face with another Greek temptation, one later called Gnosticism. The term "gnosticism" derives from *gnōsis*, the Greek word meaning "knowledge." The Gnostic viewpoint held that salvation was for the few who had special, advanced insights into divine things. And so it was in the Christian community addressed by John. The secessionists, motivated by their advanced knowledge and superior airs, set out to convert the faithful away from the unsophisticated ideas of the *old* apostle, who had it all wrong.

It is important not to underestimate the power of such ideas in a world permeated by Greek thought. Those with the new ideas not only saw themselves as the real heroes in the Christian community, but many others also perceived them in that role. Thus they "were causing considerable uncertainty" in the churches regarding "the true character of Christian belief and whether the members of the church could truly regard themselves as Christians" (Marshall, p. 14).

It is in relation to that point that John's emphasis on Christian assurance (1 John 5:13) in his first letter takes on special meaning. He had no doubt that faithful church members could "know" that they were right with God (1 John 2:5; 3:14, 19, 24; 4:13; 5:13, 19, 20). In that context mutual love among believers took on a special importance, since that love would bind them together and strengthen them both individually and collectively against the trauma they now faced from the assaults of the deceivers. "Watch out for yourselves," the apostle urges, "that you do not lose what we have worked for, but that you may receive a full reward" (2 John 8).

The situation in 2 John 7-9 is not merely ancient history. To the contrary, the church faces it today. The Christian church has always experienced tension between those who have "new light" and "advanced ideas" more in harmony with modern or postmodern culture than the Bible and those who in faith rely on the inspired instruction of God. The exact form may change across time, but "advanced" philosophic thinking always lurks just around the corner. In fact, it is closer than that. Nearly every church has its new light, in touch with the times missionaries who would move the rest of the church into a "more mature faith." But at such times what "seems and claims to be progress may be fatal error" (Westcott, p. 229).

That brings us to the crucial question of how we as Christians can tell the difference between genuine advances in Christian knowledge and the deceptive ideas of those who "run ahead." Dealing with that question is where John is consistently at his best. His answer is invariably to go back to "the beginning" and compare all new ideas to the apostolic witness and message eventually recorded in the 27 books that make up the New Testament. Therein is the searching truth by which we can and must evaluate all other knowledge. Faithfulness to the apostolic witness coupled with the strengthening love of the Christian community are central aspects in helping sincere believers maintain a healthy faith and life that will guide them to the end so that they might "receive a full reward" (2 John 8).

3. A Lesson in Hospitality

2 John 10-13

[10]If anyone comes to you and does not bring this teaching, do not receive him into your house and do not speak a greeting to him, [11]for the one who speaks a greeting to him participates in his evil deeds.

[12]Though I have many things to write to you, I did not want to do so with paper and ink. But I hope to come to you and to speak face to face, that our joy may be full.

[13]The children of your chosen sister greet you.

Shut the door in their faces" seems to be pretty brutal advice coming from the one we think of as the apostle of love. What are we to make of such an attitude? Before we turn to that question, we need to take a look at the practice of hospitality in the first century.

G. C. Findlay points out that the Romans excelled all other ancient peoples in three things—"in military discipline, in civil law, and in *road-making*" (Findlay, p. 29). Through them the Romans won and built up a world dominion that lasted for centuries. Their road-building did much to link Southern and Western Europe, North Africa, Asia Minor, and the Near East in a network of highways that made travel in the Roman period more feasible than in any time before the modern era. The journeys of the apostle Paul and the rapid spread of Christianity would have been impossible without that system and the *Pax Romana,* or Roman peace, which made travel relatively safe.

By traveling from one town to another, Christians began to fulfill the Great Commission of Christ to take the gospel to all the world (Matt.

28:19, 20). But while Roman roads may have been good, the comforts of the modern hotel were unknown. W. M. Ramsay informs us that "the ancient inns were little removed from houses of ill-fame" and the church could not expose its members "to the corrupt and nauseous surroundings of the inns kept by persons of the worst class in existing society" (in Findlay, p. 31).

The solution was for Christians in the various communities to open their homes to itinerate believers. We find examples of that practice throughout the New Testament (see, e.g., Acts 16:15; 17:7; 21:8, 16; Rom. 16:23; Heb. 13:2).

The problem with the hospitality system was that it was prone to abuse. Thus in John's letters and other early Christian documents we find discussions on how to discriminate between true and false "prophets" and traveling teachers. The *Didache,* a Christian document that developed soon after John wrote his letters, stated that traveling teachers are to be welcomed "as you would the Lord." But if they teach false doctrine, stay too long, ask for money, or don't practice what they preach they are to be rejected. Therefore, the *Didache* counsels Christians that "everyone 'who comes in the name of the Lord' is to be welcomed. But then examine him, and you will find out . . . what is true and what is false" (*Didache* 11, 12).

John here faces a similar situation. And in his particular case he warns and even commands his readers not to receive into their homes or even to greet those who do not believe that Christ did not become incarnate in human flesh (2 John 10, 11).

"Why be so difficult?" you may be saying to yourself. Because the message of those particular missionaries sought to destroy the heart of the Christian message. John argued in his first letter that to deny that Christ came in the flesh undercut the meaning of His atoning sacrifice on the cross. The subtlety of the false teachers not only led to disobedient living (1 John 2:4) but to a life of lawlessness (1 John 3:4) and a total blindness to sin (1 John 1:8, 10). Thus their Christological heresy removed everything of significance from Christianity. To John such teachers represented antichrist. Denying the incarnation in the slippery Greek philosophic world in which he existed was the heresy of all heresies. It made both Christ and Christianity into meaningless nothings.

So why not show such teachers hospitality? Because to do so was to express approval of their teachings and also to support them financially as they destroyed the church. By welcoming such travelers church members participated in their "evil deeds" (2 John 11).

But why could one not at least greet them? Because, Craig Keener points out, "greetings were an essential part of social protocol at that time, and the greeting ('Peace be with you') was intended as a blessing or prayer to impart peace" (Keener, p. 749). John wanted no part in blessing such people. They denied the Christ for which he had given his life and were destroying the church he was struggling to maintain, so he would not compromise with them in the least way.

John's position is clear enough. But how should we relate to his counsel in the twenty-first century? After all, intolerance is out and acceptance is in vogue. I would suggest that the very limitless tolerance of our day is a reason that we should carefully think through 2 John's teaching on boundaries.

William Barclay claims that the answer requires a recognition of the extremely dire situation of the church in Asia Minor at the end of the first Christian century. "There was a time," he writes, "when it was touch and go whether the Christian faith would be swamped and destroyed by the speculations of those pseudo-philosophic heretics. The actual existence of the faith was in peril," a situation without "parallel in western civilization" (Barclay, p. 168). Thus the counsel of 2 John 10, 11 is for his time and not a universal teaching for the church in more relaxed circumstances. Along that line, one student of 2 John sees the counsel in verses 10 and 11 to be an emergency regulation and points out that "emergency regulations make bad laws for less troubled periods" (Thatcher, p. 521; cf. Dodd, pp. 151, 152).

That understanding of John's injunctions is helpful in some ways, but it isn't fully adequate to help the church protect itself from the ongoing onslaught of forces that continually seek to erode its doctrinal and ethical foundations.

Leon Morris takes a firmer stand than Barclay on the doctrinal issues, but claims that "John does not mean that common courtesy is not to be extended to a doctrinal opponent," even though it couldn't be expressed in the apostle's time since it would be interpreted as expressing "appreciation of his message" (Morris, "2 and 3 John," p. 1272). John Stott holds a similar position. While respecting the apostle's "concern for the glory of the Son and the good of human souls," he points out that "John is referring to teachers of false doctrine about the incarnation, and not to every false teacher." Thus 2 John "gives us no warrant to refuse fellowship to those, even teachers, who do not agree with our interpretation of apostolic doctrine in every particular" (Stott, pp. 216, 217).

Tom Thatcher puts forth a workable approach to applying the counsel of 2 John 10 and 11 to our day when he writes that "any real application of 2 John to the situation of the modern church must recognize that John would consider dialogue on . . . two issues to be dangerously illegitimate" (Thatcher, p. 522). And what are those nonnegotiable issues? The facts of the incarnation of Christ as an historic reality and the need to accept Jesus' teachings as the foundation of Christian faith and practice. Without those two foundational premises there can be no Christianity or Christian dialogue with others. To give up those teachings or to soft pedal them in cross-religious dialogue, John would undoubtedly hold if he were alive today, would be a betrayal of Christianity and an acceptance of the doctrinal platform of the antichrist.

Before leaving 2 John, we need to briefly examine his closing remarks in verses 12 and 13. John realized that writing a series of short letters would not be nearly as helpful as a personal visit from him. He had worked with people and problems enough in his long life to realize that a written message is subject to the limitations of space and is easily misunderstood. The apostle knew that he needed to have a face to face ("mouth to mouth" in the Greek) discussion to make himself clear and to answer important questions. But he was also aware of the frailty of his age and the demands on his time. So a letter would have to do until he could make a personal visit (verse 12).

The letter's final verse, "The children of your chosen sister greet you" (verse 13), is a simple yet heartwarming insight into the fellowship that Christians have across local congregations and even across national and ethnic borders in the universal sisterhood of churches.

Exploring
Third John

Introduction to the Third Letter of John

With 219 Greek words, 3 John is the shortest book in the New Testament. By way of contrast, Philemon with its 345 words is almost "massive."

We have little reason to doubt 3 John's relationship to 1 John, partly because 70 percent of its words also appear in the larger letter. The more serious question has to do with the relationship of 3 John to 2 John. They have both similarities and differences. Among the similarities are the facts that in each the author describes himself as "the elder" (2 John 1; 3 John 1); the recipients are those whom he loves in the truth (2 John 1; 3 John 1); they fill him with joy (2 John 4; 3 John 3); the elder desires to see both "face to face" (2 John 12; 3 John 14); and both deal with hospitality (2 John 10, 11; 3 John 5-8, 10). The similarities indicate that they have the same author.

While that is undoubtedly true, major differences do exist between the two letters. Second John is addressed to a church, while the addressee of 3 John is an individual (2 John 1; 3 John 1). While the second letter (like 1 John) has no personal names, the third has three (3 John 1, 9, 12). The second treats the problem of deceivers from outside the local church, and the third deals with a problematic leader (Diotrephes) that is inside of it (2 John 7; 3 John 9). Although 2 John seeks to discourage entertaining wrong visitors, 3 John is a commendation for proper hospitality to true teachers and a condemnation of one who refused such hospitality (2 John 10, 11; 3 John 5-8, 10). Whereas 3 John features a challenge to the elder's authority (3 John 9, 10), no such problem is evident in 2 John even though it is definitely implied throughout 1 John. And finally, while the heresy regarding Jesus Christ coming in the flesh is central to 1 and 2 John (1 John 2:22; 4:1-3; 2 John 7, 9), 3 John does not mention it at all.

Given the similarities and differences, the challenge is to determine how they might relate to each other. That task is all the more difficult because the letters are so short that they offer few interpretive clues. But before we turn to their relationship, we should take a look at the flow and content of 3 John.

The apostle's reason for writing it is the return of some individuals whom he had apparently sent to circulate among the churches. In their report to John they commend Gaius for his following the truth (2 John 3) and for entertaining the apostle's representatives (verses 5-8). The author goes on to reprove Diotrephes who rejects his authority, has been spreading malicious gossip about him, refused to welcome his representatives, and even wanted to put those out of the church who were hospitable to them (verses 9, 10). Diotrephes' challenge indicates that he is a leader in the church (perhaps self-appointed) and that a power struggle exists between him and John.

With the above facts in mind, the most probable situation is that Gaius and Diotrephes belong to the same church. Given the difficult situation, the apostle wrote the two letters at the same time: one to the church (verse 9), which he fears will not be publicly read because of Diotrephes' opposition to him, and the other to the faithful Gaius, whose loyalty he could trust (verse 1).

Some students of John's epistles reject that solution on the ground that 3 John makes no mention of the false teaching about Jesus not coming in the flesh that was so central to 2 John. But we can account for that if the apostle sent both of his two shorter letters to Gaius, who was already familiar with 1 John and the general teachings of the Fourth Gospel and would now also have the second letter, which is a specific warning to his congregation, and 3 John, in which the apostle deals with one of the problematic leaders of that congregation.

While the letters might be helpful, John realizes that they will probably not solve the problem (2 John 2-12; 3 John 3-13). So he plans to send Demetrius (3 John 12) in the hope that his presence will bring harmony.

But he apparently fears that Demetrius will encounter the same rejection by Diotrephes that the messengers of verse 3 received. In the end the aged apostle knows that he will probably have to meet the problem face to face, a topic he alludes to in both 2 John 12 and 3 John 14.

Please remember that the information we have regarding 2 and 3 John is too incomplete to "prove" the above scenario of their relationship. But that overview makes sense of all of the facts and seems to be the most probable interpretation.

The elder's purpose in writing 3 John is to commend Gaius for his hospitality to traveling missionaries (verses 5-8), to draw attention to the problematic behavior of Diotrephes (verses 9, 10), and to recommend Demetrius, whom he apparently intends to send to Gaius's congregation (verse 12).

While 3 John introduces no new theological themes, it does provide a snapshot of the dynamics taking place in at least one Christian congregation in the 90s of the first century. They include challenges to apostolic authority, a divided congregation, and (if one takes both 2 John and 3 John together) the fact that both the secessionists and the apostle were sending out their own missionaries to spread their opposing theological ideas.

In retrospect, the church in the A.D. 90s doesn't look so much different from that of the twenty-first century. Therein is the relevance of both 3 John and the three letters combined.

3 John can be outlined as follows:
   I. Greetings (1-4)
  II. Encouragements and reproofs (5-12)
      A. Encouragement for Gaius (5-8)
      B. Reproof for Diotrephes (9, 10)
      C. Commendation for Demetrius (11, 12)
 III. Closing remarks (13-15)

List of Works Cited
(see introduction to 1 John)

Part I

Preliminary Considerations

3 John 1-4

1. Lessons From a Greeting

3 John 1-4

¹The elder to the beloved Gaius, whom I love in truth.
*²Beloved, I pray that in all things you will succeed and be in health,
just as your soul prospers. ³For I rejoiced exceedingly when the brothers
came and testified of you being in the truth, as you are walking in truth.
⁴I have no greater joy than this, that I hear my children are walking in the
truth.*

And who is Gaius? No one knows for certain. The New Testament
mentions three individuals by that name—Gaius of Macedonia (Acts
19:29), Gaius of Derbe (Acts 20:4), and Gaius of Corinth (1 Cor. 1:14;
Rom. 16:23)—but we lack sufficient information to link the Gaius in
3 John to any of those individuals. A late tradition "identifies the present
Gaius with the first bishop of Pergamum" (Wilder, p. 308), an appointee
of John, but that bit of information is unreliable and adds nothing to our
search. The problem is compounded by the fact that "the name Gaius [is]
perhaps the most common of all names in the Roman Empire" (Plummer,
Epistles, p. 144).

What we do know about the man is that John loved and respected
him. It is also clear from the letter that Gaius occupied a position of responsibility and leadership in the local church. Whether that local congregation was the same as the one being manipulated by Diotrephes or a
neighboring one cannot be proved with certainty, but it is probable that
the two men were leaders of the same group of Christians.

From the letter itself we know two things about Gaius. First, that he was a dedicated Christian (verse 3). And, second, that he had been faithful in showing hospitality to traveling Christians (verse 5). John undoubtedly sees Gaius as a counterweight to the problematic Diotrephes of verse 9.

Third John is one of the few letters written to an individual in the New Testament. And as such it is representative of the kinds of secular letters that circulated during the period of the early church. One example of that style is a letter from a ship's captain to his brother: "Irenaeus to Apolinarius his brother, my greetings. Continually I pray that you may be in health, even as I myself am in health. I wish you to know that I arrived at land on the 6th of the month. . . . I greet your wife much, and Serenus, and all who love you, by name. Goodbye" (in Barclay, p. 171).

Formwise that letter is an exact parallel to 3 John. First comes the greeting, then the prayer for good health, followed by the body of the letter with news and information, and concluded by final remarks in which the writer passes on greetings to mutual friends.

And what is the moral of the story? Simply that "early Christian letters were not something remote and distant and religious and ecclesiastical; they were just the kind of letters which people wrote to each other every day in the ancient world" (*ibid.*). Said a bit differently, "short notes to friends and family did not begin with the invention of e-mail" (Yarbrough, p. 222).

> "Short notes to friends and family did not begin with the invention of e-mail."

We should note several things about the greetings section of 3 John 1-4. First, John twice uses the Greek word *agapētos* ("beloved") in the first two verses, an address he employs four times in 3 John and five times in 1 John. Thus even though the letters tend to be stern and bristling with warning and rebuke, their author has framed them in terms of endearment and affection. There is something of importance in that point for every husband, wife, parent, pastor, teacher—for all of us. Just because we are treating a serious topic does not mean that we must be unloving. We need to be like Jesus, who could rebuke the Jewish leaders with tears in His eyes and His heart filled with love (Matt. 23:37, 38).

A second aspect of 3 John 1-4 of interest is that the apostle prayed for Gaius' health as well as his spiritual journey. The word for "health" is the same one that Luke used to translate Jesus' saying that "those who are well [healthy] have no need of a physician, but those who are sick" (Luke 5:31, RSV). In his concern, John was like Jesus who in His ministry of teaching never forgot that people have bodies as well as minds and souls. True Christianity is concerned with the whole person.

A third point of importance in 3 John's greeting section is that the apostle "rejoiced exceedingly" when the visitors reported on Gaius' spiritual well-being (verse 3). In verse 4 the elder states that he had "no greater joy" than when his children walked in the truth.

> We need to be like Jesus, who could rebuke the Jewish leaders with tears in His eyes and His heart filled with love.

John understood the principle of positive reinforcement. He not only felt joy in his heart, but he went out of his way to express his positive emotions repeatedly to Gaius. One can only imagine the encouraging effect that had on Gaius. We need to learn from this interchange. All too often we "serious" Christians find it easier to find fault with others than we do to express our overflowing joy in their accomplishments. John can teach us an important lesson.

Closely related to that expression of joy is a fourth insight. Verse 4 finds John referring to his "children." In this context he probably has in mind his parishioners or even his converts to Christianity. In that he was not alone since "rabbis and philosophers sometimes spoke of their disciples as their 'children'" (Keener, p. 751).

A fifth thing to note in 3 John 1-4 is that Gaius was "walking in the truth." That is the source of the apostle's joy, and he is so pleased that he repeats the statement twice. Once again he is in the business of positive reinforcement. But his thoughts on the topic are not only for the benefit of Gaius. They are for us also. After all, the greatest joy of any parent, pastor, or teacher is to see those they have worked with "walking in the truth." And walking, as we noted earlier, signifies not merely an intellectual assent to doctrinal truth, but a way of life in harmony with truth. Thus to walk in the truth is to become like Jesus (see 1 John 2:5, 6).

A sixth vital element of 3 John's greeting section is the fact that truth mattered to John. A high regard for the importance of both doctrinal and ethical truth stands at the center of all three of his letters. That is a point that those of us who live in areas of the world where doctrine is unpopular need to seriously consider. Religious truth is vital even if the surrounding culture and most Christians reject it. Listen to the apostle John. He has some wisdom on the topic desperately needed in the easy-going religious world of the twenty-first century.

Last, we need to remember that 3 John's greeting section is about a church leader named Gaius. The apostle sees that individual as central in his struggle against Diotrephes. As a result, verses 5-8 provide further encouragement for Gaius and his ministry. It reminds us that individual believers make a difference in God's work here on earth. People in general may not know who we are (as in the case of Gaius) but God does. And He not only knows us by name but He wants to use us for His work. With that in mind, we need to keep our eyes and ears and hearts open so that when God calls we will be ready to answer in the spirit of young Samuel, who responded with the words "Speak; for thy servant heareth" (1 Sam. 3:10, KJV).

Part II

Encouragements and Reproofs

3 John 5-15

2. Hospitality in Action

3 John 5-8

⁵Beloved, you act faithfully whenever you provide a service for the brothers, especially when they are strangers ⁶(who have testified of your love before the church), whom you do well to send on their way in a manner worthy of God. ⁷For they go out on behalf of the Name, accepting nothing from the Gentiles. ⁸Therefore we ought to provide hospitality to such people, so that we may be co-workers with the truth.

The return of the traveling "brothers" who "testified" of Gaius' "being in the truth" and "walking in truth" (verse 3) sets the stage for the rest of 3 John. The travelers not only brought good news about him (verses 5-8) and bad news regarding Diotrephes (verses 9, 10), but their report helped John plan his course of action for the future (verses 11-14).

The good news about Gaius begins in verse 5, in which the elder commends him for providing hospitality to Christians during their journeys. The commendation goes out of its way to point out that his hospitality even went to "strangers." The letter does not identify them, but it is probable that they were the very individuals who "testified" regarding Gaius' faithfulness in verse 3. The first part of verse 6, which I take to be parenthetical, reinforces that conclusion. There the strangers have "testified of your love before the church." In its context, the most natural meaning of that passage is that Gaius had cared for the needs of the travelers that reported to John (and who may have been dispatched by him to check out the situation) and had sent them on their way well supplied for their trip. *The New English Bible* captures that interpretation by rendering 3 John 5,

6 as follows: "My dear friend, you show a fine loyalty in everything that you do for these our fellow-Christians, strangers though they are to you. They have spoken of your kindness before the congregation here." At the opposite pole from their report of Gaius is that regarding Diotrephes, who refused to welcome the intinerants and used his authority to keep others from doing so (verse 10).

In John's few words about Gaius in 3 John 5-8 we find several important things about early Christian hospitality to other Christians and especially to those traveling on behalf of the gospel. The passage also supplies insights into missionary work in the late first century church. The two topics are intertwined.

As to missionary work, it is clear from 3 John and the New Testament in general that local churches took very seriously Christ's mandate to go to all nations to teach what He had commanded them (Matt. 28:19, 20). We get a glimpse of that dynamic activity in the outline of the book of Acts, in which right before His ascension Christ commanded His apostles (meaning those who are sent) to "witness" in ever widening circles from "Jerusalem and in all Judea and Samaria and to the end of the earth" (Acts 1:8, RSV).

The book of Acts presents one slice of that ongoing missionary activity, especially in the ministry of Paul. The spread of Christianity is one of the wonders of the ancient world. Within a couple short decades Paul could write in hyperbole that the gospel "has been preached to every creature under heaven" (Col. 1:23, RSV). The "every creature" part of that claim may contain a bit of literary flare, but the fact that in one generation Christianity spread through much of the known world is well established.

> "Let brotherly love continue. Do not neglect to show hospitality to strangers, for thereby some have entertained angels unawares" (Heb. 13:1, 2, RSV).

It is also true that itinerants such as Paul and Barnabas and other "strangers" journeying throughout the Roman Empire achieved that extraordinary accomplishment. Apparently the vast majority of them followed the counsel of Christ when He first sent out the 12. His advice was to take no money but "whatever town or village you enter, find out who is worthy in it, and stay with him until you depart." Among His general principles were that they were to "give without pay" and "the laborer deserves his food" (Matt. 10:8-14, RSV).

Christ also had instruction for those who would be supplying hospitality: "He who receives you receives me, and he who receives me receives him who sent me. He who receives a prophet because he is a prophet shall receive a prophet's reward, and he who receives a righteous man because he is a righteous man shall receive a righteous man's reward. And whoever gives to one of these little ones even a cup of cold water because he is a disciple, truly, I say to you, he shall not lose his reward" (Matt. 10:40-42, RSV).

Thus it was that the symbiotic relationship between traveling missionaries and hospitable hosts was the engine that drove Christianity to the far corners of the world. That thought brings us to the lessons that we can glean from 3 John 5-8 on the topic.

One is that such hospitality was an active practice in the A.D. 90s, as is evident from John's commendation of Gaius. But we also learn from those verses that the traveling missionaries expected to be granted hospitality from believers wherever they labored. Such hospitality was not the responsibility of "the Gentiles" or nonbelievers (verse 7), but of the churches. And the hosts were not only to care for them while they labored in their area, but were also "to send" them "on their way in a manner worthy of God" (verse 6), probably meaning "to send them on their way in a manner befitting those who serve the living God" (Kruse, p. 223).

> ### The Meaning of Hospitality
>
> "'Hospitality' conveys the idea of getting up under something so as to lift it up. That's a good picture of what hospitality is all about. We welcome people into our homes or apartments or dorm rooms for the purpose of taking a load off them and raising their spirits. We become their servants" (Barton, p. 148).

Third John 7, 8 supplies three reasons why it is appropriate for Gaius to send missionaries "on their way in a manner worthy of God." First, because "they go out on behalf of the Name" (verse 7). The word translated as "they go out" is an interesting one, because the apostle also uses it of the false missionaries in 1 John 2:19. They also go out or went out to spread the message of the antichrist. Those missionaries are the ones John calls "deceivers" in 2 John 7, of whom he warns Christians not to extend hospitality to. Thus, as we saw in our discussion of 2 John, Christians must discriminate between the true and the false. While they all go out, they do so with different messages. John's concern is that Christians be hospitable to those who "go out on behalf of the Name," meaning the name of Christ. Such were worthy ministers of the Lord. And they needed help, since unlike many itinerant philosophers and religious teachers of their day who fleeced their audiences, Christian itinerants were to rely on the hospitality of other Christians. It was a concept deeply entrenched in the Christian mentality that anyone who requested money (or took advantage of hospitality by staying indefinitely) was to be rejected (*Didache* 11). But by aiding those who went out "on behalf of the Name" Christians were helping to spread the gospel.

A second reason why local church members were to meet the needs of Christian missionaries was because such travelers could not expect any help from non-Christians (verse 7). Thus if they were to survive and labor in their important task they needed the aid of fellow believers.

The third reason that the missionaries were to be sent on their way well supplied was that by providing for them local believers became "co-workers with the truth" (verse 8). Just as those who were hospitable to the deceivers shared their evil work (2 John 11), so those who aided true workers for the gospel also became partly responsible for their results.

An important truth emerges here. Not all Christians have the same gifts and abilities. "It is significant that John does not ask Gaius to intervene in the controversy by confronting Diotrephes himself. Christians are called to different roles, and Gaius has done enough if he stands firm for Jesus Christ and provides John and his couriers an entrée into the community" (Burge, pp. 245, 246). God will use his firmness in the truth and his gift of hospitality to further His cause.

William Barclay writes along that line when he notes that "a man's circumstances may be such that he cannot become a missionary or a preacher. Life may have put him in a position where he must get on with a secular job, and where he must stay in one place, and carry out the routine duties of life and living. But where he cannot go his money and his prayers and his practical support can go; and, if he gives that support, he has made himself an ally of the truth. It is not everyone who can be, so to speak, in the front line; but every man by supporting those who are in the front line can make himself an ally of the truth." And when we firmly grasp that concept, "all giving to such a cause must become, not an obligation, but a privilege, not a duty, but a delight" (Barclay, pp. 175, 176).

May God help His church in our day to learn how to work together better, and each of us as individuals to discover how best to use the talents that He has given us.

3. Perversity in Action

3 John 9, 10

⁹I wrote something to the church; but Diotrephes, the one who loves to be first among them, does not accept our authority. ¹⁰Therefore, if I come I will bring up his deeds which he does, disparaging us with malicious words. And not being satisfied with that, he does not receive the brothers, and he forbids those who desire to do so and puts them out of the church.

Diotrephes was a tough customer. I don't know of any pastor or administrator who would like to have this guy in their church or jurisdiction. From a reading of the verses it is impossible to determine if he has a theological problem. On the other hand, it is extremely clear that Diotrephes has an authority issue. At the heart of that difficulty, John claims, is his love for the first place (verse 9). Or as G. C. Findlay puts it, "pride of place was the sin of Diotrephes" (Findlay, p. 58).

He definitely had power in the congregation, since he could remove people from fellowship (verse 10). Beyond that, he had a powerful antipathy for John. But why? we need to ask. Is it only because he saw John as a challenge to his dominance? Or is there a deeper issue?

Most students of 3 John conclude that Diotrephes had no direct connection with the antichrists and their denial of the incarnation. The primary support for that position is the fact that 3 John does not repeat the incarnational concerns of 1 and 2 John.

But that argument from silence is inconclusive at best. After all, John could have written both of his shorter letters at the same time, sending 2 John to Diotrephes, but fearing that he would not read it to the congregation since he "does not accept our [i.e., my] authority" (3 John 3:9). Thus the "I wrote something to the church" (verse 9) would be 2 John. And why wouldn't Diotrephes present it to the church? Perhaps in part because he favored the theology of the antichrist that was obviously making an impact on the churches in John's jurisdiction. If that is the case, then John would most likely have sent both 2 John and 3 John to Gaius at the same time—2 John to lay out the theological difficulty and 3 John to outline to Gaius his course of action in dealing with the problem and to encourage him to remain in the camp of the faithful in the ensuing struggle.

Tom Thatcher suggests that the key to the problem between John and Diotrephes might just lie in the relationship between Diotrephes and the antichrist party. After all, he points out, even though 3 John does not specifically deal with the doctrinal issue, "most scholars would agree that the situation described somehow arose from the Antichrist conflict." And, he continues, "within this historical context . . . one must question the common distinction between 'doctrinal' and 'ecclesial' disputes. Since John's authority is based on his claim to be a 'witness' to key elements" in the theological controversy over the incarnated Christ, "any challenge to that authority would inherently imply doctrinal deviation" (Thatcher, p. 536).

While we cannot prove the involvement of theological issues in the conflict between John and Diotrephes, it is highly probable. And it would go a long way in fueling the tension between the two men.

But even though the text does not specify that Diotrephes participated in theological deviance, it is very clear regarding his actions related to authority. Those problems are four in number.

To begin with, he is "the one who loves to be first among them" (verse 9). How paradoxical that John in his old age would have to face

> **Is There a Diotrephes in Every Chruch?**
>
> "Diotrephes represents the tares amidst Christ's wheat; he is the prototype of the diseased self-importance, the local jealousies and false independence, that have so often destroyed the peace of churches, making unity of action and a common discipline amongst them so difficult to maintain" (Findlay, p. 52).

an aggravated case of the same spiritual disease that had almost destroyed him in his youth. It must have seemed a million years earlier that his mother had gone to Jesus to obtain the two key places in His kingdom for her boys (Matt. 20:20, 21), and it truly had been a lifetime ago that he and Peter had struggled over who would be the greatest. His willful soul hadn't liked the words that the greatest would be the servant of all (Matt. 20:26), but he had eventually grasped their full impact after the crucifixion. Following his conversion on the topic of wanting to be first, John had become the loving servant par excellence. Through Christ he had gained the victory. But now six decades later he had to face the problem anew in Diotrephes.

Of course Diotrephes wasn't the last to suffer from the disease of self-importance and wanting to be at the center. In one form or another every human being has struggled with an assertive desire to be the first or the best or the most. That desire is the mother and father of all other sins. It is in that context that Jesus told His disciples that "if any man would come after me, let him deny himself and take up his cross and follow me" (Matt. 16:24, RSV). The crucifixion of one's "self" stands at the heart of Christianity.

> ### The Diotrephes Solution
>
> "The warfare against self is the greatest battle that was ever fought. The yielding of self, surrendering all to the will of God, requires a struggle; but the soul must submit to God before it can be renewed in holiness" (E. White, *Steps*, p. 43).

Diotrephes' second problem related to authority is that he refused to accept John's leadership. The "our authority" in the Greek text is undoubtedly a plural of authoritative position and thus correctly rendered as "my" in the Revised Standard Version. The reason for Diotrephes' lack of respect for John's authority is not clear. It may have been personal dislike, a desire to maintain local control of church affairs, just plain prideful stubbornness, or all of the above. But while we don't know the motivation, the reality of his insubordination is evident. Diotrephes was the top person, and he wasn't taking orders from anyone, especially a distant old man who, he may have surmised, had lost touch with the advancing truth of the times.

A third authority issue is Diotrephes' "disparaging" of the apostle "with malicious words" (verse 10). The word I translated as "disparaging" is difficult to render in English. But its sense is "to indulge in utterance that makes no sense, *talk nonsense (about)*, *disparage*" (Bauer, p. 1060). It is also used of "babbling . . . hence of making empty, groundless accusations" (Marshall, p. 91). At any rate, the apostle was on the receiving end of some pretty cruel language aimed at undermining his position. Unfortunately, that has often been the fate of Christians down through history. The evil one will do anything to discourage us. Perhaps like John we shouldn't see it so much as a reflection on us as it is on those who are spiritually sick.

The fourth point of conflict concerned Diotrephes' rejection of John's instruction to care for missionaries. Whether it was purely an authority issue or whether he disliked their theology makes little difference. In his refusal to show hospitality he "deliberately defied 'the elder'" (Stott, p. 231).

Beyond that, he expelled those from the church who did want to follow John's counsel regarding hospitality. Here was a troublemaker of the first order. And he was apparently a major officer if not *the* chief one in the congregation. Some of us get discouraged when we see corruption in the church today and conclude that it has gone to pot. Think again. The devil has always managed to get his tares into the wheat field. It was so in the days of John. And it is so in our day. In such circumstances we need to keep our eyes on the Lord of the church rather than on its problems.

One student of 3 John has written that "it is noteworthy that the elder's censure [of Diotrephes] appears comparatively mild." He goes on to suggest that John "was determined not to fight a battle of words and descend to his opponent's level" (Marshall, p. 91).

While that is undoubtedly true, the apostle wasn't finished with Diotrephes yet. Hanging in the background is the not so veiled threat: "If I come I will bring up his deeds" (verse 10). One supposes, following Christ's counsel in Matthew 18:15-17, that John would first try to settle the issue privately, and if that didn't work he would meet Diotrephes with two or three witnesses (one of whom might be the faithful Gaius and perhaps Demetrius whom we will meet in 3 John 12).

But if those tactics were inadequate John would have no choice but to "tell it to the church." If that failed, of course, Diotrephes himself would have to be put out of the church. Such is the procedure for handling disciplinary problems that Jesus had personally taught John and the other disciples so many years before.

4. Moving Into the Future

3 John 11-15

[11]Beloved, do not imitate the evil but the good. The one who does good is of God; the one who does evil has not seen God. [12]Demetrius has testimony from everyone, and by the truth itself. And we also testify, and you know that our testimony is true.

[13]I had many things to write to you, but I do not want to write to you with pen and ink. [14]But I hope to see you soon, and we will talk face to face.

[15]Peace to you. The friends greet you. Greet the friends by name.

Third John 11 turns away from the problematic Diotrephes and back to Gaius. "Do not imitate the evil," counsels the apostle, "but the good." Why the advice at this juncture? Possibly because John fears that the milder Gaius might come more directly under the influence of the forceful Diotrephes.

Now, imitating other people isn't all bad. In fact, all of us do it. The Bible tells us that we should imitate Christ (1 John 2:6). The other major option is to follow the model of the devil. Those two perspectives dry up the true alternatives. All else consists of variations of those two role models. In 3 John Diotrephes provides the model for those choosing the route of the evil one. John will present the counter model in verse 12 in the person of Demetrius.

Verse 11 with its advice on imitation is good counsel for all of us. But it was especially important for Gaius during a trying time. John had expressed his joy in his uprightness and faithfulness in verses 1-4. He had no

221

question where Gaius stood. And although he had no doubts regarding the man's current standing, he judged it wise to reinforce him.

"The one who does good is of God," but "the one who does evil has not seen God" (verse 11). The lesson is clear: people's character and daily life are outward indications of their relation to God. And on that count the domineering Diotrephes has so far failed.

But the apostle has a man who has succeeded in the doing good realm. And that brings him to Demetrius in verse 12. It is the first mention of him in John's correspondence. And readers have two questions about this person whose character and faithfulness John so highly attests to—namely, who is he? and why is his name dropped into the letter without warning?

The second of those questions is more difficult to answer than the first. Bible students have put forth two major candidates for his identity. The first is Demetrius the silversmith of Ephesus (the location of John's headquarters), who opposed Paul over the issue of the selling of images of the goddess Artemis and eventually stimulated the riot that drove the apostle out of the city (see Acts 19:21-20:1). Now it is possible that Demetrius the silversmith became converted at a later date, but we do not have a shred of evidence that he did so. But if he had become a Christian he certainly would have needed the strong testimony that the apostle provides in 3 John 12.

The same can be said for the second candidate. Demas (a shortened form of Demetrius) also had a difficult past. He had once been an associate of Paul, but had forsaken him because he loved the present world (Col. 4:14; Philemon 24; 2 Tim. 4:10). Perhaps Demas returned to the faith. Some think so. The *Apostolic Constitutions* (VII: 4:46, c. 350-380), for example, reported that John later appointed him bishop of Philadelphia. But we have no certain knowledge of any such conversion. But if he had been, he also would have certainly needed firm testimony to his trustworthiness, just as Paul the former persecutor did after his radical change (see Acts 9:26, 27).

As attractive as those two suggestions may be, when it comes right down to it we cannot identify the Demetrius of 3 John 3:12. Fortunately, we are in a stronger position when it comes to why John introduces him at this juncture in the letter. Not only is Demetrius a good example of doing good (verse 11), it is "virtually certain that he was the bearer of the letter" (Marshall, p. 93). In addition, "it may be that Demetrius is the elder's 'front man' (whose task it was to prepare the congregation for the elder's visit)" (Kysar, p. 146). Thus, since he would be arriving in Gaius' community, he would need hospitality.

That thought brings us to the outburst of commendations of Demetrius' character. "The tone of the testimonial" in verse 12 "implies that he is not well known to Gaius" (R. Brown, p. 722). Even though Gaius had a reputation for his hospitality (3 John 5-8), in the present difficult situation the apostle apparently felt that a letter of commendation was necessary.

The testimonial itself reflects the author's Jewish background, in which one established truth on the basis of three witnesses (see Deut. 19:15; 1 John 5:8). The testimonials to Demetrius' character were outstanding. First, he has the good word from "everyone" who knows him. Second, "the truth itself" speaks in his behalf, meaning that he is in harmony with Christian standards. And thirdly, John added his voice to the chorus of praise, reinforcing his commendations with "you know that our testimony is true" (3 John 12). Gaius may not have known Demetrius, but he knew John. The apostle is asserting that his word can be trusted in spite of any insinuations of Diotrephes to the contrary (see 3 John 10).

The elder closes his short letter with concluding remarks similar to those found in 2 John 12, 13—a strong inference that the two letters were composed at the same time. The first thing he tells Gaius is that he wasn't going to solve the problem by writing a long letter. The opening salvos of his attack on the problem facing the church were the penning of 3 John (and probably 2 John) and the sending of Demetrius, but the core of his solution lay in a personal visit not only to strengthen Gaius in a "face to face" conference (verse 14) but to confront Diotrephes with his evil actions in the same manner (verse 10). The apostle may have had "many things to write" (verse 13), but being a pastor at heart he knew that personal interaction was what was really needed if there was to be reconciliation.

John's final remarks in verse 15 begin with "peace," a greeting adopted from the Hebrew *shalom*—a word expressing a wish for general well-being, but one infinitely enriched by the resurrection of Jesus. "Peace be with you" was Jesus' greeting to His disciples when He first appeared to them after arising from the tomb (John 20:19, 21, 26, RSV). And in that Christian *shalom* believers to this day find a comfort second to none from the person who won the victory for them and extends to each the blessings of present grace and eternal life.

Third John's last words are greetings from one friend to another, indicating that each is to be addressed by name. There is something special in that. As Christians we are not just part of a faceless herd that makes up the church. No! God cares for us as individuals. He also knows us by name.

Well, we have finished our reading of John's letters. And we may not have found 2 and 3 John to be altogether comforting. But they have a vital message for us. They demonstrate "that life was not always rosy in the early church, and we should not idealize that period of the development of the Christian movement." The "letters also show . . . that there was genuine concern for orthodoxy [correct doctrine] and orthopraxy [correct practice] near the end of the first century in the Johannine community." The fact that the letters are "brutally honest about flaws in the churches" and point out ways in which problems can be solved justify the place of these short letters in the biblical cannon (Witherington, p. 596).

The bad news is that churches can still be as problematic as they were 2,000 years ago. The good news is that God understands and is still willing to work with mixed-up people who struggle to move forward in what are sometimes divided Christian communities. Thus His "postcard epistles" have value for each of us in our day.

Exploring
Jude

Introduction to the
Letter of Jude

Jude has a bad press! Very bad!

William Barclay writes that "for the great majority of modern readers to read the little letter of Jude is a bewildering rather than a profitable undertaking" (Barclay, p. 183).

Donald Guthrie notes that perhaps more than other New Testament books, "the Epistle of Jude is assumed to have little or no permanent value and is . . . virtually excluded from the practical, as distinct from the formal, canon of the many sections of the church" (Guthrie, p. 926).

Let's face the facts. When is the last time you heard a sermon preached from Jude? Have you *ever* heard one?

After announcing that he was going to preach a series on the book of Jude, one pastor reports, "someone came up to me and asked what on earth I could get out of the book that would be of any use to anyone!" (Gardner, p. 145). After all, who wants to hear about "nether gloom," "angels in chains," and somebody named Enoch? It just doesn't look as if Jude has much for those of us who live in the twenty-first century.

But don't give up too soon. Though Jude's style may seem strange to our ears, he has a vital message that is timeless and needed.

Author, Date, and Recipients

The writer introduces himself as "Jude, a slave of Jesus Christ and brother of James" (Jude 1). Since Jude was such a common name in the New Testament era, the key to unlocking his identity is his relationship to

227

James. He assumes that everybody knows the latter's identity. The only Jew in the New Testament with that kind of recognition, since James the Son of Zebedee was martyred early on (Acts 12:2), is the leader of the Jerusalem church (Acts 12:17; 15:13; Gal. 2:12). In Galatians 1:19 we find that that same James is Jesus' brother.

Thus if Jude is the brother of James, he is also the brother of Jesus. That equation is in harmony with the gospels. In Mark 6:3 we find James listed first and Jude third among the four brothers of Jesus. Matthew 13:55 puts James first and Jude fourth. Those are the only two mentions of Jude by name in the New Testament outside of Jude 1.

Now it is true that Jesus' brothers rejected His ministry before His resurrection. Thus it was no accident that on the cross Jesus committed His mother to the apostle John's keeping. John was probably His cousin (see Knight, p. 208) and the closest next of kin in the faith (John 19:26, 27). But His brothers were converted soon after the resurrection. Acts 1:14 identifies Jesus' mother and His brothers as being among those in the upper room right after Jesus' ascension. And 1 Corinthians 9:5 speaks of the brothers of the Lord in connection with the apostles. But aside from those texts and Jude 1 all of Jesus' brothers except James disappear from the text of the New Testament. Two of them, however, have letters preserved in the canon. And in their letters both of the brothers call themselves "a slave" of Jesus Christ (James 1:1; Jude 1).

But if they were Jesus' brothers, why didn't they say so? The traditional answer is "humility." Perhaps remembering their treatment of Jesus during His earthly life, they felt no need for pride.

Given the rather disdainful and highhanded attitude of Jesus' brothers toward Him in the gospels, it is probable that they were Joseph's sons by a prior marriage and thus older than Him. That, however, cannot be proven from the Bible. But no matter what the exact relationship, the brothers' age factor alone indicates that the book of Jude probably couldn't have been written any later than about A.D. 65-70. Once again, however, the exact date is not evident from the book itself. On the other hand, we do know that it couldn't have been written too early since it treats problems that arose only in the later New Testament period.

As to its destination, the book provides no specific information. But given its use of Old Testament history and Jewish literature, the recipients were undoubtedly Jewish.

Jude's Problem

The reason for most of the content of Jude is that false teachers had made their way into the church and had succeeded in gaining a following (verse 4). The book does not spell out their precise relationship to the Christian community, but they appear to have gained entrance through flattering (verse 16) and other deceptive means (verse 4). But once in they began to create division (verse 19) among the membership.

As we read Jude we need to remember that the letter is not written to the infiltrators, but about them as the author warns the faithful of their presence, tactics, claims, and problems. While the author has a great deal to say about them, "it is difficult to form a clear picture of their doctrine" because "the references to it in the Epistle are obscure" (Wikenhauser, p. 488). In place of a clear definition we have lists of their personal characteristics and items illustrative of their beliefs.

Among their personal characteristics is the same sort of ungodly (verse 15) antinomianism or lawlessness that John had to deal with (see 1 John 3:4; 2:2-6). Along that line, they

1. are led by animal appetites (verse 10).
2. walk according to their own desires and passions (verses 16, 18).
3. defile their flesh (verses 8, 23), perhaps indulging in the "unnatural lust" of Sodom (verse 7, RSV).
4. use the free grace of God as an excuse for licentious carousing (verses 4, 12).
5. lack any care for others as they only look out for themselves (verse 12).
6. disseminate their teaching for gain (verse 11).

They not only lived lawless lives, but rejected authority outside of themselves, probably on the ground that they believed that they were spiritually superior to others and had prophetic dreams directly from God (verse 8). Among their blasphemous actions, they not only despised the leadership of the church but also that of Christ (verse 4), the heavenly angels (8-10), and even God (verse 11). In short, they were their own authority for belief and action.

While all those things were bad enough, Jude goes on to label them as "blemishes," "waterless clouds," "fruitless trees," "wild waves," "wandering stars," "grumblers," "malcontents," "boasters," "flatterers" for advantage, "scoffers," dividers, and "worldly people devoid of the Spirit" (verses 12-19, RSV).

And beyond all of those things, their denial of Christ (verse 4) almost certainly included a rejection of the Christian understanding that God had become incarnate in Jesus. That widespread heresy flowing out of Greek philosophic thought regarding the inherent evilness of matter was the same one that plagued the churches targeted by 1 and 2 John. John's letters highlighted the connection between denying the incarnation and the rejection of His moral teachings.

Most students of Jude point out the fact that the people he writes against have many of the characteristics of what will become Gnosticism in the second century. Thus "emphasis on knowledge [*gnōsis*], which emancipated them from the claims of morality; arrogance towards 'unenlightened' church leaders; interest in angelology; divisiveness;" and licentiousness all fit that pattern. "The later Gnostics perverted the grace of God into licence, confident that the true 'pneumatic' [spiritual person] could not be affected by what the flesh does. They thought they had no duty to civil or ecclesiastical authorities—had they not been delivered from the old aeon [age] and its powers? They were, moreover, antagonistic to eschatology," believing they already possessed the divine nature. Thus they had no need for a future transformation at the Second Advent (Green, pp. 43, 44).

While the practices and attitudes of the problematic invaders in Jude had many Gnostic characteristics, it is incorrect to fully identify them with that later heresy. It is more accurate to see their attitudes and beliefs as being part of those "streams that flowed into later Gnosticism" (Bauckham, p. 12).

Even though the "superior" individuals Jude writes against may have had no interest in eschatology, they would not escape it. According to him, they already stood condemned (verse 4) and would reap certain judgment in the end (verses 5-16).

Jude's Purpose

Some documents have more than one purpose. Such is the Epistle of Jude. He has a Purpose and a purpose.

His Purpose appears in verse 3, in which he states that he had been "extremely eager" to write to them of "our shared salvation." That is what he wanted to do.

But dealing with the problem troubling his church and the people causing it derailed Jude's intentions and sent him down another track. "I found it necessary to write appealing to you to contend for the faith which was once for all delivered to the saints" (verse 3, RSV), he pens. Here we have the purpose that dominates the bulk of his letter. He seeks to warn his orthodox but somewhat shaky Christian readers of the dangers of becoming bewitched by the false teachers. His aim is pastoral and redemptive. Richard Bauckham points out that "Jude's denunciation of the opponents, because of the serious danger they pose to his readers, is accompanied by a genuine pastoral concern not only for those they have led astray but even for the opponents themselves" (in Freedman, vol. 3, p. 1103).

And that is where Jude's forceful, dynamic style comes in. Barclay suggests that while a reading of the little book with all of its Jewish allusions might be quite strange to us, it would have "hit those who read and heard it for the first time like a hammer-blow and like a trumpet call to defend the faith" (Barclay, p. 183). The letter was thus a wake-up call in every respect— to the orthodox, lest they get deceived; and to the heretics, that they faced sure and certain judgment. In addition, at the end of his letter Jude provides priceless advice on how to maintain faith in the face of error and apostasy.

Jude's Major Themes

One may wonder how a book of 25 verses could have themes. But it does. And they come in two flavors— positive and negative, often intertwined in Jude's exposition.

1. *The Fatherhood of God and the*

> ## The Letter's Accomplishments
>
> Jude achieves three goals:
> "(1) It identifies the false doctrine and its adherents as one with the infidels of all ages.
> "(2) It demonstrates the full extremity of their perversion and the degradation to which they have sunk in their twisting of the truth.
> "(3) The faith of the true believer is pointed toward the longsuffering of God and the maintenance of His promises" (W. White, in Tenney, vol. 3, p. 733).

Lordship of Christ. Jude's opening and closing verses both focus on the fatherhood of God and Jesus Christ as His representative. The Father is the lover of His children (verse 1) and their "Savior" (verse 25). The author presents God the Father as the "sender" or "active agent" in saving his readers. Thus the Father "is not an austere or absent God, but a God very much involved in their lives" (Davids, p. 30).

Jude also strongly affirms the Lordship of Christ. It is "through Jesus Christ our Lord" that God effects the plan of salvation (verse 25, RSV). Verse 4 sets forth Jesus as "our only Master and Lord," while verses 17 and 21, respectively, put Him forth as the sender of the apostles and the fountainhood of mercy.

Lordship, of course, calls for a response. Thus "Christians owe obedience to Christ as Lord for his work for their salvation, a salvation whose completion is based on a lifetime of obedience (v. 21). By contrast, immorality perverts the moral order of creation, which Christ enforces, and denies his leadership, leaving the person who sins vulnerable to judgment (vv. 4, 8-16)" (Watson, p. 479).

2. *Apostolic authority.* Related closely to the fatherhood of God and the Lordship of Christ is the authority of the apostles that they sent into the world. Jude urges his readers "to contend for *the faith which was once for all delivered* to the saints" (verse 3, RSV). In verses 5 and 17 he twice more appeals to the apostles' teaching that his readers had received when they became Christians.

Here we find an emphasis on the authoritative teaching of the apostles that was also present in John's letters (1 John 1:1-4; 2:7, 13, 14, 24; 3:11; 4:1-6). The sad fact is that as the church grew older more and more strange ideas crept in to pervert the doctrines of God's word as found in the oral teachings of the apostles and eventually in their writings.

The ensuing conflict would eventually lead to a church structure above that of a grouping of local congregations in an attempt to protect the purity of the apostolic faith. Thus F. W. Danker observes that the picture presented in Jude "reflects the common conflict between orthodoxy and heresy that we find depicted also in the Johannine letters, the Pastorals [Timothy and Titus], and 2 Peter, and that ultimately led to solidification of the role of the bishop as theological arbiter" (in Bromiley, vol. 2, pp. 1154, 1155).

3. *The connection between doctrine and morality.* Correct and incorrect per-

spectives on such theological mainstays as the identity and lordship of Christ and the coming judgments divide the faithful and the unfaithful in Jude. He presents direct lines running from proper theology to healthy action and errant theology to unhealthy behavior. Thus those who denied lordship and impending judgment felt no need of accountability and became the lords of their own lives.

4. *"Keeping" for the future.* The verb "keeping" occurs five times in the 25 verses of Jude. And, as you might guess, everyone is being kept for something. On the one hand are those who are being "kept" in Jesus (verse 1) whom God will guard from falling until the Second Advent (verse 24). On the other hand are those being kept for judgment (verses 6, 13).

Humans of course have a part in keeping. Some keep themselves in God's love (verse 21), while others like the evil angels of old do not keep to faithfulness (verse 6). In Jude God's keeping is always tied to human response.

5. *The certainty of judgment to come.* Clearly related to "keeping" is Jude's pervasive teaching on future judgment, which dominates the center of the book. And like nearly everything else in Jude, judgment comes in two varieties. For the wicked it will be darkness, gloom, and punishment (verses 7, 13), while for those keeping themselves in Christ it will be "glory with rejoicing" (verse 24). But to both those who deny future judgment and to those who anticipate it with joy Jude has one message: judgment will come.

6. *The redemptive activity of Christians for others.* Believers, as we have noted several times so far, are never passive in Jude. They have a part in the action. In verse 3 the author tells them "to contend" for the faith and in verse 22 that they need to try to convince some who doubt. And then in verse 23 Jude commands his readers to "save some" by snatching them out of the fire. Thus Christians apparently have a work for heretics. All true believers have a redemptive function in the mission of God.

The Relation of Jude to 2 Peter

Have you ever read Jude and 2 Peter at the same sitting? Try it, and you will discover a remarkable amount of overlap in the two letters. Of the 25 verses in Jude, parts or all of 19 of them appear in 2 Peter. The similarities run from subject matter, vocabulary, and phrasing to even the order in which ideas are presented. Most telling are the parallels between 2 Peter 2:1-18 and Jude 4-16 "where both are inveighing against trouble-makers and bringing virtually indistinguishable charges against them. The imagery they use to describe these people, and often the very words (including several uncommon ones), are the same. In both letters the errorists are castigated as followers of Balaam, and in both the doom in store for them is likened to the fate of the rebellious angels and that of the Cities of the Plain [i.e., Soddom and Gommorah]" (Kelly, p. 225; see Schreiner, pp. 416, 417 for a graphic presentation of the parallels). While the simularities are most intense in those passages, they don't end there, but run throughout the documents.

The extent of the overlap has led to endless discussions on whether Jude borrowed from 2 Peter, or vice versa, or whether both used the same source. We probably can't solve the problem with the amount of data we have, but the most likely solution is that 2 Peter borrowed from Jude.

Equally important to the likenesses of the two letters are their differences. Not only do the two change words or use them with different nuances, but each has its own theological agenda and audience. Thus what we find is not "copying," but rather an adaptation of the shared materials to meet the needs of social contexts that are similar in some respects yet quite different in others.

Jude's Use of Apocryphal Books

The short letter of Jude is the only New Testament book to cite a Jewish apocryphal work. It is certain that he used 1 Enoch and the Assumption of Moses and probable that he employed the Testament of Naphtali in verse 6 and the Testament of Asher in verse 8.

Jude used 1 Enoch the most, citing 1 Enoch 1:9 in verses 14 and 15 almost verbatim and utilizing 1 Enoch 60:8 in verse 14 in his description of Enoch as being "the seventh from Adam." He also draws from 1 Enoch in his portrayal of the fallen angels in verses 6-13.

That usage of uninspired materials has caused some to doubt the value of Jude. But there is no real difficulty here. He is not citing Enoch and the other works as Scripture, but as highly respected religious works of his day with which many of his readers were familiar. He incorporated material from them because he found some of the things they had said to have a direct relationship to the issues he was facing at the time. Even in his citation of Enoch in verses 14 and 15, Jude is not claiming divine inspiration for 1 Enoch, but "seems rather to be recognizing that what Enoch had said has turned out to be" true "in view of the ungodly conduct of these false teachers" (Guthrie, p. 915).

Outline

While some biblical books are difficult to outline, that is not true of Jude. In good letter fashion the book moves from the initial greetings to a body that lays out its argument step by step and then to a conclusion that contains both admonitions for believers and a doxology.

I. Introduction, 1-4
    A. Greetings, 1, 2
    B. Reason for writing, 3, 4
II. The ungodly and their doom, 5-16
    A. Past lessons, 5-7
    B. Character of the ungodly, 8-13
    C. Certain doom of the ungodly, 14-16
III. Admonitions for true believers, 17-23
IV. Closing doxology, 24, 25

Relevance for the Twenty-first Century

Jude's strange little book is surprisingly relevant for our day. It is at its heart a passionate defense of the Christian faith and morality in the face of a pluralistic and permissive society whose values had begun to invade the church. Thus Jude faced the same sorts of dynamics that confront the church in the post-modern, post-Christian societies of the West.

And in the face of those challenges Jude tells of how God keeps and protects and cares for His people even as they encounter a breakdown of doctrine and morals in the Christian community. The book of Jude not only holds up the forthcoming ultimate hope of a final reckoning that will bring joy to God's people, but it informs believers that they can learn from history and explains how they can safeguard their faith during unfriendly times.

But above all, the core of Jude's relevance is found in its confidence-building message that God loves His church and will "keep" those safe who trust in Him.

List of Works Cited

Barclay, William. *The Letters of John and Jude*. 2nd ed. The Daily Study Bible. Edinburgh: Saint Andrew Press, 1960.

Barnett, Albert E. "The Epistle of Jude: Introduction and Exegesis." In *The Interpreter's Bible*. Nashville: Abingdon, 1957, vol. 12, pp. 315-343.

Barton, Bruce B., et al. *1 Peter, 2 Peter, Jude*. Life Application Bible Commentary. Carol Stream, Ill.: Tyndale House, 1995.

Bauckham, Richard J. *Jude, 2 Peter*. Word Biblical Commentary. Waco, Tex.: Word, 1983.

Beale, G. K., and D. A. Carson, eds. *Commentary on the New Testament Use of the Old Testament*. Grand Rapids: Baker, 2007.

Bigg, Charles. *A Critical and Exegetical Commentary on the Epistles of St. Peter and St. Jude*. International Critical Commentary. New York: Charles Scribner's Sons, 1905.

Blum, Edwin A. "Jude." In *The Expositor's Bible Commentary*. Grand Rapids: Zondervan, 1981, vol. 12, pp. 379-396.

Bray, Gerald, ed. *James, 1-2 Peter, 1-3 John, Jude*. Ancient Christian Commentary on Scripture. Downers Grove, Ill.: InterVarsity, 2000.

Bromiley, Geoffrey W., ed. *The International Standard Bible Encyclopedia*. 4 vols. Grand Rapids: Eerdmans, 1979-1988.

Charles, J. Daryl. "Jude." In *The Expositor's Bible Commentary*. Rev. ed. Grand Rapids: Zondervan, 2006, vol. 13, pp. 539-569.

Charlesworth, James H., ed. *The Old Testament Pseudepigrapha*. 2 vols. New York: Doubleday, 1983.

Craddock, Fred B. *First and Second Peter and Jude*. Westminster Bible Companion. Louisville: Westminster John Knox, 1995.

Davids, Peter H. *The Letters of 2 Peter and Jude*. Pillar New Testament Commentary. Grand Rapids: Eerdmans, 2006.

Earle, Ralph. *Word Meanings in the New Testament*. Grand Rapids: Baker, 1986.

Freedman, David Noel, ed. *The Anchor Bible Dictionary*. 6 vols. New York: Doubleday, 1992.

Gardner, Paul. *2 Peter and Jude*. Focus on the Bible Commentaries. Fearn, Ross-shire, Great Britain: Christian Focus, 1998.

Green, Michael. *The Second Epistle General of Peter and the General Epistle of Jude*. 2nd ed. Tyndale New Testament Commentaries. Grand Rapids: Eerdmans, 1987.

Guthrie, Donald. *New Testament Introduction*. 4th ed. Downers Grove, Ill.: InterVarsity, 1990.

Hillyer, Norman. *1 and 2 Peter, Jude*. New International Biblical Commentary. Peabody, Mass.: Hendrickson, 1992.

Johnston, Robert M. *Peter and Jude: Living in Dangerous Times*. Bible Amplifier. Boise, Idaho: Pacific Press, 1995.

Josephus, Flavius. *Josephus: Complete Works*. Trans. William Whiston. Grand Rapids: Kregel, 1960.

Kelly, J.N.D. *A Commentary on the Epistles of Peter and Jude*. Thornapple Commentaries. Grand Rapids: Baker, 1969.

Knight, George R. *Matthew: The Gospel of the Kingdom*. Bible Amplifier. Boise, Idaho: Pacific Press, 1994.

Kraftchick, Steven J. *Jude, 2 Peter*. Abingdon New Testament Commentaries. Nashville: Abingdon, 2002.

Lenski, R.C.H. *The Interpretation of the Epistles of St. Peter, St. John, and St. Jude*. Minneapolis: Augsburg, 1966.

Lucas, Dick, and Christopher Green. *The Message of 2 Peter and Jude: The Promise of His Coming*. Bible Speaks Today. Downers Grove, Ill.: InterVarsity, 1995.

Luther, Martin. *Commentary on Peter and Jude*. Grand Rapids: Kregel, 1990.

Manton, Thomas. *Jude*. Crossway Classic Commentaries. Wheaton, Ill.: Crossway, 1999.

Mayor, Joseph B. *The Epistle of St. Jude and the Second Epistle of St. Peter*. Grand Rapids: Baker, 1979.

Moffatt, James. *The General Epistles: James, Peter, and Judas*. Moffatt New Testament Commentary. Harper and Row, n.d.

Moo, Douglas J. *2 Peter, Jude*. NIV Application Commentary. Grand Rapids: Zondervan, 1996.

Neyrey, Jerome H. *2 Peter, Jude*. Anchor Bible. New York: Doubleday, 1993.

Reese, Ruth Anne. *2 Peter and Jude*. Two Horizons New Testament Commentary. Grand Rapids: Eerdmans, 2007.

Robertson, Archibald Thomas. *Word Pictures in the New Testament*. 6 vols. Grand Rapids: Baker, 1960.

Rogers, Cleon L., Jr. and Cleon L. Rogers III. *The New Linguistic and Exegetical Key to the Greek New Testament*. Grand Rapids: Zondervan, 1998.

Schreiner, Thomas R. *1, 2 Peter, Jude*. New American Commentary. Nashville: Broadman and Holman, 2003.

Tenney, Merrill C. *The Zondervan Pictorial Encyclopedia of the Bible*. 5 vols. Grand Rapids: Zondervan, 1976.

Wand, J.W.C. *The General Epistles of St. Peter and St. Jude*. Westminster Commentaries. London: Methuen, 1934.

Watson, Duane F. "The Letter of Jude." In *The New Interpreter's Bible*. Nashville: Abingdon, vol. 12, pp. 471-500.

Wheaton, David H. "Jude." In *The New Bible Commentary*. 3rd ed. Grand Rapids: Eerdmans, 1970, pp. 1274-1278.

White, Ellen G. *Steps to Christ*. Mountain View, Calif.: Pacific Press, 1956.

Wikenhauser, Alfred. *New Testament Introduction*. New York: Herder and Herder, 1958.

Part I

Setting the Stage

Jude 1-4

1. Greetings and Warning

Jude 1-4

> [1]*Jude, a slave of Jesus Christ and brother of James,*
>
> *To those called, loved in God the Father and kept in Jesus Christ.* [2]*May mercy and peace and love be multiplied to you.*
>
> [3]*Beloved, being extremely eager to write to you concerning our shared salvation, I found it necessary to write to you to encourage you to struggle for the faith once for all delivered to the saints.* [4]*For certain men have slipped in secretly, those who long ago were written about for this condemnation, ungodly persons who pervert the grace of our God into ungodly lust and deny our only Master and Lord, Jesus Christ.*

What a delightful introduction. You can discover a lot from how people introduce themselves. The first thing Jude tells us about himself is that he is a slave to Christ.

Many modern translations soften the word "slave" by rendering it as "servant." But the Greek *doulos* primarily means "slave." Jude is not only a servant of Christ, but he belongs to Him. The modern word "servant" doesn't capture that idea adequately. It is one thing to be a servant to somebody, while it is quite another to be owned by that person.

Jude wants us to know that he is the slave of Christ. That thought has several ideas related to it. First is the truth that "having been rescued by Christ from slavery to sin and death, Christians now belong wholly to Him as His slaves" (Kelly, p. 242).

The book of Romans, in which the author also introduces himself as a "slave" of Christ (Rom. 1:1), expands that understanding. Concepts related to slavery stand at the heart of that larger book, and they help us to understand the implications of Jude. When Paul talks about redeeming sinners in Romans 3:24 he uses the vocabulary of the marketplace. "Redemption" in his day meant to buy at the market, particularly to purchase a slave. Central to the apostle's life and message was the fact that he had been redeemed by the blood of Jesus on Calvary's cross.

The idea of a Christian's slavery to Christ rises again in Romans 6, in which Paul tells his readers that every human being is a slave to either Satan or Christ, that all people belong to someone, that no person is a totally free agent, and that every individual becomes the slave of either "sin, which leads to death, or of obedience, which leads to righteousness" (Rom. 6:16, RSV).

But slavery to Christ in the New Testament presents a paradox. That is, slavery to Christ is not bondage, but rather the only way one gains freedom. It will climax in eternal life (verse 23). Thus for Paul and Jude slavery is good news. It implies not only ownership and obligation but also privilege.

It is the idea of the privilege of being Christ's slave that we want to look at now. The privilege side of slavery derives from the fact that slaves represent their owners. Thus, Peter Davids points out, in the culture of the Roman Empire "highly placed imperial slaves had tremendous authority, for they represented their master, Caesar. While technically they held only the social rank of slave (i.e., a social zero), because of whose slaves they were they were to be treated with respect, for to disregard Caesar's slave doing Caesar's business was to disregard Caesar" (Davids, p. 34).

> Jude was the brother of James (Jude 1);
> James was the brother of Jesus (Gal. 1:19);
> therefore,
> Jude was the brother of Jesus.

That aspect of authority also appears in Jude 1. It is no accident that Peter (2 Peter 1:1), Paul (Rom. 1:1), James (James 1:1), and Jude (Jude 1) referred to themselves as the slaves of Christ and that Moses and Joshua called themselves servants of God (Ex. 14:31; Deut. 34:5; Joshua 1:1, 2).

They represented God, and as such, they had a right to speak and be listened to. Thus Jude is announcing that his words are authoritative.

If Jude's reference to himself as the slave of Christ contained nuances of both humility and delegated authority, his labeling of himself as James' brother tends more toward the humility only pole. We noted in the introduction that being a brother of James meant that he was also a brother of Christ, and that neither James nor Jude explicitly calls himself a brother of Jesus. The best reason for that is one of humility. But it is one thing to be humble about a relationship to the divine/human Jesus Christ and quite another to be so in connection with a purely earthly older brother who is more famous than one's self.

By announcing that he is the brother of James, Jude identified himself as a person content to be in second place. In that respect he is much like Andrew, who was known as "Simon Peter's brother" (John 6:8, RSV). It is easy to be resentful in such a situation. No normal human likes to live in the shadow of a sibling more powerful, famous, and visible. But not so with Jude. His introduction of himself as the brother of James has something special about it. He had apparently learned the life of dying to self (Matt. 16:24-26) and of servanthood to others (Matt. 20:26) that Jesus had so much to say about during His earthly ministry. Jude was humble in spite of the fact that he represented the King of the universe. Here is a lesson we can all learn from.

Moving beyond Jude's description of himself, verse 1 addresses the letter's readers as:

1. "called"
2. "loved"
3. "kept"

Each of those words indicates God's initiative in the plan of salvation. The Greek word for "called" is the same as that used in Matthew 22:3 to invite people to a joyous feast. It is a word often attached to God's people in both testaments. Thus God called Israel to be His special people in the Old Testament and Christians to fulfill the same role in the New. As a result, "in describing his readers as 'called,' Jude is in effect reminding them of their high privileges" as God's sons and daughters (Hillyer, p. 232). And we must never forget that "calling" in the Bible is always at the initiative of God.

God not only calls, He also loves His people. That love, in fact, is the reason for His call. We see the connection between God's calling and His love in Deuteronomy 7:6-8, in which we read that "the Lord your God has chosen you to be a people for his own possession. . . . It was not because you were more in number than any other people that the Lord set his love upon you . . . but it is because the Lord loves you . . . that the Lord has . . . redeemed you from the house of bondage" (RSV).

Just as the Father's calling is based on His love, so is His keeping or guarding of His people. The good news here is that "the Christian is never left alone; Jesus Christ is always the sentinel of his life and the companion of his way" (Barclay, p. 206).

Thus Christians are "called," "loved," and "kept." And "loved" and "kept" are perfect participles in the original Greek, indicating a past act with continuing effects. Thus those whom God calls He continues to love and keep. Christians are not merely the objects of the Father's care in the past, but they still are and will always be so in the future.

The three little words that tell Christians that they are called, loved, and kept are at the center of what salvation is all about. God always takes the initiative in loving, calling, and keeping. Our human part is that of acceptance and response.

In the introduction to Jude we discussed the fact that what he really wanted to do was to write a letter regarding their "shared salvation," but that he had had to change his plans due to the arrival of certain disruptive individuals who had infiltrated the church and threatened to lead some astray (Jude 3).

We especially need to note several important points regarding Jude's remarks about the newly arisen and problematic situation. First, his letter was one of encouragement to his faithful readers. The fact that they needed reassurance suggests that they might be in danger of slipping themselves. Thus Jude's urgent letter and his emphasis on the "keeping" power of God. His readers must continue to trust the One who had sustained them thus far.

Their safety was in knowing, heeding, and struggling for, or defending, "the faith once for all delivered to the saints." The word translated as "struggle" is a forceful one, used for striving in such activities as wrestling or an athletic contest. It is an active and aggressive word. The contest was serious and needed all of their energy. And what were they to heed and defend? "The faith" was the apostolic teaching that lay at the foundation of not only their personal religious experience, but of Christianity in general. All true Christianity, from Jude's perspective, must be grounded in the apostolic witness that we now have recorded in the New Testament.

The problematic people whom Jude writes about had "slipped in secretly." Thus while they may have appeared to be faithful members, Jude is issuing a wake-up call that they were indeed wolves in sheep's clothing (Matt. 7:15) and that his readers needed to be on double guard.

They may have looked orthodox to the casual observer, but, Jude notes, they were ungodly individuals who apparently perverted God's free grace as an excuse for immoral actions. After all, the idea ran, if God is going to forgive anyway, why not sin so that He can be more gracious? Paul had faced the same perverted logic in Romans 6:1. His response was that no Christian could live in sin (Rom. 6:2-11). Jude shared the same perspective, indicating that to live a sinful life was to deny the lordship of Christ. He had caught the truth that our lives show whom we are following.

Part II

Character and Doom
of the False Teachers

Jude 5-16

2. Three Dreadful Examples

Jude 5-7

> *⁵Now I want to remind you, though you once knew all these things, that the Lord, having saved a people out of the land of Egypt, afterward destroyed those who did not believe. ⁶And angels who did not keep their own domain, but left their own dwelling place, He has kept in eternal chains under darkness for the great day of judgment. ⁷Just as Sodom and Gomorrah and the cities around them, in like manner these having indulged in fornication and having gone after different flesh are set forth as an example, undergoing the punishment of eternal fire.*

Not a pleasant paragraph.

But the message is clear enough. First, once-saved-always-saved is a shaky teaching in the light of history. And second, judgment will be the lot of those who rebel against God.

Jude starts out gently enough. Wanting "to remind" his readers of things that they already knew, he presents three biblical examples that illustrate the consequences that await those who depart from God's will.

William Barclay points out that in order to comprehend the first two examples we need to understand that "the evil men who were corrupting the Church did not regard themselves as enemies of the Church and of Christianity; they regarded themselves as the advanced thinkers, as a cut above the ordinary Christian, as the spiritual aristocracy and elite. They regarded themselves as the leaders and not the corrupters of the Church" (Barclay, pp. 213, 214). As a result, Jude selects his first two examples to demonstrate that even if people receive the greatest advantages, they may still fall away into utter disaster.

The first example features those Israelites destroyed after God had "saved" them out of the land of Egypt (Jude 5). Jude utilizes the most impressive story of Israel's past. What greater deliverance could there have been than that of a band of powerless slaves from the hands of the world's most powerful nation? By His providential care God had brought His people through the sea and across the forbidding Sinai desert. Why? Because He loved them and wanted to bless them.

But some disbelieved and perished. Here Jude undoubtedly has in mind the experience recorded in Numbers 13 and 14, in which the vast majority of the nation rejected the report of Caleb and Joshua and accepted that of the other spies. The latter claimed that the people of Canaan were so great and strong that there was no hope of conquering them.

Here was evidence of a clear lack of faith in God. He had already "saved" them from things far worse, and here at Kadesh-barnea, on the very borders of the Promised Land, they disbelieved and disobeyed. The result was destruction in the wilderness (Num. 26:64, 65).

That was a story that haunted both the mind of Paul (1 Cor. 10:1-11) and the writer of Hebrews (Heb. 3:18-4:2). And it was proof that even the most privileged person can turn blessing into disaster. Or as John Bunyan put it in *Pilgrim's Progress*, there is a way to hell even at the gates of heaven. In Jude's mind that lesson was one that both his faithful readers and also the "superior" dissidents needed

> "Let therefore none presume upon past mercies, as if he were now out of danger" (J. Wesley, in Moffatt, p. 232).

to grasp, since his illustration implies that they had been "formerly 'orthodox,' who had experienced divine redemption" (Charles, p. 553).

The lesson in Jude's second example (Jude 6; cf. 2 Peter 2:4) is also clear enough, but it has generated more theological discussion than the first. Most interpreters read the passage through the eyes of 1 Enoch, a book that Jude was quite familiar with. First Enoch 6, 7 identifies the "sons of God" who saw the beauty of "the daughters of men" and married them in Genesis 6:1-4 as fallen angels. The result of those unions was that "the women became pregnant and gave birth to great giants" (1 Enoch 7:2).

That interpretation of Jude 6 has largely captured the imaginations of past commentators on Jude, but it has a number of problems. For one thing, Robert Johnston points out, "in Numbers 13:33 the Nephilim are said to be giants; if Numbers is referring to the same race as Genesis 6:4, that would imply that those people somehow survived the Flood. A further problem facing this Jewish tradition is that Jesus seems to say that angels do not have sex (Matt. 22:30)" (Johnston, pp. 157, 158). A sensible alternative interpretation to Genesis 6:4 is the one found in the context: that the "sons of God" are the descendents of Seth as opposed to those of Cain.

If that is so, then the "angels who did not keep their own domain" of Jude 6 must have an alternative explanation. Barclay suggests one focusing on "the fall of the angels as due to pride and to rebelliousness" (Barclay, p. 216). Central to that interpretation is Isaiah 14:12-14:

> "How are you fallen from heaven,
> O Day Star, son of Dawn!
> How you are cut down to the ground,
> you who laid the nations low!
> You said in your heart,
> 'I will ascend to heaven;
> above the stars of God
> I will set my throne on high; . . .
> I will ascend above the heights of the clouds,
> I will make myself like the Most High'" (RSV).

That passage coupled with Ezekiel 28:13-17, which again alludes to Lucifer's downfall in terms of pride, and Revelation 12:7-9, which describes a war in heaven in which Satan falls, provides a biblically sound approach to the interpretation of Jude 6.

In spite of the various interpretive issues that exist, the message of Jude 6 is plain: if angels who were privileged to dwell in the presence of God's glory could become lost and are subject to a negative verdict on judgment day, there will be no hope of escape for mere mortals. And here the allusion to pride in the fall of the angels is certainly appropriate, since it is that same sort of pride that had infiltrated the lives of the dissidents whom Jude is combating.

The author's illustration in verse 7 shifts away from the certainty of judgment on the "saved" and privileged insiders to the certainty of judgment on obvious sinners. The most notorious example that Jude could find in the Old Testament was the destruction of Sodom and Gomorrah. No event in biblical history made a more profound impact as an example of human sin and divine judgment than did that of the destruction of the cities on the plain. Scriptural history is littered with the residue of that incident. Thus we find Deuteronomy 29:23; 32:32, Isaiah 1:9; 3:9; 13:19, Jeremiah 23:14; 49:18; 50:40, Lamentations 4:6, Ezekiel 16:46, 49, 53, 55, Amos 4:11, Zephaniah 2:9, Matthew 10:15; 11:24, Luke 10:12; 17:29, Romans 9:29, 2 Peter 2:6, Jude 7, and Revelation 11:8 reflecting on the sin and fate of Sodom and Gomorrah. It was the Illustration of illustrations for the connection of sin with judgment.

We should note two specific things about Jude 7. One is that its sin was sexual lust and perversion. Jude probably chose the illustration and its wording because it reflected one of the characteristic sins of the intruders that he sought to expose. In other places he notes that they "defile the flesh" (verse 8, RSV), live on the animal level (verse 10), "boldly carouse" (verse 12, RSV), and follow their own passions (verse 16)—all phrases signifying sexual aberrations.

According to Jude 7, Sodom and her sisters (and presumably the invaders of Jude's target audience) were fornicators and had "gone after different flesh." The word "fornication" is a compound intensive that suggests "excessive immorality" (Rogers, p. 606). Thus the *New American Standard Bible's* rendering of the word as "gross immorality." The "different flesh" found in Jude 7 can also be translated as "strange flesh," or "unnatural, not of God's appointment" (Wand, p. 202). The closest parallel in the New Testament is in Romans 1:26, 27, in which men and women give themselves over to "dishonorable passions" and "unnatural" same-sex relationships (RSV).

Genesis 19:1-11 tells the story of the wickedness of Sodom, in which the men of the city surround Lot's house and demand that he surrender his two male guests so that they can "gang rape" them (Gardner, p. 183). Homosexuality in their minds was apparently preferable to heterosexual activity since they turned down Lot's offer to supply his daughters for their pleasure (Gen. 19:8-11). Jude 7 labels their sexual preference as "strange," or "different," or "unnatural" because it did not follow the created order of men and women who had been physiologically made for each other in terms of both pleasure and procreation. Thus the wickedness of the Sodom event was not in the fact that it was "gang rape," but that it was an "unnatural" and "dishonorable" approach to sex that substituted same-sex relationships for heterosexual ones (cf. Rom. 1:26, 27).

The second thing that we should note about verse 7 is that the cities were destroyed for their perversions and were obliterated by fire from heaven with eternal results. One can tour the Dead Sea area today without seeing a trace of the cities, although there is evidence of an environment destroyed by fire.

Jude 5-7 presents three powerful illustrations of the facts that judgment follows sin and that there are no privileged refuges from those consequences. Those lessons from the pen of Jude are for both his faithful audience and those seeking to seduce them into heresy and sin.

Before moving to verses 8-10, we should note in passing that all three of the illustrations that Jude 5-7 uses are examples of group sin. Here, Paul Gardner points out, were entire communities that had accepted wrong ways of thinking and acting. What

Eternal Fire

"Sodom and Gomorrah were destroyed by fire. Their fire is eternal in that their destruction was complete, and, unlike most burned cities in Palestine, they were never rebuilt" (Davids, p. 53).

had at one time been unacceptable had become acceptable. "We must never underestimate two pressures which come on us as Christians. The first is that we are tempted to excuse and eventually accept that which the world around us accepts in terms of sexual behaviour, and the second is that we begin to accept uncritically what some Christians do and gradually bow to peer pressure to the extent that we begin to justify actions that would have been unacceptable a few years before" (Gardner, p. 187). One of the imperatives of the little book of Jude is for Christians to take a hard look at the teachings of the Bible, a firm gaze at what today's society and even at times the church is willing to accept, and "to struggle for the faith once for all delivered to the saints" (Jude 3). The bottom-line lesson of Jude 5-7 is that God means what He says in all areas of our lives.

3. A Crisis in Authority

Jude 8-10

> *8Yet in the same manner these dreaming ones also defile the flesh on the one hand and on the other reject authority and despise the glorious ones [angels]. 9But Michael the archangel, when he disputed with the devil in arguing about the body of Moses, did not dare to pronounce a slanderous accusation, but said, "The Lord rebuke you." 10But these men despise whatever they do not understand, and what they do understand is by instinct like irrational animals. By these things they are destroyed.*

In verses 8-13 Jude turns from the lessons of the past to the subjects of his letter and demonstrates that they are both impure and presumptuous. "Yet in the same manner" (verse 8) is a direct continuation of verse 7, in which the Sodomites received eternal punishment for their perverted actions. "The words stress the surprise that, in spite of God's clear punishment of such behaviour in the past, these men have still dared to follow their ungodly example" (Wheaton, p. 1276).

Jude 8 brings three charges against the dissident leaders in the author's community:

1. They "defile the flesh."
2. They "reject authority."
3. They "despise the glorious ones."

Each of those charges directly relates to the three illustrations of verses 5-7. Thus

1. their defiling of the flesh is the problem of the Sodomites (verse 7).

2. their rejection of authority parallels the same problem among the rescued Israelites (verse 5).

3. their despising of the glorious ones reflects the problem of those angels who did not keep to their proper place (verse 6).

Central to Jude 8 is the rejection of authority. Here we have a core issue among those whom Jude wrote against. In place of the apostolic authority as represented by "the faith once for all delivered to the saints" (Jude 3), they were apparently substituting their own, which supposedly came through prophetic dreams. Such a rejection led to each of their other problems.

But a deeper concept underlies the word I have translated as "authority." A literal rendering is "lordship." The plain fact is that in denying the authority of one's master, an individual is in essence also rejecting the master as lord and refusing the person's right to be ruler of their lives. It is in that context that Jude's proclamation in verse 4 takes on fuller meaning. In that verse the "ungodly persons . . . pervert the grace of . . . God into ungodly lust and deny our only Master and Lord, Jesus Christ." Thus what they are spurning in Jude 8 is the lordship of Jesus and His authority in their lives. The foundational problem with the dissidents in the book of Jude is that they themselves had become the lord of, and authority for, their own lives. They were not just rebelling against Pastor Jude, but against Christ Himself.

The "glorious ones" that they despised in Jude 8 are God's angels. "Glory" in Jewish thought originally belonged to God alone. But eventually "the 'glory of God' came to be associated with the angelic cohort that surrounded God, and they were considered to share in this glory" (Kraftchick, p. 42; cf. Kelly, p. 263).

A major question, of course, is why they rejected and despised God's angels. The best answer is that the law was "delivered by angels" (Acts 7:53, RSV; cf. Gal. 3:19; Heb. 2:2). And that law, as we have already seen, Jude's dissenters, who were a law unto themselves, had refused to accept. Thus denying the lordship and authority of Jesus was intrinsically linked to the rejection of His angelic messengers.

Jude 9 with its discussion of Michael disputing the devil over the body of Moses appears to be a bit esoteric to most modern Christians, but the story would have been familiar to many of the letter's first readers. Here we find a story partly based on the Bible and partly on a popular Jewish work of the first century. The biblical basis for the story is Deuteronomy

34:1-6, which describes Moses' death and burial. The apocryphal Assumption of Moses expands the story. That version finds the archangel Michael sent to bury the body. The devil, who argues that Moses' body belongs to him because it consisted of matter and because Moses was a murderer, opposed him. After all, didn't he slay the Egyptian who he saw smiting a Hebrew (Ex. 2:11, 12)?

The question most modern readers ask when reading this story concerns the identity of Michael the archangel. The concept of archangel appears in the New Testament only in Jude 9 and 1 Thessalonians 4:16, in which the archangel announces the Second Advent. Michael is the only archangel named in the Bible, and in the New Testament his name occurs only in Jude 9 and in Revelation 12:7, which pictures him as leading the angels of God against the devil. Daniel 12:1 also speaks of Michael, describing him as a "great prince" who has charge of God's people (RSV). Although Zechariah 3:1-5 mentions neither Michael nor an archangel, the scene is one of dispute between "the angel of the Lord" and the devil, in which verse 2 identifies "the angel of the Lord" as "the Lord." And, interestingly, His remark to Satan in the struggle is "The Lord rebuke you" (Zech. 3:2, RSV), the exact words found in Jude 9. For these reasons among others, many Christians have identified Michael with Christ.

But the identity of Michael, while it may be of interest to modern readers, is not the crucial point in Jude's illustration. His focus is on the complex theory of angels found in first century Judaism. Jewish sources, for example, have a seven-layered hierarchy of angels, with Michael being the leader of the top rung, the seven archangels (see Freedman, vol. 4, p. 811).

In that context "Jude's point is that, if the greatest of the good angels refused to speak evil of the greatest of the evil angels, . . . then surely no human being may speak evil of any angel" (Barclay, p. 221).

That thought fits nicely as a lead-in to Jude 10, in which Jude tells his readers that the troublemakers "despise whatever they do not understand." That clause makes two points. The first, from verses 8 and 9, is that while Michael had been so careful in rebuking the devil, these people not only scorn authority and lordship in general, but "despise the glorious ones," or angels. Second, they are really ignorant of spiritual things—"they do not understand" (verse 10). That ignorance stands in stark contrast to their supposed spiritual superiority related to their "dreaming" (verse 8).

Jude 10 continues on to let readers know that even though the troublemakers may have been unenlightened about spiritual things, they were not ignorant of everything. To the contrary, they functioned on the animal level by following their instincts. The rationality they so highly prized was beyond them. It was by living on the animal level and being informed by their lusts and appetites, Jude claims, that "they are destroyed."

Commenting on verse 10, Fred Craddock writes that "apparently these disturbers of the church found all divine intervention, whether as revelation or providence or judgment, to be intrusive violations of their freedom, and therefore they blasphemed the angels as agents of such interventions. But, says the writer, they are thereby showing their ignorance and their kinship with brute creatures who follow base instincts, totally oblivious to any higher order of being or quality of living. It seems to be possible . . . for a human being to be so preoccupied with satisfying physical appetites that the other faculties of mind and heart and spirit atrophy until the image of God fades past recognition" (Craddock, pp. 140, 141).

So what else is new under the sun? Sin began with Eve's rejection of God's lordship and authority back in Eden. The same problem plagued Jude's readers. And it is still thriving in our day. At its foundation, the problem of sin is one of authority. To put it in stark terms, either we accept the sovereignty of God and let Him be "our only Master and Lord" (Jude 4) or we reject it and become the masters and lords of our own lives. Of course, the Bible tells us that that second option is in actual fact a delusion—that those who reject God actually come under the authority of the devil. But the "good news" of Satan's leadership is that he is more than happy for people to live on the level of their animal appetites and lusts. Here we find the root of all addictions, whether they be related to sex, alcohol, or anything else. Jude had it right when he wrote that "by these things they are destroyed" (verse 10). Rejecting divine lordship and authority comes with a heavy price.

The author's antidote is to return to God's authoritative Word, "the faith once for all delivered to the saints" (verse 3) and eventually recorded in Scripture. In summary, human lives are shaped and molded by authority and lordship. And it is up to every one of us to determine who will be in charge of our personal and individual existence as we journey through life.

4. Illustrated Lostness

Jude 11-13

¹¹Woe to them! Because they walk in the way of Cain, and for gain they abandon themselves to the error of Balaam, and perish in the rebellion of Korah. ¹²These are hidden rocks in your love feasts as they feast with you without fear, caring for themselves; waterless clouds, carried about by winds; fruitless trees of autumn, twice dead, uprooted; ¹³wild waves of the sea, casting up the foam of their own shame; wandering stars for whom the black darkness has been kept forever.

With verses 11-13 Jude shifts his strategy. In verses 5-10 "he portrayed the false teachers simply as sinners, in vv 11-13 he portrays them as false teachers who lead people into sin." That shift in emphasis was necessary because "many of Jude's readers no doubt found the false teachers impressive and persuasive." Thus he had to portray the false teachers in a different light that would reveal their real character (Bauckham, pp. 79, 92).

> " 'The way of Cain' is to rely upon one's own works and scoff at the true good works; it is to circumvent and ruin those traveling on the right road, just as these very ones are doing" (Martin Luther, p. 295).

Jude uses a series of eight graphic images to accomplish his purpose. The first three find him employing Jewish history as a source of illustrative examples of the wickedness of the false teachers. Cain stands at the head of Jude's historical list. He, of course, is notorious as being the first murderer (Gen. 4:8). And while "it is doubtful that Jude thinks that the false teachers whom he excoriates are actual murderers" (Beale, p. 1076), it is undoubtedly true that Cain was an unloving person who cared nothing for others. Hebrews 11:4 presents him as the opposite of a person of faith. And Jewish thought depicts Cain as a cynical materialist who reject's God's authority and has no concern for the well-being of others. Thus Josephus, the first-century Jewish historian, tells us that the first murderer accumulated "much wealth" and was "injurious to his neighbours." But even more to the point of Jude's concern was the fact that Cain "became a great leader of men into wicked courses" (Josephus *Antiquities* 1. 2. 2).

And that is precisely the author's point. The false teachers were not only devoid of love, but they were leading others to "walk in the way of Cain" (Jude 11).

> ### Snapshots of Evil
>
> "In these three pictures from the OT we see three leading characteristics of the errorists. Like Cain they were devoid of love. Like Balaam they were prepared in return for money to teach others that sin did not matter, [and thus were] leaders in sin. Like Korah they were careless of the ordinances of God and insubordinate to church leaders" (Rogers, p. 607).

Jude's second example is Balaam. The false teachers, he tells us, had abandoned themselves "to the error of Balaam" (Jude 11). And just what was that error? We discover the answer in the book of Numbers. Chapters 22-24 find Balak attempting to bribe Balaam, a prophet, to curse the people of Israel. He refuses bribes five times, but Balak knows his man. Eventually, though, Balaam succumbs to temptation, leads Israel into immorality and the worship of Baal (Num. 31:16; 25), and comes to a violent end (Num. 31:8). The Balaam lesson is simple enough. A covetous person, he was prepared to sin to gain a reward. But even more to Jude's point, he stands for one willing to teach others to sin—the greatest sin of all.

Jude's third historic example is Korah, known for his rebellion against the leadership of Moses (Num. 16:1-35). To reject Moses' authority, of course, was to spurn that of God. Like Korah, these men had not only opposed the duly appointed leadership of the church, they were teaching others to do so. That problem not only troubled Jude's readers, but is reflected in John's letters and in 1 Timothy 1:20, 2 Timothy 3:1-9, and Titus 1:10,

11; 3:10, 11. Once again, it is in the line of Jude's theme to pick out an example who came to a violent end in a judgment of God (Num. 16:35).

In verses 12 and 13 Jude moves from his three historical examples of the perversity of the false teachers to five graphic metaphors from nature of their problematic traits. As James Moffatt puts it, "sky, land, and sea are then ransacked for illustrations of their character" (Moffatt, p. 239).

His first snippet claims that they are like "hidden rocks in your love feasts." That translation is quite different from "spots" (KJV) or "blemishes on your love feasts" (RSV), translations influenced by the wording of 2 Peter 2:13. But Jude 12 uses a quite different Greek word even though most of its letters are the same. The idea in Jude is that the false teachers are like hidden rocks covered with water and only awaiting unwitting mariners to get hung up on them (see Robertson, vol. 6, p. 191). Thus Joseph Mayor's reading: "When they take part in your love-feasts they cause the shipwreck of the weak by their wantonness and irreverence" (Mayor, p. 73).

Love feasts in the early Christian church were dinners that accompanied the Lord's Supper. They were designed to be a time of sacred fellowship in which the rich and the poor could share what they had with each other. But in such places as Corinth problems soon began to surface in the *agapē* feasts. There they soon caused division rather than union, with some eating too much and becoming drunk, while others went hungry (1 Cor. 11:17-22).

Something of the same was happening among the Christians that Jude wrote to. The false shepherds may have appeared to be nice Christians as they participated in the love feasts, but they were really treacherous "hidden rocks" who had secretly infiltrated (Jude 4) the fellowship for the purpose of spreading their false teachings. Meanwhile, like the problematic individuals in 1 Corinthians 11, they only cared for themselves, rather than playing the part of good shepherds who first fed and cared for the sheep. Given their animal appetites as reflected upon in Jude 8, 10, and 16, their feasting was probably of the "carousing" type as suggested by the Revised Standard Version's rendering of verse 12. *The Message* is even more explicit, describing their feasting as "carousing shamelessly, grabbing anything that isn't nailed down." And all of that "without fear" (Jude 12) or pangs of conscience.

Beyond being treacherous hidden rocks, Jude labels them as "waterless clouds." If you have ever been in a drought, you know the joy that comes when you see some dark, solid clouds on the horizon. You know their meaning—the arrival of much needed rain. How happy the community is as the clouds approach and the winds pick up. But how devastated it is as the clouds pass by, leaving no life-giving moisture in their wake.

So are the false teachers in Jude's sights. Like clouds they appear to bring a blessing, but leave none. A waterless cloud is worse than useless. "Here," writes Michael Green, "is a graphic example of the uselessness of teaching which is supposedly 'advanced' and 'enlightened' but has nothing to offer the ordinary Christian for the nourishment of his spiritual life. I find this a solemn warning to those who, like myself, are professional theologians. We must constantly ask ourselves if our studies and knowledge are benefiting anybody at all" (Green, p. 190).

"Fruitless trees" don't appear to be any more helpful than "waterless clouds." But these trees aren't merely fruitless but "twice dead" and "uprooted" (verse 12). If, as Jesus suggested, one recognizes a prophet by his or her fruit, these teachers are outstanding because of their total lack of fruit. But how can anyone even hope for any positive spiritual fruit from people who are "dead." Once again, they might have the appearance of something to offer in their teachings, but in fact they have nothing of value.

> "The false teachers are
> - as dangerous as sunken rocks,
> - as selfish as perverted shepherds,
> - as useless as rainless clouds,
> - as dead as barren trees,
> - as dirty as the foaming sea, and
> - as certain of doom as the fallen angels"
> (Green, p. 192).

Jude's fourth metaphor is that the false teachers are like "wild waves of the sea, casting up the foam of their own shame" (verse 13). That metaphor borrows from Isaiah 57:20, which reads, "But the wicked are like the tossing sea; for it cannot rest, and its waters toss up mire and dirt" (RSV). The author's meaning is that the false teachers are as dangerous and out of control as the wild waves of the sea, which will eventually break down any defense if they pound on it long enough. And what do they have to offer? Nothing but scum and dirt.

Last, the false teachers are like wandering stars. In a world without compasses, the stars guided travelers on both land and sea. They could find their way by taking bearings on the stars fixed in the sky. But a wandering star was useless. It was lost itself, and thus couldn't guide anyone else.

Jude's closing thought in verse 13 is that "the black darkness has been kept [for them] forever." We met that same darkness in verse 6, in which it represented the darkness in which God keeps the rebellious angels until the "great day of judgment." As always, Jude pictures the journey of the false teachers to be heading in one direction—darkness, judgment, and eternal loss. They have reservations on the train of doom that cannot be cancelled unless they change their ways. Meanwhile, Jude in no uncertain terms warns the rest of us not to get on the same vehicle.

5. A Few More Evildoer Thoughts

Jude 14-16

¹⁴And Enoch, the seventh from Adam, prophesied about these men, saying, "Behold, the Lord came with ten thousands of His holy ones ¹⁵to execute judgment against all and to convict every person of all their ungodly deeds which they impiously did and of all the harsh things which ungodly sinners have spoken against Him." ¹⁶These are grumblers, faultfinders, walking according to their own lusts, speaking arrogant words, flattering people for the sake of gain.

Jude 13 closed with a promise of judgment. Verse 14 supplies a "prophecy" from Enoch to confirm that judgment.

Bible readers are familiar with Enoch. We first meet him in Genesis 5:21-24, in which we discover that he fathered Methuselah and that he walked with God, who "took him," apparently meaning that he was translated to heaven without experiencing death. We next encounter him in Luke 3:37, in which we discover that he is the seventh from Adam and an ancestor of Jesus. Then Hebrews 11:5 confirms the fact that Enoch went to heaven without seeing death because he pleased God as a person of faith. Other than those few glimpses, the biblical record is silent regarding this hero of the faith.

Jude, of course, tells us that he "prophesied" concerning future judgment. The problem is that the prophecy is not in the Bible, a fact that takes us to the Jewish apocrypha, which had much to say about that Old Testament saint. The three books of Enoch contain 108, 73, and 48 chapters and, to say the least, greatly amplify the supposed events of his life and teachings. The prophecy of Jude 14, 15 is taken from 1 Enoch 1:9, which reads, "Behold, he will arrive with ten million of the holy ones in order to execute judgment upon all. He will destroy the wicked ones and censure all flesh on account of everything that they have done, that which the sinners and the wicked ones committed against him."

Jude's utilization of 1 Enoch has caused a great deal of discussion. Some have wondered if that means that 1 Enoch is also divinely inspired, or, at the other extreme, if Jude is not inspired since he attributes a "prophecy" to an uninspired book. Others argue that Jude wasn't quoting 1 Enoch, but that they were both citing the same reliable source (see Lenski, p. 640).

While those are interesting discussions, the solution is much simpler. "The fact is that Jude, a pious Jew, knew and loved the Book of Enoch and had grown up in a circle and a sphere where the Book of Enoch was regarded with respect, and even reverence; and he takes his quotation from it perfectly naturally, knowing that his readers would recognize it, and that they would respect it. Jude is simply doing what all the New Testament writers do, and which every writer must do in every age, he is speaking to men in language which they recognized and understood" (Barclay, p. 231). Modern Christian authors do the same thing when they quote an inspiring or informative statement from another Christian, or even a non-Christian, author. Citing recognized literature of the day still "remains one of the most important elements in the communication of Christian truth" (Green, p. 193).

Of course, there remains the issue that Jude 14 says that Enoch "prophesied." But that does not necessarily mean that the New Testament writer is citing him as Scripture. To the contrary, Jude "seems rather to be recognizing that what Enoch had said has turned out to be" true "in view of the ungodly conduct of these false teachers" (Guthrie, p. 915). That is, their ungodly actions will certainly call forth a judgment that will be executed at the Second Advent. In that sense, Enoch's prophecy still holds for false teachers and evil doers in the twenty-first century. We should also recognize that Enoch's prediction is quite in harmony with the teachings of both testaments which put forth a day of the Lord that will hold the wicked accountable.

Jude 16 moves on to one final catalogue of evil characteristics of the false teachers. Given what he has already said, it doesn't seem as if he could have missed anything. But just in case he did, Jude offers another list of five characteristics.

First, they are "grumblers." Here we have the very same Greek word so often used in the Greek translation of the Old Testament (the Septuagint) for the murmurings of the children of Israel against Moses as he led them through the wilderness. It is also the same Greek root employed in Luke 15:2, in which the scribes and Pharisees complained about Christ eating with sinners. The grumblers against Moses' leadership, of course, left their bones in the desert. God frankly told all "who have murmured against me" that "your dead bodies shall fall in the wilderness," (Num. 14:29, RSV). As we might expect, those who murmured against Christ will also have a problematic future.

With the grumblers we are right back to Jude 8 and the rejection of authority. Jude is circling back for one more verbal shot at a core problem of the false teachers—their denial of God's authority both in His word and as it is delegated to leaders in the church on earth. Unfortunately, the tribe of grumblers has not died out. Its citizens have filled the halls of history from the time of Moses to Jude and from Jude's era to ours.

The second characterization of the false teachers is that they are "faultfinders." The word I translated as "faultfinders" is a rare one that appears only here in the New Testament. In many ways it is similar in meaning to "grumblers." But with "faultfinders" we find a distinct em-

> ## A Sixth-Century Distinction Between Grumblers and Faultfinders
>
> "Grumblers are people who mutter against others under their breath, whereas malcontents [faultfinders] are those who are always looking for ways in which they can attack and disparage everything and everybody" (Oecumenius, in Bray, p. 255).

phasis on "complaining of one's fate" (Earle, p. 456). It is used of a person who complains about every situation. Some days it is too hot, and others it is too cold. When it is summer, they long for winter, but when it is winter they pine for summer. What the faultfinder needs to recognize is that such an attitude is an insult to God who provides us with all things.

Whatever the full distinction between grumbling and faultfinding might be, one thing is certain—that the false teachers must have a serious problem along that line since God hit them twice on the same charge. That double whammy ought also to be a wake-up call to those of us today who make a habit of grumbling and faultfinding. From the biblical perspective, it puts us into some bad company with a certain future that may not be according to our liking. Perhaps it's time for an inventory of our personal habits in this realm.

The third characteristic in Jude's list is "walking according to their own lusts." We encounter a vital lesson here at the very heart of the false teachers' problem. After all, becoming a Christian means to follow Christ in all things. These teachers are either retreating from their prior commitment to Christ or they never had one. But one thing is certain: "they have found another master to *follow*—themselves" (Lucas, p. 211) and their lustful desires. And with that thought we are back to verse 8, with the rejection of authority, and verses 7 and 10, with their mention of perverted sexual appetites and the mindless submission to animal instincts. Jude is nailing down his case through varied repetitions of the same charges. He desperately wants his readers to see the dangers clearly.

The fourth characteristic is "speaking arrogant words" or being "loud-mouthed boasters" (RSV). The false teachers speak with arrogant pride, a problem undoubtedly related to their attitude of spiritual superiority toward the members of the church and its leaders. "Instead of using their voice to praise God and to encourage others, they are busy sounding off about themselves" and *their ideas* (Reese, pp. 63, 64). Or as Richard Bauckham puts it, "they express their arrogant, presumptuous attitude toward God, their insolent contempt for his commandments, their rejection of his moral authority which amounts to a proud claim to be their own moral authority" (Bauckham, p. 99).

Last, the false teachers are not above "flattering people for the sake of gain" or to flattering "others for their own advantage" (NIV). The implication here is that the false teachers were willing to do just about anything to gain converts to their theology and its lifestyle. Many people let down their guard in the face of flattery. That response creates just the opening that such unethical teachers sought.

How much stronger our churches would be today if we as Christians were more discriminating. With Jude 16 in hand we need to recognize that grumbling and faultfinding are signs of an ungodly life. And it is possible to detect even the most deceitful, flattering people if they reflect ungodly lifestyles and attitudes. Building the power of discernment is what the letter from Jude is all about.

On the other hand, if we turn Jude 16 on its head and do just the opposite of grumbling, faultfinding, following our own lusts, arrogant talking, and deceptive flattering, we will be on the path to what developing a Christian character is all about.

Part III

Admonitions for True Believers

Jude 17-23

6. The Characteristics of Error

[17]But you, beloved, must remember the words predicted by the apostles of our Lord Jesus Christ; [18]they said to you, "In the last of time there will be scoffers walking according to their own lusts for ungodly things." [19]These are the ones who create divisions, worldly-minded, not possessing the Spirit.

Verses 5-16 presented a tour de force of the dangerous traits of the false teachers. Jude left no stones unturned as he exposed their characteristics to those whose fellowship they had secretly invaded (verse 4). He climaxes his exposition of the false teachers with a thundering prediction of their forthcoming judgment at the Second Advent in verses 14 and 15.

Then in verses 17-23 Jude shifts his exposure of the heretics from the descriptive mode of verses 5-16 to that of more directly admonishing those still loyal to "the faith once for all delivered to the saints" (verse 3), even though his description of the false teachers remains as the background of his remarks. In verses 17-19 Jude frames his focus in terms of the characteristics of evil, while verses 20-23 transfer the perspective to the characteristics of good.

Jude begins his admonishments with a follow up to the prediction of judgment to come in verses 14 and 15. There he built upon the words of 1 Enoch, but in verse 17 he reminds his readers of the predictions of the apostles. "Remember," he tells them, "the words predicted by the apostles."

"Remember" is the first imperative in Jude, but it will not be the last.

271

The imperative mood dominates the next few verses, thus indicating his shift from description to admonishing.

At this point a lesson on remembering will be helpful. "Remembering in the Scriptures does not involve mere mental recollection, as when we remember a person's name that we had temporarily forgotten. Remembering means that one takes to heart the words spoken, so that they are imprinted upon one's life" (Schreiner, p. 477). That concept is evident in verse 5, in which Jude reminds his readers that those people whom God "saved" out of Egypt who were not faithful were afterward destroyed. The imperative to remember in the Bible has implications for how one thinks and lives. Thus it is back in Exodus 20, in which God commands His people to "remember the Sabbath day, to keep it holy" (verse 8, RSV). The call is not for contemplation on God as Creator, but for a life-changing experience leading to holiness. Jude's command to remember is fraught with meaning for both his first readers and for us. If God's past teachings don't make a difference in our lives we are merely playing games in the name of Christianity and are devoid of the real thing.

The remembering in Jude 17 is directly connected to "the words predicted by the apostles." The interesting thing about those "predicted" words is that they do not appear in the New Testament. And here we have something important to understand. The early church did not have a copy of the New Testament as we know it. What the earliest Christians had were oral collections of the sayings of Jesus and the apostles, some of which were gradually put into written form as the church progressed through the first Christian century. It is undoubtedly from one of those early oral collections that Jude (and 2 Peter 3:2) bases his words.

The prediction itself tells us that "in the last of time there will be scoffers walking according to their own lusts for ungodly things" (Jude 18). Two items deserve special mention in that verse. First, Jude and the other Bible writers believed that they were living "in the last of time" or "the last days." Their understanding goes back to a Jewish belief that divided history into two great eras—the age of the past and the age to come. When Jesus announced at the beginning of His ministry that the kingdom of heaven was arriving (Matt. 4:17), He was announcing that the age to come was at hand. Thus the belief that the world had entered "the last of time." That period began with the ministry of Jesus the Messiah and would continue until His return at the Second Advent which will bring the kingdom of heaven to its fullness. Thus the interim between the two advents of Christ are "the last days" or "the last of time."

The apostles had predicted that scoffers would arise in that period. Second Peter 3:3 picks up the same prophecy, but he specifically applies it to those who deny the Second Advent (verse 4). Jude gives no hint that that form of scoffing was a problem among the false teachers with whom he dealt. What seems to be clear from the text is that they scoffed at or mocked or made fun of those "who refused to go with them in the path of their own lusts; men who still had scruples and 'old-fashioned' or 'puritanical' standards, unlike the superior, spiritual Christians such as themselves, who were exploiting their Christian freedom! The false teachers were claiming to be so Spirit-filled that there was no room for law in their Christian lives. They claimed that grace was so abundant that their sin (if so it must be called) provided greater occasion for it (cf. v. 4). They claimed that the salvation of the soul is what matters, and that what a man does with his body is immaterial, for it is bound to perish. Those who fussed about sexual purity seemed to them astonishingly naïve" (Green, p. 196).

Jude 19 moves on to tell us that the false teachers are "the ones who create divisions" or as "one old English translation reads, 'These are the makers of sects'" (Manton, p. 197). Charles Bigg suggests several ways in which they probably created divisions in the church. One was that the false teachers "attached themselves to the rich," one of the implications of verse 16 with its "flattering people for the sake of gain" (Bigg, p. 339). The rich would have been the educated church members. Thus one line of division would have been based on socio-economic factors. And, if what took place in 1 Corinthians 11 is any indication of the situation in Jude's area, that division probably crept into the *agapē* feasts he mentions in verse 12, with part of "hidden rock" function of the false teachers to be their engineering of the unity feast as an event in which the rich were well fed while the poor went hungry. Thus they could even turn an occasion aimed at unification into one that fractured the church. Another line of division would be over the rejection of authority, both divine and churchly, by the false teachers in Jude 8.

But it appears that we find the foundational ground for divisions hinted at in Jude's use of the Greek words that I have translated "worldly-minded" and "Spirit." Both Paul (1 Cor. 2:14-16) and James (James 3:15) make a distinction between spiritual and unspiritual or worldly individuals. The words they use are *pneumatikoi* and *psuchikoi*, which respectively mean those who have the fullness of the Spirit and are thus spiritual, and those individuals governed by the natural life of this world. Edwin Blum suggests that what we have in the accusation of Jude 19 may be a foreshadowing of the later Gnostic practice of "classifying" individuals "into groups of initiates ('spiritual') and lesser ones" or *psuchikoi* (Blum, p. 394), based on the superior *gnōsis* or knowledge of the spiritual group. Thus the church would separate into the camps of the sophisticated ones who looked with a smirk ("scoffing") on their faces at the lesser group, and those who weren't enlightened and thus had all kinds of outdated ideas regarding behavior and doctrine.

With that picture in mind, verse 19 takes on fuller meaning. When Jude asserts that the false teachers are "worldly-minded" and devoid of the "Spirit" he is reversing their teachings. "'It is you,' he thunders at them, 'who are the *psuchikoi*, the fleshly and flesh-dominated; it is you who possess no *pneuma* [spirit], no real knowledge and no experience of God,'" (Barclay, p. 238). Jude is telling the false teachers that although they picture themselves as being the truly religious people, in actuality they have no religion at all. They were people of the world who lacked the Holy Spirit and the spiritual life that comes from the Spirit. While they had a form of religion, it was one that in their desire to sin they had twisted to fit their needs. Such is the end of their religious tragedy.

One of the difficult facts of religious life 2,000 years later is that the church still struggles with those so-called spiritual intellectuals who are critical of everything and create divisions. The only safety for any of us is to examine the fruits of those who give such impressions in the light of "the words" handed down "by the apostles" (Jude 17) that reflect "the faith once for all delivered to the saints" (verse 4). Whether we like it or not, we have no choice but to "test the spirits" of those whom we come in contact with to see "whether they are of God" (1 John 4:1, RSV; cf. 1 Thess. 5:19-21). That is a Christian obligation rather than an option. And in the process of such testing the book of Jude is both valuable and enlightening.

7. The Characteristics of Goodness

Jude 20-23

²⁰But you, beloved, building yourselves up in your most holy faith, praying in the Holy Spirit, ²¹keep yourselves in God's love, earnestly waiting for the mercy of our Lord Jesus Christ unto eternal life. ²²And have pity on those who doubt. ²³And save others, snatching them out of fire; and on others have pity with fear, hating even the garment defiled by the flesh.

In verses 20-23 "Jude comes to the main purpose of his letter, which is to give his readers positive instructions about how, in the situation in which they find themselves, they are to 'carry on the fight for the faith' (v. 3)" (Bauckham, p. 117). Whereas the letter up to this point has focused on the characteristics and problems of the false teachers, in these four verses Jude presents his readers with something they can do.

Centering on the virtues of faith, hope, love, and prayer, Jude's instruction to his readers deserves our careful attention. One could hardly go wrong by following the counsel in Jude 20-23.

His first injunction is for the faithful to build themselves up in "your most holy faith" (verse 20). Here we find the building metaphor so prominent in other parts of the New Testament (1 Cor. 3:9-15; 2 Cor. 6:16; Eph. 2:20-22; 1 Peter 2:4-10). Building themselves up suggests the completion of a structure on a foundation already laid. "That foundation is for Jude 'your most holy faith.' Upon that foundation alone can the edifices of Christian character and the Christian fellowship be securely erected." By way of contrast is the foundation of those who are guided by "only their dreamings (vs. 8), instinct such as irrational animals possess (vs. 10), [and] their own ungodly passions (vs. 18)" (Barnett, p. 338).

Faith in Jude undoubtedly includes the apostolic teachings "once for all delivered to the saints" (verse 3), but that doctrinal deposit never stands alone in biblical thought. Faith at its heart is a relationship with that Lord who gave His apostles the doctrinal teaching that they in turn passed on to the church. Thus building on the "most holy faith" includes both a relationship and an understanding of truth.

Jude's second injunction is to pray "in the Holy Spirit" (verse 20). The battle against the false teachers of Jude's day and in all other times in history will never be won by argument. As Paul so graphically notes, Christians "are not contending against flesh and blood, but against the principalities, against the powers, against the world rulers of the present darkness, against the spiritual hosts of wickedness in the heavenly places" (Eph. 6:12, RSV). In the spiritual warfare between good and evil we need God's strength. As James Moffatt puts it: "Prayer is love in need appealing to Love in power" (Moffatt, p. 243). Another author suggests that "prayer is the key in the hand of faith to unlock heaven's storehouse" (White, p. 94). But in the war against spiritual darkness, human prayer is not adequate. It must be prayer "in the Holy Spirit," a teaching that implies that Jude's readers are empowered by the Spirit, since they can pray in Him, while the false teachers are without the Spirit (verse 19).

> ### The "To Do's" of Jude 20-23
>
> 1. Build oneself up in faith.
> 2. Pray in the Spirit.
> 3. Keep in God's love.
> 4. Wait on Christ's mercy.
> 5. Pity those wavering.
> 6. Love sinners by seeking to save them.
> 7. Hate sin.

Jude's third injunction is that Christians need to keep themselves in God's love (verse 21). With "keep" we find a word that Jude uses again and again. We first came across it in verse 1, in which Christians are "kept in Jesus Christ." The concept but not the same Greek word shows up again in the letter's closing verses, which indicate that God is able to preserve His children from falling (verse 24). "Here," Douglas Moo writes, "we find the typical two sides of the New Testament approach to the

Christian life. God has done all in Christ that we need to be saved; yet we must respond to God if we are to secure our salvation. God 'keeps' us; we are to 'keep ourselves.' Both are true, and neither can be sacrificed without missing something essential to the Christian pursuit of godliness" (Moo, p. 285). Keeping, of course, is a process rather than a once for all time event. Both Jude's first readers and ourselves need to cling to God's love on a day to day, moment by moment basis for as long as life shall last. The Christian life is a line rather than a point, and the devil is more than happy to help us get unkept at every step of life's journey.

A fourth Christian duty is to wait for Christ's mercy (verse 21). Here Jude refers to what Paul calls the "blessed hope" (Titus 2:13, RSV) of the Second Advent in which all things will be righted. Undergirding Christianity is the knowledge that this world is not all that we have. Christ will return and everybody will receive their just reward. Jude reflected on that truth in his citing of Enoch's prediction that the Lord would come with "ten thousands of His holy ones to execute judgment" (verses 14, 15). But that judgment is two-edged all the way through the Bible. For the wicked it means being cast into outer darkness (Matt. 25:30; Jude 13), but for Christians it will be the blessing of full redemption. While Christians go through life with one eye on the future, false teachers live according to their passions and lusts (Jude 8, 16) since this life is the only hope that they have. For Jude the hope of eternal life can be linked to faith, love, and prayer as one of the true marks of Christians, one that helps them stay on the path to the kingdom and out of the subtle heresies of the false teachers.

Jerome Neyrey notes that "what is unusual is that Jude describes Jesus as the dispenser of mercy" rather than God, as in most of the Bible. Neyrey is undoubtedly correct when he writes that this builds upon those New Testament passages that picture Jesus arriving to judge and hand out the rewards (see Matt. 16:27; 25:29, 30, 46; Neyrey, p. 91).

Jude 22 and 23 continue on with the imperatives of what it means to be a Christian. But here we have a problem that readers who compare several English versions will soon discover. That is, the Greek text of these two verses is uncertain. Thus translations vary. My translation accords with the best available Greek text, but, as Peter Davids points out, "this is one of the places in the NT in which scholars simply cannot state with any assurance what the original text was" (Davids, p. 99). Still, the general intent of the passages is widely agreed upon, even if that is not so for the exact wording.

The main point Jude makes in verse 22 is that Christians should be merciful people who show a caringness toward those who doubt or waiver in their Christian experience. That category represents those who have found the false teachings to be attractive, but have not yet opted to align themselves with the new theology and way of life. They have been tempted and might go either way, but they have made no firm decision for or against either Jude's viewpoint or that of the false teachers. This group represents potentially fruitful ground in the "struggle for the faith once for all delivered to the saints" (Jude 3).

A less promising category in the struggle are those who have already decided for the false teachers and are, so to speak, already in the "fire" (Jude 22). They need to be snatched from the flames since they have already committed themselves to the ways of the false teachers. Thus they constitute a category of people more difficult than the doubters, but there is always hope through God's grace. The task of the Christian in such situations is to move forward in faith, praying in the Holy Spirit for a breakthrough in the hearts and minds of those thoroughly confused spiritually.

But it is the third group that represents the really difficult cases. That category relates to the attempt to convert the false teachers themselves. But here the faithful must "pity with fear" (verse 23). Because of the power of the personalities of the false teachers and the subtleness of their arguments, the rescuers themselves are in danger as they undertake such a precarious task. But, Jude states, they still need to try. There is a wideness in God's mercy that is almost beyond our imagination. He loves even His enemies (Rom. 5:8, 10; Matt. 5:43-48). Thus "even to the worst heretic, even to those most far gone in error, even to those whose beliefs are most menacing and dangerous, the Christian has a duty that is binding" in reaching out to others for their salvation (Barclay, p. 242). But they must do so in recognition of their own weaknesses with both eyes open and their faith intact, constantly "praying in the Holy Spirit," and earnestly keeping themselves in God's love (Jude 20).

That brings us to Jude's final injunction in his categorization of Christian goodness. Even as people do all they can to save and love sinners, they must at the same time hate sin. They must genuinely hate "even the garment defiled by the flesh" (verse 23), which is another way of saying that the contaminating power of sin is so strong that anything that has even come near it is dangerous to a Christian's well being. Yet believers must still reach out in mercy to even the most aggressive sinners. But they must do so only in fear for their own spiritual journey and with a firm connection to God. They may "have God on their side, but they must remember not to attempt anything in their own power lest they too fall prey to the false teachers' lies" (Barton, p. 261).

Part IV

Closing Doxology

Jude 24, 25

8. Glory to God!

Jude 24, 25

[24]Now to the One who is able to keep you from stumbling and to present you without blame before the presence of His glory with great joy, [25]to the only God, our Savior through Jesus Christ our Lord, be glory, majesty, dominion, and authority before all time and now and forever. Amen.

What a positive ending to a largely negative letter! Here we have in all probability the only two verses of Jude that many people know. And with good reason. Few passages in the Bible unite the saving power of God with His glory and majesty more forcefully than Jude 24 and 25.

Central to these climatic verses of a tension-filled letter is the word "keep." Keeping has had a prominent place throughout. We first met it in verse 1, in which believers are "kept in Jesus Christ." Thus the letter begins and ends with God's salvational preserving power. On the other side of the ledger are those who are kept for a far less pleasant judgment (verses 6, 13).

Keeping in Jude also has a human side. Some people keep themselves in God's love (verse 21), while others like the evil angels of old do not hew to faithfulness (verse 6).

In Jude God's keeping is always tied to human response. But the power of God is always primary. And that's good, because it is dangerous to live as Christians in a world permeated with false teachings and seductive morals. And it is also "a hazardous thing to try to rescue men for the gospel out of such an environment" as portrayed in Jude 23. After all, "if you get too near the fire, it will burn you," and "if you get too near the garment stained by the flesh, it will defile you" (Green, p. 205). In such a world Christians can praise God who is able to keep us from stumbling into a life of rebellion if we stay connected to His power.

The word translated as "stumbling" is of interest in its own right. The ancient world employed it of both a sure-footed horse which does not stumble and of a person who does not fall into error. It would be wonderful if there were such individuals who could live that kind of life under their own steam. Yet the sad reality, as Paul forcefully points out, is that all have stumbled and fallen into sin (Rom. 3:9-20, 23). All, therefore, are subject to the judgment of condemnation (Rom. 6:23). But the good news is that not only can God restore stumblers—He has the power and desire to preserve them from falling. That theme is highlighted in Psalm 121, in which we read that God "will not let your foot stumble; he who guards you will not sleep. . . . The Lord is your guardian, your protector. . . . The Lord will guard you as you come and go, now and forevermore" (verses 3, 5, 8, REB). Paul picks up that thought in 1 Corinthians 1:8 when he writes that "He will also keep you firm to the end, so that you will be faultless on the Day of our Lord Jesus Christ" (GNT). The best of news is that God who "began a good work" in us is able to "bring it to completion at the day of Jesus Christ" (Phil. 1:6, RSV).

According to Jude 24, believers are not only kept from stumbling, but will be presented "without blame before the presence of His glory." "Without blame" is another biblical word pregnant with meaning. The Old Testament uses it of a sacrificial animal without spot or blemish and therefore fit to be offered to God. The amazing truth is that God through Christ's work can take damaged goods and transform them into beings appropriate for the presence of God.

Here is a cause for "great joy" (Jude 24) for both God and His people. Peter Davids notes that such joy is not a private one but public. It is an eschatological term, appropriate to the festivity surrounding God's final deliverance of His people. "The picture," Davids writes, "is that of a festival in the presence of God, a sea of people singing, praising, and dancing in joyous celebration in the very presence of the God they had served on earth" (Davids, p. 111). Revelation 19 features the same joyous occasion as the marriage supper of the Lamb. What a day of rejoicing that will be.

Jude 25 puts the climactic focus on God and Christ. As the epistle comes to an end, we want to shout "Amen" with Jude for God's delivering and preserving power and for His kingly glory, majesty, and authority. "He is the King with ultimate power and authority for he is the 'only God'" (Gardner, p. 229).

Glory to God forms the final note in Jude's letter. Why? Because the Father is Savior through Jesus, the two working unitedly in history's greatest search and rescue operation.

Jude has nothing but praise for the divine Godhead. All the prophet can think of as he brings his letter to a close is shouting out his heartfelt feelings regarding the eternal "glory, majesty, dominion, and authority" of the one who is able to solve the sin problem and rescue those who have faith in Him. All credit is due to "God, our Savior."

And all that Jude can add to his final doxology is the word "amen." Using that word at the end of his letter is the same as if he was shouting "Yes!" to all that God through Christ has done for His people and will still do in the future. And as we close our study of Jude's short letter we need to join him in his great shout of praise and adoration. To God "be the glory, majesty, dominion, and authority" forever and ever! Amen.

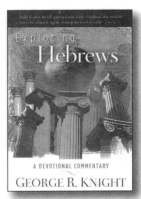
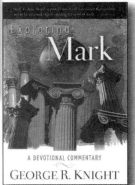
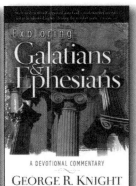
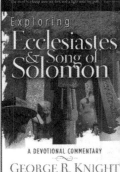

LIBRARY OF
ADVENTIST THEOLOGY
SERIES

There is no more important topic than God's plan of salvation for a lost world. In these noteworthy books George R. Knight considers the very heart of the Christian message—God's work *for* us in justification—and also explores His work in us.

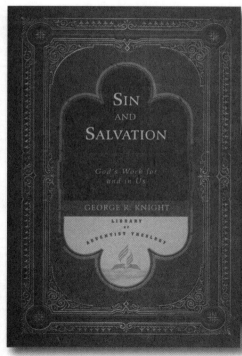

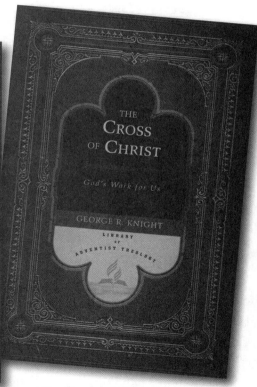

Sin and Salvation, Book 2
Hardcover, 208 pages.

The Cross of Christ, Book 1
Hardcover, 158 pages.

Why does George Knight say **this is the most important book** he's ever written?

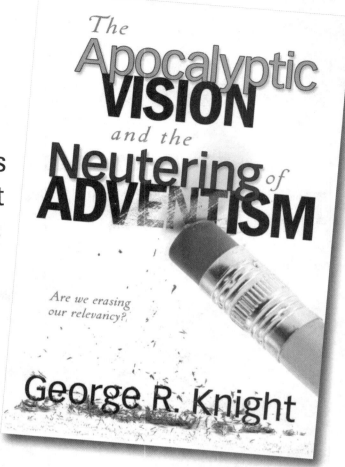

Does the Adventist Church have any reason for existence if it has lost that which makes it different from all the rest of Christianity?

Why were the early Seventh-day Adventists so passionate about evangelizing the world?

How can we rekindle in our own lives that passion for spreading the gospel?

Could a revitalization of the apocalyptic vision provide the answer as the world and the church move toward the Second Coming?

Accept Knight's challenge to go back to your roots for the answers. (But beware—you may have to uproot yourself from the pew to be truly Adventist!) Paperback, 112 pages.